NAVAJO INFANCY
An Ethological Study of Child Development

A Volume in the Series

BIOLOGICAL FOUNDATIONS OF HUMAN BEHAVIOR

Melvin Konner / Richard Wrangham, Series Editors

NAVAJO INFANCY
An Ethological Study of Child Development

James S. Chisholm

Aldine Publishing Company
New York

Grateful acknowledgment is made to Harvard University Press for permission to adapt Figure 1.1 from E. O. Wilson's "Sociobiology" (1975) and to the New York Academy of Sciences for permission to redraw Figure 1.2 from C. H. Waddington's "A Catastrophe Theory of Evolution" (in Waddington, 1975).

Aldine Publishing Company
200 Saw Mill River Road
Hawthorne, New York 10532

Library of Congress Cataloging in Publication Data

Chisholm, James S.
    Navajo infancy.

    (Biological foundations of human behavior)
    Bibliography: p.
    Includes index.
    1. Navajo Indians—Children. 2. Indians of North
America—Southwest, New—Children. 3. Child development
—Southwest, New. I. Title. II. Series.
E99.N3C48   1983   305.2'32'08997   83-12258
ISBN 0-202-01169-0

Printed in the United States of America

For
Dine dóó bą ałchiní yazhi dóó
Madelene

CONTENTS

Preface   *ix*

1 DEVELOPMENT IN AN EVOLUTIONARY CONTEXT

The Process of Adaptation   *1*
Ontogeny and Phylogeny   *12*
Adaptability and Development   *24*
Summary   *39*

2 THE ENVIRONMENT OF NAVAJO INFANCY

Perturbations in the Environment of Navajo Infancy   *41*
The Navajo   *42*
Cottonwood Springs   *51*

3 THE CRADLEBOARD

The Cradleboard and Swaddling in Cross-Cultural Perspective   *71*
Previous Studies of the Cradleboard   *79*
The Hypotheses: Does the Cradleboard Affect Navajo Child
   Development   *87*

4 THE RESEARCH

Anthropology and Ethology in Child Development Research   *93*
The Samples   *97*
The Methods   *108*

5 THE BEHAVIOR OF NAVAJO AND ANGLO NEWBORN INFANTS

The Analysis of Brazelton Scale Data: Methods and
   Rationale   126
Prenatal Influences on Navajo-Anglo Group Differences in
   Newborn Behavior   130
Discussion and Conclusion   135

6 NAVAJO AND ANGLO CHILDREN'S FEAR OF STRANGERS

Similarities and Differences in Navajo and Anglo Fear of
   Strangers   142
Environmental Correlates of Navajo Fear of Strangers   152
Discussion and Conclusion   156

7 MOTHER–INFANT INTERACTION AND THE CRADLEBOARD

The Immediate Effects of the Cradleboard   164
Some Situational Determinants of Cradleboard Use   172
The Longer-Term Effects of the Cradleboard   174
Discussion and Conclusion   198

8 THE DETERMINANTS OF MOTHER–INFANT INTERACTION

Deriving the Determinants   199
Navajo Neonatal Behavior and Mother–Infant Interaction in
   the First Quarter   203
The Child's Opportunity for Interaction with Others   206
Discussion and Conclusions   212

9 SUMMARY AND CONCLUSIONS: DEVELOPMENT AS ADAPTATION

Summary   215
Synthesis and Implications   225

Bibliography   251
Index   265

PREFACE

The opposition between nature and culture to which I attached much importance at one time now seems to be of primarily methodological importance.

Claude Levi-Strauss
The Savage Mind

In the pages to follow a variety of topics and issues are discussed. Although this book is about the Navajo and their children, it is also about social and cultural anthropology, human ethology, evolutionary theory, human biology, and developmental psychology. The real subject matter, however, is the relationship between nature and culture. Disciplinary boundaries are the bane of all disciplines, but perhaps because my father was a chemist and my mother a poet I simply grew up with a fascination for conceptual bridges. The book, then, is about how the process of development might constitute a phylogenetic and ontogenetic bridge between nature and culture.

Chapter 1 describes the process of adaptation and outlines the evolutionary biological reasons why the process of development constitutes an important adaptive mechanism, especially for K-selected species. This chapter also argues that an evolutionary approach to the process of development would predict increasing degrees of behavioral plasticity during development in K-selected species, especially our hominid ancestors; this argument is juxtaposed to the growing suspicion in developmental psychology that early experience and constitution may affect later behavior only under the most stable environmental circumstances. Chapter 2 describes the Navajo, concentrating on those aspects of the Navajo environment (social and physical) which seem to have been the most stable over the years and which are most likely to affect child development. Chapter 3 focuses specifically on the cradleboard, an aspect of the environment of Navajo infancy that has considerable theoretical interest, since one set of theories and data suggest that it should have long-term effects on behavior while another set suggests that it should not. Chapter 4 describes my research, including use of the techniques of human ethology and assessment of the behavior of newborn infants. Also included is research on a group of Anglo-American infants who were also using the cradleboard. This chapter compares and contrasts the environments of infancy that characterized both the Navajo and Anglo-American families. Chapter 5 provides a detailed description of the behavior of newborn Navajo and Anglo-American infants. It also provides an analysis of the prenatal influences on group differences in behavior that appeared and suggests that gene pool differences are not likely to be the best explanation of these differences. Chapter 6 describes the development of fear of strangers in Navajo and Anglo-American children and analyzes both within- and between-group differences in fear of strangers in terms of cradleboard use and the larger aspects of the social environment of infancy. Chapters 7 and 8 concentrate on analyses of Navajo and Anglo-American mother–infant interaction. The former describes how the cradleboard has the effects on mother–infant interaction that were predicted, but also shows that these effects seem to hold only while the infant is actually on the cradleboard. The latter focuses on how the larger social context affects both within- and between-group differences in patterns of mother–infant interaction. A summary and synthesis of my findings concludes the volume. This chapter discusses the reasons why the effects of the cradleboard do not last and why differences in the larger social context of development might be expected to have effects that last longer than those of the cradleboard. Also discussed are Navajo and Anglo differences in neonatal behavior, fear of strangers, and patterns of mother–infant interaction from the standpoint of both temperament and cultural beliefs and values about appropriate behavior. Drawing on the evolutionary approach to development presented in Chapter 1, I conclude that genetically based developmental rules are a likely explanation of why the cradleboard seems to have no lasting effect on behavioral development but that for good evolutionary biological reasons the proximate causes of group differences in children's behavior are likely to be social-cultural differences in the environment of infancy.

The field research on which this book is based was carried out during the years 1974 to 1976 in a Navajo community that I have called Cottonwood Springs. It is to the people of the Navajo Nation and Cottonwood Springs that I owe the greatest debt for this book, for they not only allowed me onto their land and into their homes, they did it with their characteristic warmth and quiet good humor. My work is dedicated to them and their children, for if I have seen anything, it is they who showed it to me.

My research was supported financially by a grant from The Harry Frank Guggenheim Foundation to Nick Blurton Jones of the Institute of Child Health, University of London, and by a grant from the National Science Foundation. I gratefully acknowledge the support and encouragement of these institutions. I am also indebted to the Research Allocations Committee of the University of New Mexico for financial aid in the preparation of this book for publication.

At every stage in the development of this work I received such support, encouragement, and very practical assistance from so many others that authorship might appropriately be shared with a long list of colleagues and friends. My name alone must be listed, however, not to monopolize any credit, but to absolve the others from my shortcomings. Even the following list of those deserving special thanks could be expanded.

To Nick Blurton Jones and Robin Fox I owe my greatest intellectual debt. In the early years of my anthropology studies at Rutgers, Robin provided the crucial environment for giving my developing interests in evolutionary theory a productive direction. Lionel Tiger and Jane Lancaster were also instrumental in this developmental process. This background provided me with an opportunity to work with Nick Blurton Jones at the Institute of Child Health in London. This was especially and continually rewarding, not the least because of the special group that Nick established in the Institute's Ethology Section. This group included Fae Hall, Rob Woodson, Elizette da Costa-Woodson, Barry Carter, John Richer, Sue Pollock, Maggie Evans, and Midge Elias.

My time at Cottonwood Springs was one of the most enjoyable two years one could hope to have anywhere. For making it so enjoyable, and for contributions of a very practical nature, I would like to quietly single out for special thanks Madelene, Joe and Nancy, Harold and Stella, Pat and Lydia, Jimmy and Emily, LeRoy and Barbara, Willie and Sue, Margo, Nellie, and Kathy, and the staff at the Cottonwood Springs Clinic.

I will also long be indebted to Berry Brazelton and Heidi Als of Boston's Children's Hospital Medical Center for introducing me to the pleasures of newborn infants and for teaching me how to make some sense out of their behavior. To John Porvaznik and the staff of the Tuba City Indian Health Service Hospital I offer many thanks for making it possible to gather my data on Navajo neonatal behavior.

V. K. Burbank, Mel Konner, and Marjorie Shostak have not only been good friends from the very beginnings of this work, but they also provided welcome advice and support during the work itself, and have continued to do so. They were also with me at the Flagstaff restaurant where I first saw an Anglo-American infant on a cradleboard. We all talked with the child's mother and father and with their encouragement I met the other infants and their parents in what became the Flagstaff comparison group. This was a delightful group of people, and their hospitality and interest have meant a great deal to me.

In the final stages of manuscript preparation a number of people provided help and encouragement that made the denouement as pleasurable as the preparation and the fieldwork. Those whom I would like to specially thank are Bonnie and Farley Sullivan, Tim Perper, Bill Powers, Linda Cordell, Scott Rushforth, Pat Draper, Henry Harpending, Louise Lamphere, and Charlie Super.

James Chisholm

1
Development in an Evolutionary Context

THE PROCESS OF ADAPTATION

IN 1859, with his *Origin of Species*, Charles Darwin initiated a paradigm shift that is not yet complete. When refinements in his theory of adaptation by natural selection have shifted this paradigm beyond the final barriers of vitalism, it will no longer be as appropriate to introduce works such as this one with the statement that the nature-culture dichotomy is false. This is a tiresome dichotomy, and in its several forms it has hindered theory and research in the life and social and behavioral sciences for too long. On the one hand, it is still too often accepted as a matter of extreme and naive faith that it is *either* nature *or* culture, that nature only proposes while culture disposes, and thought too often stops at the boundaries of academic disciplines. On the other hand, it is not enough to effect a synthesis and extension of thought across academic disciplines by acts of naive will: to argue that of course it is *both* nature *and* culture, that they go together and interact, and that man is naturally cultural may be true, but it is also to make wishful statements. If this tiresome dichotomy is to be removed from the realm of belief systems and politics and placed properly in the realm of scientific analysis, it is not enough to naively assume or deny that nature and culture interact—it must be shown how they interact.

To describe how nature and culture interact, it is necessary first to separate them in order to see how they go together. It is necessary to treat their interaction as problematical and to trace in as much detail as possible the causal pathways whereby one can logically proceed from nature to culture. The important word here is neither "nature" nor "culture," but "proceed," because in describing processes, one also provides explanations:

1

> Explanation is not achieved by description of the patterns of regularity, no matter
> how meticulous and adequate, nor by replacing this description by other abstrac-
> tions congruent with it, but by exhibiting what *makes* the pattern, i.e., certain
> processes. To study social forms it is certainly necessary but hardly sufficient to be
> able to describe them. To give an explanation of social forms, it is sufficient to
> describe the processes that generate the form (Barth, 1966:2; original emphasis).

The process that I will describe in order to proceed from nature to
culture is the process of adaptation by natural selection, and the purpose of
this chapter is to discuss the nature of this process and to show how it is
relevant both to the nature–culture problem and to theories of child development.

Levels of Explanation

There is an instructive parallel between the fields of evolutionary biology
and developmental psychology: both sciences face the task of explaining
change and continuity over time. In recent years, a number of developmental psychologists and evolutionary bologists have begun to question the
notions of stability and continuity that have been the keystones of their
respective sciences for several decades. The developmental psychologists
have begun to question the notion that early constitutional or experiential
factors are related in any simple way to an individual's later behavior and
the evolutionary biologists have begun to question the notion that early
phylogenetic events and conditions are related in any simple way to a
species' later behavior (or morphology). The developmental psychologists'
questions have arisen from the paucity of evidence that early ontogenetic
events and conditions matter very much except under the most stable
environmental conditions (see, for example, Kagan, Kearsley, and Zelazo,
1978; Brim and Kagan, 1980) and from the more positive growing theoretical recognition of the high degree of adaptability of the developing child
(see Bateson, 1976; Dunn, 1976; Sameroff, 1975; Sameroff and Chandler,
1975; Waddington, 1975a). The evolutionary biologists' questions have
arisen from the paucity of clear evidence in the fossil record for continuous
gradual evolution and from the growing theoretical recognition of the possibility that the process of adaptation by natural selection may often drive
evolution through a series of "punctuated equilibria": "Certainly the fossil
record is poor, but the jerkiness you see is not the result of gaps, it is the
consequence of the jerky mode of evolutionary change" (Gould, quoted in
Levin, 1980:883; see also Eldridge and Gould, 1972; Gould, 1977; Gould
and Eldrige, 1977; Stanley, 1979).

At the same time that there is growing discomfort over the issues of change and continuity in developmental psychology and evolutionary biology, the task of explaining both is being approached more and more in ethology with the realization that behavior must be explained at many levels simultaneously. The most elegant formulation of this explanatory approach was put forth by Tinbergen (1951, 1963) who stated that when we ask why a behavior has occurred we must in fact ask at least four separate questions: what are the factors, internal and external to the organism, that caused the behavior to occur at the moment it did (*immediate or proximal causation*)? What are the maturational and experiential factors in the organism's life history that underlie its capacity or predisposition to perform this behavior (*ontogeny*)? Does the behavior in question affect the organism's reproductive success or inclusive fitness (*distal or ultimate causation*)? What is the evolutionary history of the capacity of members of this species to perform this behavior (*phylogeny*)? Most of the barren furor of nature-culture or nature-nurture debates stems from the failure to realize that these levels of explanation are separate, but are also complementary and not mutually exclusive. In fact, a complete explanation requires complex multivariate explanations at each level and an understanding of how the explanations at each level are related to each other.

Because evolutionary biology deals with change and continuity in entire populations over millions of years, it has of necessity been most concerned with questions about phylogeny and ultimate causation—adaptation by natural selection that changes gene frequencies in populations. A species' phylogeny is its history, and the process of adaptation by natural selection is the process that generates this history. Even with our incomplete understanding of this process, it has been possible to generate an immense variety of living and social forms from an original range of fewer and more simple forms. On the other hand, because developmental psychology deals with change and continuity in the lives of individuals over only a few years, it has of necessity been most concerned with questions about ontogeny and immediate causation. However, these obvious differences in scale and scope do not prevent developmental psychology from making use of the most essential conceptual tool of evolutionary biology—the concept of adaptation by natural selection—for there is a concept of adaptation by natural selection that is not limited to changes in gene frequencies in populations. In this concept, the process of adaptation is one that occurs every day throughout the lives of individuals, and it is a concept as appropriate to questions about immediate causation and ontogeny as it is to questions about ultimate causation and phylogeny.

Development of the Phenotype

This concept of adaptation has been most clearly formulated by Slobodkin and Rapoport (1974), who arrived at their definition from the fields of
evolutionary biology and game theory. Fundamental to this and all concepts of adaptation by natural selection is the notion that adaptation is a
process involving the interaction of *genotype* (the genetic endowment of
possibilities) and environment over an all-important time dimension. One
of the more common mistakes, and not just for those with little training in
evolutionary biology, is the potentially compounding one of confusing
genotype and phenotype. Natural selection operates on *phenotypes* (the
actualization of a genetic possibility) and not directly on the genotype. As
Waddington put it: ". . . there is an essential indeterminancy in the relations between [the] phenotype and the genotype . . ." (1968:364). In the
realm of behavior, for example, the capacity of an organism to display
absolutely any behavior that it does is, by definition, located in the
organism's genotype. But natural selection does not operate on capacities
or potentials no matter how deeply coded in the organism's genotype.
Natural selection operates on the actual *expression* of behavior—which is
an aspect of the phenotype. Waddington (1968, 1975b) even suggests that
models of evolution that are formulated only in terms of the genotype may
be of limited relevance to human evolution, where the "essential indeterminancy" between genotype and phenotype is probably adaptive and has
probably been selected for. It is also commonly overlooked that an
organism's phenotype has a temporal dimension, that the phenotype develops over time. This makes it impossible to adequately describe the
phenotype without reference to a particular time or stage in the organism's
life history—from zygote to death. Or, as Lumsden and Wilson (1981) have
recently put it in their discussion of human epigenetics,

> It has become clear that the future of general microevolutionary studies lies in the
> refocusing of genetic analysis on development. This is particularly the case for
> human social behavior, the class of phenotypes most removed from the DNA
> templates (1981:238).

Epigenesis is the process of gene–environment interaction that begins
with the first translation of RNA from DNA in the zygote, continues
through all phases of embryological and fetal development, all phases of
postnatal maturation, and all phases of behavioral and cognitive development, and ends only at death. In their new book, *Genes, Mind, and
Culture*, Lumsden and Wilson treat the nature–culture problem as a gene–
environment interaction problem, and they argue that the best approach to
the nature–culture problem is through the study of development because

there are epigenetic rules that govern the development of the phenotype. An epigenetic rule is "any regularity during epigenesis that channels the development of an anatomical, physiological, cognitive, or behavioral trait in a particular direction" (1981:370). All epigenetic rules, they claim, have a genetic basis, but some are flexible, permitting the development of a wide variety of phenotypes in a wide variety of environments while others are virtually inflexible, permitting the development of variant phenotypes only under the most special environmental conditions. I will return to this discussion in the final chapter.

One example of a class of relatively inflexible epigenetic rules are those that seem to govern maturation in general and that make the rate, sequence, and timing of metabolic, neurological, endocrine, and morphologic development so environmentally stable. Stable though the development of these systems may be, however, the complex of genes that buffer them against most environmental fluctuations do not buffer them against all such fluctuations and are themselves, of course, subject to phylogenetic change. The *potential* flexibility inherent even in these otherwise relatively inflexible gene complexes can be appreciated in terms of what has been called the "operon model" (Jacob and Monod, 1961). Although strictly applicable only to prokaryote cells, it is often suggested that something analogous to the operon model will be found to operate in eukaryote cells and higher organisms (e.g., Plomin et al., 1980). To understand this model, it is important to understand that by itself the DNA molecule does almost nothing, but that it exists in a biochemical environment which not only *enables* the DNA to replicate itself, but also *uses* the information stored in the DNA to manufacture amino acids, proteins, enzymes, hormones, neurotransmitters, and so on—which go on in turn, to make more and different proteins, enzymes, hormones. In the operon model, *structural genes* are the ones that initiate the biochemical developmental processes that lead ultimately to the phenotype—the morphological and behavioral structures of the organism. At this level of ontogeny the laws of chemistry are also epigenetic rules. But these structural genes are under the direct on-off control of *operator genes,* and these operator genes are under the control of *regulator genes,* which, in turn, are sensitive or responsive to fluctuations in the biochemical environment of the cell. Not only does this arrangement mean that the actual operation of the structural genes may be influenced by extraorganismic environmental factors which influence the biochemical environment of the cell, it also provides a basis which at present is poorly understood, for the operation of natural selection to alter the rate, sequence, and timing of the development of species' metabolic, neurological, endocrine, and behavioral systems. The significance of natural selection for changes in organisms' rates of development will be dealt with in a later section, but it is worth mentioning here that there is good reason to believe that this sort of evolution can, and has, occurred: comparing the proteins and amino acids (initial products in the bio-chemical processes initiated by information contained in DNA) of humans and chimpanzees, King and Wilson (1975) determined that these macro-molecules of the two species were 99% identical. This figure means that humans and chimpanzees are separated by a genetic distance actually less than that which ordinarily separates two species of the same genus. They suggest that the obvious anatomical and behavioral differences between humans and chimpanzees are the result not of changes in structural genes, but of changes in the regulator genes which have led to ontogenetic dif-ferences in the expression of essentially the same structural genes. In a sense, then, a portion of the difference between human and chimpanzee is due to differences in epigenetic rules.

Neither the nature, number, nor degree of flexibility of human epi-genetic rules is known, but in humans and nonhuman primates it is known that learning plays a massive role in development. Undoubtedly there are epigenetic rules influencing learning, making some things "easy to learn" and other things "hard to learn" (cf. Lumsden and Wilson, 1981, especially Chapters 2 and 3), but such rules are surely among the most flexible, for human learning is clearly very highly dependent on the environment in which the learning occurred. This means that an adaptively crucial aspect of the development of the human phenotype is environmentally labile— that is, it is determined much more by the developmental history of inter-actions between organism and environment. Thus, for humans at least, the impact of natural selection has depended to a great extent on the onto-genetic, life-historical preservation of the effects of previous adaptations to the environment of development. I will return later to a discussion of this "preservation."

It has been necessary here to stress that the phenotype has a temporal dimension, that it develops, because the central point of Slobodkin and Rapoport's concept of adaptation by natural selection is that adaptation is a process that is not limited to changes in the genotype, but instead specifically includes and depends upon the organism's phenotypical, immediate behavioral responses to the environment throughout its life. A corollary of this point is that because adaptation is a process, it can best be understood by focusing explicitly on these immediate behavioral responses to "environmental perturbations." This contrasts with other strategies for studying adaptation which look for such massive responses as differential reproductive success, changes in demographic patterns, and changes in gene frequencies in entire populations.

Environmental Perturbations

For Slobodkin and Rapoport, an environmental perturbation is a departure from some mean, variance, or periodicity value of some component of the organism's environment for some period in its lifetime. Perturbations have the qualities of magnitude or force of impact, speed of onset, relative novelty, frequency, and duration. A perturbation is recognized by the organism to the extent that it perceives or experiences some stress as a result of the departure from the mean value of the environmental component.

Use of the word *stress* here does not imply a model based on pathology. Rather, Slobodkin and Rapoport's concept of the process of adaptation is a model of both the development of pathology and the maintenance of nonpathology, for two reasons. First, the distinction between pathology and nonpathology is relatively arbitrary; if pathology develops, it must develop from a state that is initially nonpathological. Second, the case can easily be made that life and development are stressful and that stress itself is normal. One current view in medicine, for example, is that health is a process "potentially measurable by the individual's ability to rally from insults, whether chemical, physical, infectious, psychological, or social" (Audy, 1971, quoted in Vayda and McCay, 1975:239). What is pathological, then, is stress (an insult, a perturbation) to which the organism cannot successfully respond. Adaptation itself is defined as a successful response to an environmental perturbation.

Successful Responses

The core of Slobodkin and Rapoport's concept of adaptation, the successful response to an environmental perturbation, is defined with explicit attention to the temporal or processual nature of adaptation: a successful response is one in which the next time the organism meets that same perturbation it can respond with less cost. Cost to the organism must be determined empirically in each particular case, but is defined generally as anything that tends to decrease the organism's capacity to make a successful response to any perturbation. This cost may be in resources consumed, energy expended, or simply time lost in adapting (responding) that might otherwise have gone to feeding, mating, caring for young, and so forth. The ultimate cost, however, is death, for when there is no more *time* for organisms to respond to environmental perturbations, adaptation proceeds on the basis of natural selection of mutations and recombinations alone. These are slow and only potentially flexible or adaptive ways of responding to the environment—nor are they available to the individual. A successful response at the level of the genotype depends on having just the right mutation occur or on there already existing in the gene pool just the right set of alleles for recombination to bring into play.

Preserving the Successful Response

In order for adaptation to occur, there must be a mechanism for preserving the successful response in the behavioral repertoire of individuals. The process of evolution is the way that natural selection makes it easier for organisms to behave in the ways that have worked best in the past; the process of adaptation includes the development of mechanisms for the preservation of these behaviors. Before some of these mechanisms are outlined, it must be stressed that it does not matter for the process of adaptation *how* a successful response is preserved—only that it *is* preserved. Further, the preservation need not be absolute but can be probabilistic.

There seem to be four general categories of preservation mechanisms. The first is well known: successful responses can be preserved directly in the genotype as, for example, innate releasing mechanisms or fixed action patterns. Responses preserved directly in the genotype are those that have been successful in removing the stress associated with perturbations that have been the most constant and widespread over many generations. The second set of preservation mechanisms would include the complex genetic and epigenetic mechanisms underlying cognition, learning, and memory. Closely related to this, but not isomorphic with it, are the third and fourth mechanisms: the third includes those factors underlying the capacity of individuals to elicit from *others* a successful response to their own perturbations and the fourth is the capacity of social organizations and cultures to store information necessary for a successful response by any member of the group.

These four broad categories of mechanisms for preserving successful responses to environmental perturbations will be dealt with in more detail in the concluding chapter, but it may be useful here to give examples of the third and fourth mechanisms. Consider an infant crying because of the stress (pain) associated with, say, a toothache. The infant's social environment will ordinarily include his or her mother, and the infant's pain cry will ordinarily elicit from her a successful response to the infant's perturbation. Her initial response will probably include cuddling and carrying and perhaps nursing—responses which are more functional in alleviating the pain than the specific problems associated with an erupting tooth but which are at least momentarily successful in removing the stress of the particular dental perturbation. It the toothache persists and the mother's responses to the infant's cries no longer serve to alleviate the child's pain, the mother might then take her child to a pediatrician, who would then respond to the child's perturbation, perhaps by prescribing some medication. In this case, the infant's social environment provided the agents of his or her successful response, and the infant's culture provided both the role of the pediatrician and the specific storehouse of pharmacologic information used to finally remove the perturbation.

A more general example can be seen in an infant growing up and learning the language of his or her cultural group. With the acquisition of this language there is now access not only to all who speak that language and from whom he or she may elicit responses, but there is also access to all information about the environment and its workings that the culture has stored. Phenotypical plasticity of response has been uniquely selected for in humans partially to the extent that the capacity to learn information stored in the environment has made possible our major adaptive mechanism— culture. According to one important interpretation, culture is a means of storing information in an individual's environment in a strikingly systematic and easily retrieved form (Goodenough, 1978).

Environmental Tracking

Regardless of how adaptive culture may be, however, it is not enough to say that humankind is unique simply because culture is biologically adaptive. One must describe the natural selective processes that produced the phenotypical, behavioral plasticity which so characterizes man and has made it possible for man to so uniquely specialize in the extragenotypical preservation of successful responses to the environment; it is necessary to outline the evolutionary theoretical reasons why there should be natural selection (in the sense of ultimate causation) for an adaptive "essential indeterminancy" in the ontogenetic effect of the genotype on the phenotype.

Slobodkin and Rapoport's notion that the process of adaptation starts with behavior is not unique. Theirs is a notion that is common to all theories of "environmental tracking." The special value of the general concept of environmental tracking here is that it provides the most basic evolutionary theoretical rationale for natural selection for behavioral flexibility or adaptability. Environmental tracking is the process whereby natural selection produces the ubiquitous "good fit" between organism and environment. In this process, organisms are seen as responding to environmental changes or perturbations in terms of mulitple, hierarchically interconnected response systems, beginning with bio- and electrochemical responses at the level of individual cells, proceeding through the range of reflexive and instinctual responses, on to slightly slower but more pervasive or long-lasting hormonal responses, then learning responses, and on ultimately, when large numbers of individuals are involved in the same perturbation, to population responses in demographic and gene pool characteristics. The immediate and quick responses, when called into play frequently and/or for long periods of time, serve to trigger the slower responses, which in turn may reset the response thresholds of the quicker responses (helping the higher responses to alleviate the stress) and/or which may themselves change. The slowest responses are the most costly to the organism because they have such far-reaching effects on the potential flexibility of all the faster responses above them in the response hierarchy.

Behavior, perhaps especially social behavior, is the best example of an environmental tracking device. Behavioral responses to environmental perturbations have been selected for in evolution because they tended to provide a high degree of response flexibility that protected the slower, deeper, and only potentially flexible response capacity latent in the gene pool. The principle of natural selection for behavioral response flexibility (the "adaptive indeterminancy") can be illustrated with the game theory analog of the process of adaptation envisioned by Slobodkin and Rapoport. The game is called Gambler's Ruin and is a bizarre card game in which all players have a

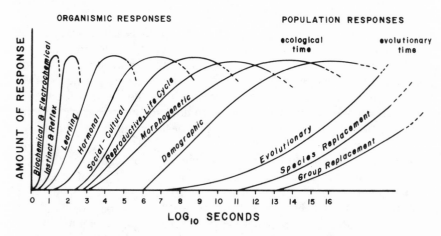

Fig. 1.1 A hierarchy of responses to environmental perturbations (adapted from Wilson, 1975:145).

fixed number of chips (limited resources), all promise to play indefinitely (no one can drop out—just as organisms ordinarily strive to avoid death), and all promise to wager something, no matter how little, on each hand (each environmental perturbation). The most bizarre rule of all is that whenever a player loses all his chips, he is dead. It is immediately obvious that there is only one sensible strategy for playing this ultimately losing game: players should minimize their bets in order to maximize their chances of simply staying in the game—the "existential game of life."

Slobodkin and Rapoport envisage natural selection for increasingly sophisticated and fine-tuned environmental tracking systems that seem to have reached their most perfect form in *Homo sapiens*. The essence of this response strategy is that the least costly, lowest stake, and quickest responses are made first. If the perturbations to which these responses are made are short or unique, and/or if the responses are successful, then stress experienced at the perturbation has been alleviated with little cost to the organism's capacity to respond successfully to the next perturbation. However, if the initial perturbation is more severe, lasting, or repeated, the quick and minimally costly responses may be called into play more often and may thus themselves become a set of perturbations that call into play slower, deeper, and less flexible response capacities. For example, panting when at high altitudes will suffice for short periods, but becomes stressful to the heart and lungs after a time. This stress serves to increase lung volume and heart pumping capacity and to alter blood chemistry, but these physiological responses are slower than the panting reflex, and more costly in the way that they consume energy over a longer period (for altering metabolic processes and anatomical structures) and in the way that they actually reduce adaptive potential because they are such slow and long-lasting responses.

Thus, in the long run, plasticity or adaptability in immediate behavioral responses to the environment will be selected for because this tends to protect and conserve the flexibility and adaptability of the slower, deeper, and more costly physiological, demographic, and populational genetic adaptive mechanisms. These latter responses are ultimately the least flexible ways of responding to the environment. There will tend to be natural selection for an "essential indeterminacy" in the relation between the genotype and behavioral aspects of the phenotype because the genotype will be altered only when the phenotypical responses (especially the behavioral ones) made at each higher level in the response hierarchy have been shown to be at least partially effective. This is because stress is itself a sort of proof that the response was effective, for the experience of stress is, so to speak, a sign of continued life—and is information that the deeper and slower response systems can "use" to alter their values. (See also Løvtrup, 1974 for a similar discussion of natural selection for adaptability.)

Seeing the process of adaptation in these terms of environmental tracking allows us to recognize that the information encoded in DNA reflects the degree to which phenotypical responses to environmental perturbations have been assimilated into the genotype, that is, the degree to which environmental perturbations have been severe enough, widespread enough, and long-lasting enough to affect the frequency with which genes are passed from one generation to the next. Visualizing the process of adaptation in these terms of environmental tracking also allows us to see that the process of adaptation is not limited to changes in the gene pool over generations, but includes and may depend upon immediate behavioral response to the environment in the lifetime of individuals. Failure to see the two ends of this scale of adaptation had made naive biological indeterminists of many psychologists and anthropologists and naive biological determinists of many biologists and sociobiologists. In their understanding of the relationship between nature and culture, naive determinists tend to assume simple models of biological cause and cultural effect because they see too few individuals, behaving the same way, in environments that are seen as too similar and too long-lasting and constant. The naive indeterminists tend to assume a largely blank slate of essentially infinite potential, and their models are simple ones of cultural cause and cultural effect because they see too many individuals behaving in different ways, in environments that are usually seen as too different, short-lived, and historically separate. But what makes both naive is not so much the extremism, the failure to appreciate the significance of gradations, but the failure to look at the process of adaptation: "the process of responding to the environmental perturbation" (Slobodkin and Rapoport, 1974:199). This process is the interaction of the genotype and the environment, but it is relevant to more than Tinbergen's third question about ultimate causation conceived only in terms of changes in gene frequency from generation to generation. Ultimately, that *is* where genotypes get altered, and natural selection is thus the ultimate "why" of the four that Tinbergen suggests, but natural selection operates on phenotypes, and phenotypes are the ontogenetic interaction of the genotype with the environment.

ONTOGENY AND PHYLOGENY

Having suggested an evolutionary theoretical rationale for natural selection for increased adaptability, we now need to discuss specific mechanisms whereby this increased adaptability could actually be selected for. We also need to examine the evidence that natural selection for this increased adaptability may have been especially characteristic of hominid evolution, for *Homo sapiens* is certainly among the most adaptable of all species. The focus in this section will thus be on fleshing out the abstract theoretical concept of environmental tracking with an analysis of evolutionary processes which could contribute to increased adaptability in our own lineage. Put another way, the purpose of this section is to suggest that there are good evolutionary biological reasons to believe that *Homo sapiens* is an animal unique by virtue of natural selection for increased adaptability.

K-Selection

To briefly reiterate, the concept of environmental tracking advanced here holds that natural selection will tend to favor increased adaptability because the sufficient and most proximate causes of behavior are generally to be found in the organism's environment while only the necessary causes, or the general capacity for the behavior, are to be found in the organism's genotype. Thus, natural selection will tend to favor phenotypes which are less strictly determined by the nature of the genotype. The question here is how might natural selection produce an adaptive causal indeterminacy in the developmental effect of the genotype on the hominid phenotype? The answer may lie in the fact that the hominid line has been under extensive *K*-selection throughout most of its evolution.

It has been recognized in evolutionary biology for some time (e.g., Dobzhansky, 1950) that organisms differ systematically in the degree to which their survival and reproductive success is a direct function of their genotypes or phenotypes. The reason for this is that natural selection has two general modes of operation and the effects of natural selection vary along a continuum. At one end of the continuum, in environments where there are periodic catastrophic rates of selection and large numbers of a species are killed for essentially random reasons, natural selection tends to select for characteristics of the organism that allow it to rapidly recover from severe population depressions. This mode of natural selection is termed *r-selection*, for it tends to maximize the organism's *rate* of increase. At the other end of the continuum, in environments where selection pressures are less random and more constant, natural selection tends to select for characteristics of the organism that improve its efficiency in exploiting resources in the environment. This mode of natural selection is termed *K-selection*, for populations in relatively constant environments are typically at, or near, the inherent *carrying capacity* of that environment. Species are said to be "*r*-selected" or

"K-selected," but no species is ever purely r- or K-selected; there is always some compromise between the two selection modes and the difference between any r-selected species and K-selected species is always relative.

Because of the different environments and the corresponding differences in the mode of natural selection, a major difference between r- and K-selected species is in their reproductive strategies. As an adaptation to periodic population "boom and bust" cycles, the essence of the r-strategy is to transmit as many copies of parental genes as possible into the next generation as fast as possible. The selection pressures and evolutionary payoff here are obvious: individuals able to reproduce more rapidly and/or in greater numbers than others are disproportionately represented in the next generation by virtue of their head start in filling available niche space. On the other hand, as an adaptation to the high levels of intraspecific competition that are ordinarily characteristic of populations at or near carrying capacity, the essence of the K-strategy is to ensure that at least some copies of parental genes are represented in the next generation. In this case, because there is no payoff in having large numbers of offspring (for this would tend to increase already high rates of intraspecific competition and endanger the survival of any offspring at all), selection pressures are for increased efficiency in the exploitation of scarce resources in relatively crowded econiches. Most fishes, insects, and rodents are examples of relatively r-selected species, while large birds, elephants, the higher primates, and especially humans are examples of relatively K-selected species. Some of the more general characteristics of r- and K-selected species are listed in Table 1.1.

In many respects, the essence of K-selection is "fewer and better offspring." Probably the most common interpretation of "better" is increased efficiency in exploitation of resources, but another is that one aspect of "better" includes more sophisticated and complex environmental tracking mechanisms and a higher degree of adaptability (the ability to make successful responses to environmental perturbations). This is because with a more constant or predictable environment, high intraspecific competition, and more density-dependent and directed mortality, natural selection is simply less random and K-selected organisms are more likely to be selected against because of some real inefficiency in the way that they respond to particular environmental perturbations. Pianka (1970), for example, notes that K-selected organisms may be generally more adaptable by virtue of their relatively large size and long life: being larger they tend to have fewer predators and are "better buffered from changes in their physical environment" (1970:49); having longer lives, they have had to develop successful responses to a wider temporal range of environmental cycles and vicissitudes.

Table 1.1 General Characteristics of *r*- and *K*-Selected Species[a]

r-selected	(←Relative→)	*K*-selected
Variable or uncertain environment		More constant or predictable environment
Recolonization of empty niches		Constant occupation of same niche
Mortality rates often catastrophic, nondirected		Mortality rates steadier, more directed
Variability in population size		Stability in population size
Intraspecific competition nil		Intraspecific competition keen
Many offspring		Few offspring
Low parental investment		High parental investment
Small body size		Large body size
High infant mortality		Low infant mortality
Short birth interval		Long birth interval
Rapid development		Slow development
Early reproduction		Delayed reproduction
Short life		Long life
Social behavior often simple or weak		Social behavior often complex

[a] After Pianka (1970); Wilson (1975).

In a similar vein, summarizing an intriguing discussion of natural selection for increased "versatility," Vermeij (1973) stresses the broad associations between efficiency, complexity, and adaptability ("independence from external conditions"):

> There is . . .often a direct functional relationship between independence from external conditions on the one hand and effectiveness of resource exploitation on the other. At the same time, a relation between potential versatility and efficiency exists in the sense that fewer adaptive compromises are necessary if more parameters controlling form can vary independently; in other words, it is easier to optimize a function by using more variables without necessarily reducing the efficiency of other structures and functions (1973:473–474).

Thus, to the extent that *K*-selection is characteristic of hominid evolution (and we have all the *K*-selected traits; but see also below), we have an evolutionary biological mechanism for natural selection for increased adaptability in *Homo sapiens*.

K-Selection and Neoteny

Probably the most pervasive way that *K*-selection has operated to produce "fewer and better offspring" has been through selection for patterns of individual development that are retarded relative to ancestral species. The natural selection for more efficient or adaptable life history strategies or developmental chronologies is well-established in evolutionary theory (e.g., Cutler, 1976; Gadgil and Bossert, 1970; Stearns, 1976) and the hormonal bases of rates of physical growth and development and sexual maturation, while imperfectly understood, are known to have a genetic component (Tanner, 1978). Retarded development is a characteristic of K-selected species and represents one dimension of their generally more complex and finely tuned mechanisms for tracking the environment through behavior. Retarded development seems to have been selected for in populations at or near carrying capacity because with a relatively long period of infant dependency and relatively delayed sexual maturity, individuals become more efficient in exploiting resources (if only because they have more protected time for learning about their environments before they reproduce).

At the same time, there is also a complex interaction between selection pressures for more efficient life history strategies and those for the other hallmark of K-selection, increased parental investment. These interactions are such that selection for retarded development would be a concomitant of selection for increased parental investment, and vice versa. For example, because there is a high positive correlation between total life span and such developmental components of total life span as length of gestation, age at sexual maturity, birth spacing, and period of infant dependency (Cutler, 1976), direct selection for prolonged periods of infant dependency and/or delayed sexual maturity will tend to be associated with increased life span. Prolonged periods of infant dependency and delayed sexual maturity will exert selection pressure for increased parental investment because parents must be vigilant for longer periods and may have to play a greater teaching role. Selection for longer life per se would also, by itself, give parents more time to invest in their offspring even well after the last one was born.

Another reason for natural selection for retarded development in some K-selected mammals stems directly from the adaptive effects of selection for increased parental investment. Goodman (1963), for example, notes that the evolution of the more efficient higher mammalian hemochorial placenta was a prerequisite for the development of the large hominid brain, for the neocortex is especially easily damaged by fetal hypoxia and a rich supply of both nutrients and oxygen is required for neural differentiation. He argues thus that the appearance of the more efficient hemochorial placenta could have engendered specific selection for delayed development in higher mammalian young. The reason for this is that the primitive mammalian epithelichorial placenta is less efficient than the higher mammalian hemochorial placenta in that the former maintains a greater separation between the maternal and fetal circulations while the latter permits more effective placental transfer by bringing the maternal and fetal circulations into more intimate contact. This constitutes greater parental investment in higher mammals with the more efficient hemochorial placenta. Goodman notes too, however, that the closer contact between higher mammal maternal and fetal circulations could well bring the maternal immune system into play as a significant prenatal environmental factor to which the higher mammalian fetus would have to adapt because any new genetic material, from whatever source, would create new fetal proteins which would more easily cross the hemochorial placenta and would thus more easily stimulate the maternal immune system to produce antibodies against the new protein. When this occurred the survival and normal development of the fetus would be increasingly problematical. Goodman suggests that under these conditions there would be selection for reduced genetic heterogeneity in early hominid populations and selection for a shortened period of gestation and/or for the postponement of the expression of new genetic material until after birth. New genetic material which was expressed only postnatally would have the selective advantage of not provoking the maternal immunological system, but postponing the expression of new genetic material until after birth would also have the effect of postponing the development of the hominid child, making him or her even more helpless at birth and requiring even more postnatal parental investment.

The selection pressures for retarded development and for increased parental investment interact in another way as well. On a *scala naturae* the *K*-selective trend toward increased parental investment is clearly evident in such major evolutionary steps as internal fertilization, internal gestation, lactation, and the development of close maternal-offspring bonding. With each of these steps there was an increase in the probability of survival of zygotes, fetuses, newborns, and infants, but there was at the same time a corresponding decrease in the total number of offspring any female could bear during her lifetime because increased parental investment, by observation and definition (Trivers, 1972), lowers the parent's ability to invest in *other* offspring. What one gains in "quality" (increased survivorship), one loses in "quantity." Consider, for example, increased parental investment through lengthening the period of gestation: by investing in a fetus for several months a mammalian female reduces the total number of offspring she might bear during her entire life if she invested in the fetus for only a few weeks. One aspect of *K*-selection for increased parental investment then is a corresponding selection pressure for a longer life during which parents may increase their reproductive potential simply by bearing and rearing more offspring.

Lovejoy (1981) suggests that this interplay between the *K*-selective pressures for prolonged development-prolonged life and increased parental investment had a determining role in early hominid evolution. His argument is that

> ... the total reproductive rate of a primate species can remain constant with pro-
> gressive increases in longevity only if the crude mortality rate is correspondingly
> reduced. Actual mortality rate is dependent on both maximum life potential, a
> genetic factor, and environmental interaction. Deaths caused by predation, accident,
> parasitism, infection, failure of food supply, and so forth, are at least partially
> stochastic events beyond the complete control of the organism. Only if mechanisms
> are developed to increase an organism's resistance to such factors can the effects of
> increased longevity be reproductively accommodated. Strong social bonds, high
> levels of intelligence, intense parenting, and long periods of learning are among the
> factors used by higher primates to depress environmentally induced mortality. It is of
> some interest that such factors also require greater longevity (for brain development,
> learning, acquisition of social and parenting skills) and that they constitute reciprocal
> links leading to greater longevity (1981:343).

In Lovejoy's model of early hominid evolution it is this reciprocal feedback between prolonged development-prolonged life span and increased parental investment that sets up the selection pressures for the later hominid evolution of bipedalism, the separation of roles by sex, human sexual morphology and behavior, the home base, the nuclear family, and the development and elaboration of male parental investment. Lovejoy points out that alternate models of human origins have tended to emphasize "singular, extraordinary traits of later human evolution" (1981:348), and one of the attractions of his model is that it derives these later, uniquely human traits from a well-established baseline of K-selection in the higher primates.

Stephen Jay Gould has also recently (1977) developed a model of human evolution that emphasizes the singular role of K-selection and retarded development. The thrust of his argument is that the most important determinant of human evolution is the increasing K-selective trend toward neoteny. Neoteny is defined as the retention of the juvenile characteristics of ancestors by their adult descendants and it is brought about by natural selection for retarded rates of somatic development. Gould is in no way arguing that ontogeny recapitulates phylogeny. Ontogeny does not recapitulate phylogeny. Because evolution is opportunistic, building on what it has already produced, the earliest embryological and developmental stages tend to be conserved while evolution adds later stages on to them. Therefore, ontogeny does not recapitulate phylogeny, but ontogeny tends to recapitulate the earlier ontogenetic stages of ancestors (cf. Konner, 1977). The effect is that the early developmental forms of ancestors and the early developmental forms of descendants tend to resemble each other more than the later, adult stages do. Gould takes pains to demonstrate that the old argument is simply silly, but he also argues that the acrimony and silliness surrounding this debate for nearly 100 years has made suspect and unfashionable various attempts to analyze the relationship between ontogeny and phylogeny. Including evidence from zoology embryology, paleontology, population genetics, and from recent research in gene regulation, Gould amply demonstrates that the study of ontogeny has a major place in evolutionary biology, and his book should also help to narrow the gulf between those geneticists who see only the determining power of the genotype and those embryologists who see only the development of the phenotype.

The cornerstone of Gould's model of hominid evolution is that there was natural selection for retarded somatic development because individuals possessing the morphological and behavioral effects of retarded development (i.e., neoteny) had a greater reproductive success and were more adaptive and efficient in exploiting resources in a highly K-selective regime. Retarded or delayed development may be accomplished by natural selection for the extension or prolongation of the *period* of growth and/or for retardation of the *rate* or growth. The effect is that the appearance of the adult form in a descendant is delayed relative to its appearance in an ancestor. Natural selection for heterochrony (changes in rates or periods of growth) may produce dramatic evolutionary changes because different aspects of morphology or behavior may develop at different rates: just as the principle of mosaic evolution describes how body parts evolve at different rates, so the principle of allometry describes how body parts may grow and develop at different rates.

The major adaptive significance of neoteny in K-selective environments stems from two related effects of retarded development. First, by postponing sexual maturity (by slowing the rate of somatic growth and/or prolonging its period), an aspect of morphology or behavior is simply given more time to grow. With more time to grow, neotenous, K-selected organisms thus tend to have long lives and large body sizes, two features that by themselves tend to "buffer" the animal against environmental perturbations (Pianka, 1970). Second, and especially significant in hominid evolution, by slowing the rate of somatic growth and/or extending its period, an aspect of morphology or behavior is also given more time to differentiate. Growth is not a unidimensional increase in size, but obviously also includes development, differentiation, and an increase in organizational complexity. Because neotenous organisms develop for relatively longer periods, morphological, neuroendocrine, and behavioral organization can proceed further than they did in ancestral forms, and this increase in organizational complexity by itself tends to increase adaptability because it increases "independence from external conditions" (Vermeij, 1973)—which is the essence and function of more sophisticated environmental tracking systems.

There are many aspects of human morphology and behavior that qualify as examples of neoteny, but one aspect of prolonged development that is most significant in this context of increased differentiation is the extension of the period of growth of the human brain. A good way to see this extended development is to look at neonatal cranial capacity as a percentage of adult cranial capacity in a number of species: in many mammals, it is virtually 100%; in rhesus monkeys it is 60%, in chimpanzees about 40%, and in humans it drops to only 23% (Gould, 1977:371–372). It has also been estimated that neonatal australopithecines had a cranial capacity somewhere between 24 and 37% of the adult—showing a degree of retarded development intermediate between the Pongids and Homo (Leutenegger, 1972 in Gould, 1977). Similarly, Holt *et al.* (1975) plotted brain weight against body weight from early in prenatal development to adult weights in four primate species, including humans. Interestingly, all four species showed the same rate of prenatal growth. However, in the three monkey and ape species, the prenatal growth rate fell off dramatically at around the time of birth while in humans, the high rate of prenatal brain growth was extended for a full 2 years after birth. Some part of this greatly extended period of growth in humans is due to the general K-selective pressure for retarded development, but a large part of it is also due to the unique selection pressure in hominids for "premature" birth so that the increasingly large head of the newborn may pass through the pelvic girdle of the mother; the pelvis, of course, is under a selection pressure for narrowing as an adaptation for bipedal locomotion [possibly also due in part to K-selection for neoteny (Gould, 1977:378)].

This great extension of the period of hominid brain growth has a number of implications. Gould, for example, suggests that extending the period of brain growth might account for some portion of the marked and sudden increase in hominid cranial capacity from an australopithecine average of only about 500 cm^3 to a modern *Homo sapiens* average of over 1300 cm^3 in only 2 million years. Gould's neoteny hypothesis is not incompatible with any of the several other hypotheses advanced to explain this sudden increase, but is an attractive candidate for primacy because, as in Lovejoy's model (Gould, 1977), brain enlargement through prolonged development follows quite automatically from the well-established baseline of high rates of K-selection in the great apes. That the australopithecines already had relatively retarded development is seen from Leutenegger's data on neonatal cranial capacity cited above, and from Mann's (1975) data on australopithecine dental wear gradients. Mann suggests that the australopithecines had already achieved an extended period of development because of a strong correlation between order of molar eruption and amount of dental wear, indicating that there was sufficient time between eruptions for such wear to occur.

Perhaps the most far-reaching implication of this K-selection for greatly extended periods of hominid brain growth lies in its effects on the ontogeny of early hominids and the reciprocal selection pressures that this neoteny itself would begin to exert. For at least 2 million years newborn hominids were presented to their social and physical environments for as long as 2 years with brains that were less mature, less developed, and less different-iated than those of their immediate ancestors, the pongids and transitional hominids. Accordingly, for 2 million years natural selection operated on phenotypes that were more flexible, more sensitive, or responsive to their social and physical environments than had earlier been the case. Common to all developmental sciences is the observation that earlier developmental stages are more open and flexible than later ones. Lynch and Gall (1979), for example, in a recent review of neurobiological concepts of developmental plasticity, concluded that the available evidence indicates that " . . . the most dramatic examples of nervous system flexibility were found in im-mature animals" (1979:138).

An analogous phenomenon is seen in the earliest phases of imprinting, where precocial birds will follow a wide variety of stimuli; in later stages, only those stimuli associated with the original imprinting object will elicit following. Similarly, children are more sensitive or responsive to the phon-ology and syntax of their first language than they are to subsequent languages. Moreover, there is a likely neurological basis for this flexibility in slowly developing organisms:

> During ontogeny, there is evidence of a progressive reduction of the capacity to form new neuronal connections and to modify existing ones. This reduction occurs at different times in different classes of neurons, so that those which are generated late in ontogeny and those which mature slowly have the greatest modifiability in the mature animal. According to this theory, the modifiability of neuronal connections in the adult is regarded as a continuation of developmental processes that are much more pronounced in embryos (Jacobson, 1969:547 quoted in Gould, 1977:401).

Thus, prolongation of the period of hominid development also prolonged the flexibility characteristic of early developmental stages into later develop-mental stages, perhaps even adulthood.

In addition to increasing and prolonging developmental flexibility how-ever, K-selection for retarded development would also have created re-ciprocal selection pressures affecting the social environment of hominid infancy in fundamental ways. With the initial K-selected prolongation of development, the best avenue to parental reproductive success would have been through increased parental investment. With the marked secondary increase in the early helplessness of the hominid infant as a result of restruc-turing the pelvis for bipedal locomotion, the best and perhaps only avenue to parental reproductive success was through even greater increases in parental investment. According to most models of human origins (e.g., Love-

joy, 1981; Gould, 1977), the only remaining avenue to increased parental investment was through increasing *male* parental investment specifically. Mammalian morphology and physiology ensured that the bulk of
parental investment (e.g., gestation, lactation) would remain the province of
hominid females, but high levels of intelligence and sociability and complex
social organizations (e.g., elaborate dominance relations, matrilineal kin
groups, some sharing and the capacity for at least transient pair bonding)
among the higher primates made it possible for males to invest significantly
in offspring through investment in females. This is a likely basis for such
uniquely hominid (or human) features as the loss of estrus, the home base,
sharing and the sexual division of labor, and the nuclear family. All of these
adaptations to prolonged development radically altered the environment of
hominid infancy by making it more intensely and constantly social. It would
be more *widely* social as well, increasing the opportunity for interaction
with others of both sexes and a wider age range: with prolonged development, younger siblings of both sexes would more frequently be born before
older siblings had acquired much independence; with prolonged life spans,
grandparents and other older adults of both sexes would more frequently
still be alive before children had acquired much independence. Prolonged
periods of development in such groups, along with the higher primate
capacity to form close maternal–infant bonds and the neotenous early flexibility and sensitivity to social–environmental learning, may have set the
stage, some 2 million years ago, for the extension of these emotional bonds
to others within the group. If one takes a behavioral ecological approach to
the evolution of extreme sociality rather than a strictly phylogenetic approach, the social carnivores may provide an instructive parallel: not only
are they among the most social of all nonprimate mammals, they are also
relatively retarded in their development. Thus it is more than just a figure of
speech to say: "Retardation is the biological basis for societal life" (Versluys
and Lorenz, 1939 quoted in Gould, 1977:403).

There are then, good evolutionary biological reasons for viewing *Homo
sapiens* as an animal unique by virtue of its phylogenetic history of natural
selection for increased adaptability. The abstract theoretical concept of
environmental tracking suggests that in the long run flexibility or adaptability in immediate behavioral responses to environmental perturbations
should be selected for because this immediate sensitivity or responsivity to
the environment tends to protect and conserve the adaptive potential of the
slower, deeper, and more costly response capacities latent in the gene pool.
The phenomenon of *K*-selection provides a specific evolutionary mechanism whereby natural selection could achieve an increase in the flexibility
or adaptability of response capacities because under *K*-selection, mortality
depends less on random factors and more on the efficiency of the organism

in a specific environment. At least in a general sense, the phylogenetic history of K-selection in the human line is very deep: mammals tend to be relatively more K-selected than other classes, primates tend to be relatively more K-selected than other orders, and the fossil hominids may have been relatively more K-selected than other primate families are now. Certainly, modern humans are among the most K-selected of all species. Perhaps the most widespread and significant mechanism whereby K-selection tends to increase adaptability is that of retarded development. With K-selected, neotenous retardation of somatic development, hominid infants were not only simply given more protected time for learning, they were also better able to learn, being presented to their environments for longer periods in a state that was less final, less differentiated, and at the same time, more sensitive, more responsive, and more flexible. Under these developmental conditions (for a minimum of 2, and as many as 10 or 15 million years), the survival of the hominid infant depended more and more on steadily increasing and complex forms of female and male parental investment. At the same time, because the hominid infant was in such a relatively unfinished, sensitive, responsive, and flexible condition for longer periods, natural selection on hominid infants and juveniles (which must have been intense) would have been increasingly on the developmental effects of their early sensitivity, responsivity, or flexibility. Being more sensitive or responsive to their early environments, and living in increasingly complex, intense, and permanent social (and cultural) environments, the survival of hominid infants would depend more and more on their capacity to be socialized. This provides a quantum increase in adaptability by making it possible to preserve adaptive responses to environmental perturbations in the individual's social-cultural environment.

These developmental conditions in early hominid phylogeny would also provide fertile ground for operation of the phenomenon of genetic assimilation. First described by Waddington (1953), genetic assimilation is an ontogenetic process whereby a change in the developmental environment may produce dramatic changes in adult phenotypes which persist even if the developmental environment returns to its preexisting state. In his classic experiment Waddington showed that if normal *Drosophila* flies, who have a distinctive, species-typical pattern of veins on their wings, are subjected to heat stress as pupae, they will develop without the normal wing-vein pattern. After exerting artificial selection for this new, abnormal pattern of wing veins, Waddington found that the deviant phenotype appeared consistently in large numbers of flies, and he was able to isolate a strain of *Drosophila* showing the abnormal pattern even when they were not subjected to heat stress as pupae. Thus, the new trait is said to have been genetically assimilated. This is not an example of Lamarckian inheritance, for what Waddington was doing was selecting for the gene complex that *permitted* the development of the new pattern of wing veins; as these genes became more numerous through Waddington's selection, they permitted development of the new wing-vein pattern even in the environment in which it would not previously develop. In the same manner, even a gradual change in the environment of early hominid development could result in a dramatic change in hominid ontogeny. Lumsden and Wilson put it this way:

> By cultural experimentation and the continual exploration of new environments, protocultural species are likely to test the potential of the genes that prescribe epigenetic rules of behavior and to produce novel responses. . . . When these responses confer selective advantage, the genes possessed by individuals tend to shift into a new frequency distribution, prescribing epigenetic rules that channel development toward a new response (1981:244).

The increase in early hominid parental investment might well have created an environment where the retardation of development conferred a selective advantage on infants and children who could better enculturate themselves. Because of the adaptability accruing from more sophisticated and complex cultural patterns, the genes allowing retarded development would be likely to be widely assimilated.

ADAPTABILITY AND DEVELOPMENT

This evolutionary biological view of human phylogeny as one of long and intense natural selection for greater behavioral adaptability through delayed development has a number of implications for theory and research in child development, especially cross-cultural child development, the discipline best suited to the study of the ontogeny of human adaptability. The purpose of this section is to discuss some of these implications and thereby to establish points of contact between theory in evolutionary biology and theory in child development.

The most immediate yet general implication of this view is the central notion that behavioral plasticity or adaptability is probably the most vital and far-reaching survival mechanism of *Homo sapiens* in that it thus provides both a reason for focusing research on the nature and determinants of adaptability and a powerful rationale for models of human development that emphasize such adaptability in the developing child. Because adaptation is seen in terms of hierarchically interconnected environmental tracking systems, that is, a process that is not limited to changes in the genotype over generations, but includes, may depend upon, and begins with the most immmediate behavioral responses of individuals to environmental perturbations, it is thus possible to view the process of development itself as one of adaptation. This in turn makes it logical to employ an evolutionary biological strategy in child development research. The essence of this strategy is simply to determine what the environment will "do" to the child if the child does not perform a particular behavior in question. The steps in this sort of research are: (1) the identification of environmental perturbations; (2) the analysis of the relative success of these responses in alleviating the stresses associated with the perturbation; and (3) the analysis of the mechanisms whereby the successful responses are preserved. In principle, the value of this approach to human development is that it would provide empirical data on just how adaptable the human infant is; we know that the human infant is highly adaptable, but we also know that the human infant is not a *tabula rasa*. Knowledge of the determinants of developmental adaptability, and of the limits to this adaptability, would have great implications for theory and research in evolutionary biology, child development, anthropology, and other sciences concerned with the nature-culture problem. It would also, of course, have immense practical implications for early intervention programs, social and educational policy, and clinical developmental psychology.

Perturbations in Attachment

Because adaptation is a process occurring over time, it is necessary to study the responses of individuals to real environmental perturbations rather than to take relatively arbitrary before and after measures, the choice of which is usually based on hypothetical models. There are a variety of pathways to a successful adaptation and many, if not most, adaptations represent a compromise between two or more environmental perturbations (cf. Tinbergen, 1965). Thus, in order to study adaptation, it is first necessary to identify a perturbation—a departure from some mean value of a component of the environment that is experienced by the individual as stressful. For a number of reasons (many of which will be developed in greater detail in the next two chapters), one of the most likely places to identify a developmental perturbation is in the interaction of mother and infant during the process of attachment formation.

In attachment theory, certain disruptions or difficulties in mother–infant interaction are likely to constitute a developmental perturbation for the infant because they interfere with the attachment process. In John Bowlby's (1969) view, in the "environment of evolutionary adaptedness" of the higher primates and the hominids, predator pressure was sufficiently severe, constant, and widespread to ensure that mothers and infants were in close physical proximity. From the infant's point of view, this proximity was brought about through a set of environmentally stable, "high stake," genotypically determined emotions which provided the impetus to a series of behaviors which had the set-goal of proximity to mother. These behaviors are the so-called attachment behaviors: crying, clinging, sucking, following, and smiling. (Robson [1967] suggested that mutual gazing with mother also be added to this list.) Bowlby interprets the dynamics of mother–infant interaction and the development of attachment in systems theory terms: various qualities of the mother and her behavior, and of the child's environment (including his or her internal, physiological environment) are innate sign stimuli for the perception of a situation as fit or not to activate one or another of a range of behavioral subsystems to reach this genotypically determined set-goal of proximity to mother or other attachment figure. The infant's appearance, behavior, and state may, in turn, act as releasers or reinforcers for further maternal care or interaction.

When there are problems or perturbations in mother–infant interaction, the attachment bond may be distorted and the child is placed at risk for the subsequent development of a variety of emotional and behavioral problems. Bowlby (1965, 1969, 1973, 1980) has been repeatedly explicit about the long-term sequelae of disrupted attachment relationships in infancy, and has suggested that some adult predispositions to anxiety, depression, fear, or anger may stem from "anxious attachment" in infancy. In extreme cases of deprivation, the absence of mutually responsive interaction and severely disturbed attachment may be precursors of failure to thrive, childhood schizophrenia, infantile autism, and even death.

Ainsworth and her colleagues (Ainsworth et al., 1978) have emphasized more than Bowlby the quality of the mother–infant intereaction itself rather than its metric quantification and dissection into component parts. From extensive research with the "strange situation test" (Ainsworth et al., 1971; Ainsworth et al., 1978), it has been shown that a determinant of the major dimensions of individual differences in patterns of attachment is the mother's "sensitivity" or "responsiveness" to her child. Ainsworth and her colleagues have been less concerned than Bowlby and others about specifying the long-term effects of disrupted attachment, but in documenting the determinants of individual differences in patterns of attachment they have clearly shown short-term effects strongly suggesting that early perturbations in mother-infant interaction could have long-term effects.

The strange situation test is a standardized laboratory observation procedure in which mothers and their infants (typically 12–18 months old) interact under a variety of conditions. The test consists of seven 3-minute episodes in which the infant is observed, for example, as he or she explores the novel room environment with the mother present, as the mother leaves the room, as she returns to the room, and as he or she reacts to a stranger with and without the mother present. This test has been extensively used and validated (e.g., Sroufe and Waters, 1977; Waters, Wippman, and Sroufe, 1979) and has consistently revealed three major dimensions of individual differences in attachment patterns. Infants in the first group are characterized as having "secure attachments" to their mothers (Ainsworth calls this Group B). These infants are clearly interested in mother and enjoy interacting with her, they respond with clear signs of protest when she leaves the room and clear signs of pleased greeting when she returns, and they are able to use her as a "secure base" from which to explore the room. Infants in the second group are characterized as having "anxious/avoidant attachments" to their mothers (Ainsworth's Group A). These infants tend to avoid contact with mother after she returns to the room or tend to ignore her attempts to initiate interaction. These infants also may show normal levels of exploration of the room, but show little desire for proximity to mother or for interaction with her. Infants in the third group are characterized as having "anxious/resistant attachments" to their mothers (Ainsworth's Group C), and tend to resist contact or interaction with mother on her return to the room, and/or they may fail to be comforted by her presence after she returns, and they show little or no inclination to explore the strange room.

Not only have these three basic patterns of attachment been replicated in several studies, Ainsworth and her colleagues have also shown that early patterns of mother–infant interaction are related to each of the three patterns. Briefly, infants judged securely attached at 12 months in the strange situation test had mothers who, during the child's first year of life, were ranked highest on sensitivity to, acceptance of, cooperation with, and accessibility to their children. In contrast, mothers of the other two groups were ranked lowest on sensitivity, cooperation, and accessibility. Mothers of the "anxious/avoidant" and "anxious/resistant" infants differed, however, on how accepting they were of their children; mothers of the "anxious/ avoidant" infants scored low on acceptance while the mothers of the "anxious/resistant" infants scored higher on acceptance. The differences between these two groups of infants is perhaps best summarized in Ainsworth's words:

> To the extent that a baby's interaction with his mother has been characteristically disturbed by her rejection of him, he responds to the stresses of the strange situation with defensive proximity-avoiding behavior, which competes with and tends to block off all attachment behavior. To the extent that mother-infant interaction has been made disharmonious through maternal interference or ignoring, but in which maternal rejection is either moderate or very well masked, a baby seems unable to defend himself, reacting with great distress in the separation episodes and with ambivalence to his mother in the reunion episodes (Ainsworth, Bell, and Stayton, 1971:49).

While there has been some debate over the definition and measurement of attachment and in the actual scope of the concept itself (e.g., Weinraub, Brooks, and Lewis, 1977; Parsley and Rabinowitz, 1975), increasing numbers of researchers have taken the view that the human infant is socially competent at birth and phylogenetically endowed with the capacities to elicit behaviors from caregivers that result in increased proximity and/or progressively longer or more complex social and verbal interaction (e.g., Bell, 1968, 1974; Brazelton, Koslowski, and Main, 1974; Stern, 1974; J. S. Watson, 1967, 1972). Thus, in spite of disagreement on some particulars, there seems to be a widespread concensus that " . . . socialization results from reciprocal mother-infant responsiveness' (Ainsworth, Bell, and Stayton, 1974;118).

Ainsworth and her students and colleagues have explored many of the short-term sequelae of maternal sensitivity and responsiveness in early interactions and of the corresponding individual differences in patterns of attachment. Many of these short-term effects demonstrate that less-than-optimum early interactions and attachment could diminish the infant's capacity to successfully respond to subsequent developmental tasks or perturbations. Many of these short-term effects also suggest how much selection pressure there might have been for the maternal and infant behavioral capacities underlying the development of secure attachment. They have shown, for example, that mothers who were highly responsive to their infants' cries have infants who cried less as they developed and who were also more communicative in other modes (e.g., lability of facial expression, gesture, and nonfret vocalization) (Bell and Ainsworth, 1972). They also showed that infant obedience to mothers' commands was positively correlated with maternal sensitivity and responsiveness (Stayton, Hogan, and Ainsworth, 1971). Both of these findings are relevant to a consideration of the evolution of human attachment: not only would higher rates of infant crying be of possible significance in predation, it is known to be characteristic of children at high risk for abuse (Freidrich and Boroskin, 1976; Frodi, 1981; Lynch, 1975; Richards, 1976). Egeland and Sroufe (1981) have recently shown that early maltreatment (abuse and/or neglect) is significantly more likely to lead to "anxious/avoidant" or "anxious/resistant" attachment than is normal mothering in a sample of impoverished, high-risk mothers. Because of the relationship between crying and maternal sensitivity/responsiveness, the latter could also be quite directly related to the infant's capacity for language development and thus enculturation, for Shaw (1977) has shown that language-delayed children often have a history of irritable and excessive crying. Connell (1976), examining the relationship between attachment and language development, found that infants judged securely attached at 12 months had, along with their mothers, longer vocabulary lists at 18 months than did the mothers and infants in the two "anxiously" attached groups. Main (1973), in a similar study of attachment and cognitive development, found that those infants who were securely attached at 12 months were significantly advanced over the "anxiously" attached infants on the Bayley Scales of Mental Development at 20.5 months. Infant obedience, language development, and general cognitive functioning would have had, and may still have, direct survival implications as well as implications for the child's ability to socialize or enculturate himself through his growing capacity to internalize adult commands or directions by categorizing them into general "rules and recipes" for appropriate cultural behavior.

These studies, along with Waters' (1978) evidence for the stability of individual differences in attachment, suggest that the later effects of the early experiences that contribute to any particular pattern of attachment are not ephemeral and that there is good reason to expect that the disruption of early mother–infant interaction could constitute a developmental perturbation for the child because of the way that these effects tend to decrease the child's capacity to successfully respond to subsequent developmental tasks and perturbations. Thus, to study adaptation, and to thereby begin to outline human environmental tracking systems and the nature and determinants of adaptability in human development, disrupted early mother–infant interaction can be initially identified as a likely perturbation.

Adaptability and Continuity in Development

For the study of development as adaptation, however, the identification of a perturbation cannot be left only to high theoretical expectations or previously published research results. In spite of such high expectations and previous reports of developmental continuity, it has proven notoriously difficult for child development to demonstrate consistently the effects of early experience (or constitution) on later behavior. One of the reasons for this failure is that with few exceptions, child development theory and research design have given too little credit to the child's adaptability—his or her ability to make successful responses to environmental perturbations. To study adaptation the effects of early experience must be sought immediately after the experience itself and followed longitudinally. Seeking the effects of early experience immediately after the experience itself will at least rule out the distinct possibility that the immediate response (the immediate effects of the early experience) may actually prevent any long-term sequelae because the immediate response is a successful response to an environmental perturbation. Thus, for studying adaptation, it is necessary to look for behaviors that constitute a successful response to a perturbation immediately after the onset of the perturbation.

The questions of continuities in development and the effects of early experience on later behavior have especially concerned developmental psychologists over the past few years. Many studies have simply failed to demonstrate such effects in spite of otherwise sound theoretical expectations and many more have failed to replicate previous reports of continuities and later effects, especially when the replications were conducted cross-culturally. Jerome Kagan (Kagan, Kearsley, and Zelazo, 1978; Kagan, 1980, 1981) has recently reviewed the issues and data surrounding the questions of continuities and the effects of early experience and has argued that for the most part there is insufficient evidence to justify developmental psychology's emphasis on early experience as a major determinant of later behavior. He argues instead that biological maturation (especially neuro-endocrine maturation) accounts for more stability and continuity in development than early experience by itself. He suggests that maturational forces will tend to ensure similar developmental pathways in spite of variability in early experience. To illustrate his position he presents an intriguing quote from Freud, who, he says, was moving toward a similar biological-maturational view toward the end of his career:

> The phylogenetic foundation has so much the upper hand over personal accidental experience that it makes no difference whether a child has really sucked at the breast or has been brought up on the bottle and never enjoyed the tenderness of a mother's care. In both cases the child's development takes the same path (Freud, 1964:188; quoted in Kagan, 1981:61).

In addition to Kagan's argument that there is simply a dearth of evidence for the effects of early experience on later behavior, Bateson (1976), Dunn (1976), and Sameroff (1975; Sameroff and Chandler, 1975) have all recently explored the possibility that one reason for the lack of such evidence for later effects is that there has been virtually no attempt to locate and describe hypothetical "developmental control mechanisms." In a passage strikingly similar to Freud's, Sameroff puts the problem this way:

> Despite the great variety and range of influences on development, there are a surprisingly small number of developmental outcomes. Evolution appears to have built into the human organism regulative mechanisms to produce normal developmental outcomes under all but the most adverse of circumstances (1975:283).

Perhaps the best example of how development produces normal outcomes under a great variety and range of influences is the apparent capacity of any human infant to learn any culture. Just as bands of Japanese macaques and chimpanzees, for example, have local protocultural traditions which infants of these species learn (Itani and Nishimura, 1973; McGrew, 1977), there is no reason to doubt that even at the earliest stages of hominid evolution there were analogous cultural differences between hominid groups and that hominid infants had to learn their own group's particular variety of culture. Throughout human evolution the environment of infancy has included social and cultural diversity. Cross-cultural studies of child development have traditionally emphasized this diversity almost exclusively (cf. LeVine, 1970) and together with class, ethnic, and simple individual differences within one society, the evidence for variability was so strong that the conclusion that the child was a *tabula rasa* seemed inescapable. But the *tabula rasa*, even if it existed, would, by definition, have to be part of the human genotype. To the extent that human infants are able to develop normally under a great range of circumstances, they can be said to demonstrate a high degree of plasticity in their capacity to respond successully to perturbations in their environments. The fact that any child can apparently learn any culture would seem to be a good example of the kind of optimal strategy of evolution outlined by Slobodkin and Rapoport. Plasticity of response itself may be the defining quality of the human genotype, selected for because this plasticity simply made it possible for infants to learn a culture that was itself successful in storing information that allowed individuals to make successful, adaptive responses to environmental perturbations. Thus, what was once considered evidence for the *tabula rasa* is now better considered evidence for adaptability.

In any case, the *tabula rasa* does not exist. While the infant has a great capacity to learn that is essentially genotypically determined, this capacity is not infinite but seems to follow epigenetic rules (cf. Lumsden and Wilson, 1981, especially Chapters 2 and 3). At one level the infant's behavior is limited by simple physiology and maturational stage; infants are not so plastic, for example, that they can ignore hunger pains. At a higher level, the infant seems to be the bearer of the phylogenetically determined capacity to respond to internal and external stimuli such that an attachment is formed between him and an attachment figure. One of the major contributions of attachment theory is the impetus it has given to empirical research which has shown that far from being a *tabula rasa*, the child is fully an interactor in his or her own right who has a significant influence on the behavior of others (Bell, 1968, 1971, 1974; Lewis and Rosenblum, 1974). At a still higher level, it may also be that the infant is the bearer of phylogenetically determined capacities to influence these others in such a way that he also influences the direction or trajectory of his development.

The evidence for developmental control mechanisms, or the capacity of the child to direct his or her own development, is limited, but developmental psychologists have recently begun to see the potential value of Waddington's (1975a) concept of the "epigenetic landscape." The epigenetic landscape is a model of developmental processes which respond to environmental perturbations in such a way that they tend to "push" the developing organism back onto the normal trajectory or pathway of development. Waddington developed his concept of epigenesis to model embryological tissue differentiation: early in embryological development one bit of tissue has the potential to develop into a wide variety of organ systems, but as development progresses, that bit of tissue becomes more and more "canalized" by the epigenetic landscape. Waddington conceived of the bit of tissue as a ball rolling down a valley which had smaller valleys branching off it. At the top of the valley, the ball *could* roll into any of the smaller branching valleys, but as it rolls down one valley, further "choices" are denied it, and at the end of the last valley (a particular organ system) the ball comes to rest and development is complete. Waddington does not specify what the slopes and valleys actually represent, but generally describes them as mechanisms that influence development. He goes further to suggest that if the system of valleys that guide the rolling ball on its normal

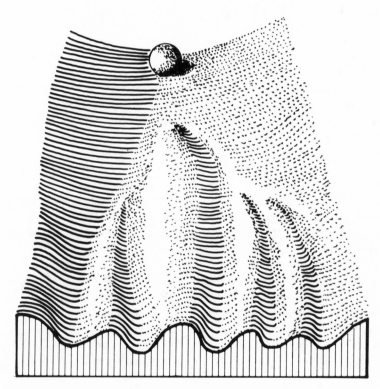

Fig. 1.2 Waddington's epigenetic landscape (redrawn from Waddington, 1975:259; by permission, New York Academy of Sciences).

developmental course is affected by an environmental perturbation (in his extended metaphor this is represented by a landslide in one of the valleys), there will be a tendency for the ball to roll up and around the blockage to return to the same path further down the valley.

Without question, Waddington's developmental metaphor is still only a metaphor, but is does have the virtue of helping us visualize what is currently the best example of a possible developmental control mechanism in action. In describing the phenomenon of "catch-up growth," Prader, Tanner, and von Harnack (1963) showed that if a child's ordinarily highly predictable growth trajectory were disrupted by some perturbation (e.g., disease, malnutrition), when the perturbation was removed the child would undergo a period of rapid "catch-up growth" during which the growth curve would be steeper than normal until it reached the point where the child would have been had he or she not become ill or malnourished. At this point growth velocity diminished and the normal growth trajectory was resumed.

In general terms, Bateson, Dunn, and Sameroff (like Lumsden and Wilson, 1981) suggest that there may be genotypical "rules" for development and that developmental processes may be to some extent predetermined and self-correcting in a way analogous to the phenomenon of catch-up growth. These rules of development may operate by laying out relatively unvarying developmental stages (e.g., Piaget, 1950) that tend to ensure that the child has the cognitive processes needed to handle the information concerning his environment as that environment itself changes as the child's abilities to learn and store information about the environment also increase. As the child's information processing capacities change according to these hypothetical rules, so too does the child's environment by virtue of his new abilities to know it and interact with it. The rules may also operate through the operation of feedback processes whereby the child compares the feedback from his environment to some "genotypically stored" representation of preferred values for that environment (cf. Bischof, 1975b). The behavioral adaptability or plasticity of the child is, so to speak, the raw material, the genotypical capacity to respond to his environment and its perturbations in such a way that he can establish for himself an optimum interaction with his environment that is at least partially defined by these preferred values. This optimum may be a particular growth curve or pattern of mother-infant interaction that we gloss under the term "attachment," and the response flexibility, the capacity of the child to rebound from environmental perturbations, provides the means for following an alternate pathway to the optimum height, weight, or interaction. With the view of the child as an actor able to influence the behavior of others around him and therefore also able to influence his own relationship with his environment, the observed plasticity of the child, the observed diversity of developmental outcomes, and the observed adaptability of children in spite of this diversity are beginning to suggest that except in the most extreme cases the child's development may be canalized, at least partially, by the child himself through the operation of epigenetic rules, and that there may be a variety of pathways to the state of adaptation.

In child development research there have not been enough longitudinal studies of sufficient length and detail to see very clearly how the concept of developmental control mechanisms might be applied to social-behavioral development, but there are a few suggestive studies (many of which are reviewed by Sameroff, 1975; Sameroff and Chandler, 1975; Dunn, 1976). For example, Werner and her colleagues (1971) followed the 670 children born in one year on the island of Kauai from birth to 10 years of age. As numerous retrospective studies had shown, severe congenital and perinatal stress factors were related to a variety of psychological and social difficulties at 20 months. By 10 years, however, these effects had disappeared—but only in children born to higher socioeconomic status (S.E.S.) families. The continuities revealed in many retrospective studies were not replicated, and the reason seems to be that there was something different about the interaction of the child with its environment in the higher S.E.S. families that counteracted the early deficits, whereas in the lower S.E.S. environments these deficits were unaffected or exacerbated. Werner and her colleagues did not focus their research on the behavior of the child as he or she interacted with caregivers so they could not specify how the child might have influenced his or her own development. In order to determine whether the child is using the influence he is known to have on the behavior of others, and therefore on aspects of his environment, the focus of research must be on interactive behavior. This must be the focus too if we wish to explore the development of environmental tracking systems and the notion that the child himself responds to environmental perturbations in such a way that he actually seeks for himself the short-term developmental path that will return him to the long-term, normal species path.

The possibility of developmental control mechanisms might even be implicit in some of the data on individual differences in attachment, where a powerful theory predicts that insensitive/unresponsive mothering and anxious attachment can have significant later effects and where numerous studies have actually documented such effects. As Dunn (1976) has noted, if maternal sensitivity/responsiveness is so crucial to the development of secure attachment and if secure attachment is a state that has been so crucial for infants' survival or at least normal development throughout human evolution, how is it that only about a third of Ainsworth's original sample of mothers were judged to have this all-important quality of sensitivity/responsiveness and how is it that only 57% of the infants could be judged to be securely attached? In other strange situation samples the number of infants judged securely attached reaches 73% (Aisworth et al., 1978) but in at least one only 39% were so judged (Tolan and Tomasini, 1977). It is not impossible that middle-class mothers in America are under such stress that between 27 and 61% of their infants fail to establish secure attachments, but it seems much more likely, as Dunn suggests, that the long-term effects of "insensitive" or "unresponsive" mothering are not completely relevant to the child's fitness and that children may have means of compensating for early anxious attachment. Long-term follow-up studies are needed, but it seems doubtful that the mental health profession or natural selection could now identify just those 43% of Ainsworth's original sample who were judged to be anxiously attached.

Thus, in spite of the fact that attachment theory so strongly suggests that mutually insensitive and unresponsive mother-infant interaction can constitute a significant developmental perturbation, and in spite of so many studies showing at least short-term effects, we must still reckon with the troublesome facts that anxious attachment does not always produce clear later effects, that the entire significance of early experience for later behavior is being questioned, and that the infant, who influences the behavior of others, may at the same time influence the direction of his or her own development. By studying development as adaptation it is possible to reconcile these apparently opposing positions. Following Bateson's (1976) argument on developmental control mechanisms, we need not discard the mutual responsiveness theory simply because it does not invariably have clear long-term effects:

> . . . a developmental control mechanisms whose preferred value drifts should not be dismissed as an irritating example of variability in biological material. Instead, the environmental conditions in which those drifts take place should be closely scrutinized since the modification in preferred value may have some obvious functional significance (1976:418).

It is possible, for example, at least in principle, that in some particular environments the behaviors underlying the classification of "anxious attachment" may represent an adaptive, short-term, alternate pathway to long-term appropriate developmental outcomes. What is needed is a very precise description of the environment of development, for if epigenetic developmental control mechanisms exist, they would come into operation when some "phylogenetically normal" developmental path or trajectory was blocked. It is necessary to know the adaptive significance of one developmental path in one environment and of another path in some other environment. In other words, one must identify perturbations in the environment of infancy, for it is these perturbations that block developmental pathways and that provide the stimuli to which children may respond adaptively.

But one must clearly go well beyond identification of the perturbation and describe and analyze the response of the child to the perturbation, for not only is the child's response the first step in the process of adaptation, it might also be the first step on an alternate pathway to normal development. Certainly it is only in this way that the very existence and nature of these hypothetical developmental control mechanisms could be determined.

Adaptability and the Social Context of Development

If one is going to study the response of the child to environmental perturbations one must consider the possibility that the success of the response may not depend only on the child, but that he or she may elicit a successful response to the perturbation from others and indeed, that interaction with others in the child's wider social context may counteract the effects of the perturbation. Until the late 1960's, a major focus in child development research was on the effect of parental attitudes and behavior on the growing child. In the past decade a new focus was on the effect of the child's behavior on his or her caretakers. The impetus for this paradigmatic shift stemmed primarily from Bowlby's emphasis on the biological survival value of infant attachment behavior and from Bell's (1968) argument that it was not inherently more parsimonious to attribute causal power to parental behavior than to infant behavior whenever the two were correlated. In the past few years, however, especially among anthropologists studying child development, there has been a growing awareness that neither the *tabula rasa* thesis nor the Bowlby-Bell antithesis are sufficiently broad in scope and that more attention should be directed toward describing the effects of the larger social context on early mother-infant interaction. While the most proximate determinant of the nature of mother–infant interaction may be the actual behavior of mother and infant, mothers and infants do not exist in social vacuums and data are accumulating to show that the nature of their interaction may be systematically influenced not only by the child's very opportunity for interaction with different numbers of others but also by the opportunity for interaction with others of different age/sex/kinship identities in certain social settings. Thus, to study the response of the infant to perturbations in mother–infant interaction, one cannot view their interaction in a social vacuum but must instead document the effects of the wider social context on their interaction and how interactions with others besides mother may affect the infant's response to perturbations in mother–infant interaction and how interactions with others may counteract the effects of these perturbations by providing an adaptive, alternate short-term pathway to normal developmental outcomes.

Of the several studies observing that the nature of mother–infant interaction is at least partially a function of variables that cannot be recorded in their interaction itself, those by John and Bea Whiting and their students and colleagues are most notable. For example, in their summary analysis of socialization data from each of the Six Cultures studies, Whiting and Whiting (1975) report that a major determinant of child behavior was the "status of the target," that is the age/sex/kinship identity of the person with whom the child was interacting. There was a strong, cross-cultural correlation between the status of the target and certain types or styles of interaction (e.g., interaction with infants was nurturant, interaction with parents was intimate-dependent and nonaggressive). From these and other findings, the Whitings argue that the primary socializing effects of parents and other caretakers is not so much in their direct, face-to-face effect on the child, but instead in their power to assign the child certain tasks or otherwise place him or her in certain social settings where the child will be surrounded by others of certain age/sex/kinship identities and where the child will thus tend to have a preponderance of certain types of interaction. In a more recent formulation of their approach, B. Whiting (1980) argues that knowing the age/sex/kinship identities of potential interactors in the social settings which occupy most of the child's time will allow one to predict characteristic patterns of interpersonal behavior. She argues further that there are a limited number of types of behavior that are satisfying in any interaction with certain age/sex/kinship statuses and that these patterns of interactive behavior are readily learned—more by trial and error than by explicit reward and punishment. Fundamental to the Whitings' approach is the fact that their data clearly demonstrate that the major determinants of the child's social setting, and thus his or her most characteristic types of interaction, are the subsistence ecological variables that determine group size and composition, daily activities, and the workloads of caretakers.

In addition to the age/sex/kinship identity of potential interactors, the simple number of others available for interaction may also be expected to affect the nature of early interactions, not only because the number may affect the age/sex/kinship distribution, but also because the number determines the child's opportunity for any interaction at all. In a study of infant development among the Logoli of Kenya, for example, Munroe and Munroe (1971) found that in large households infants were held significantly more often than in smaller, less dense households. Also, the larger the household, the more quickly someone (not necessarily the mother) responded to the child's cries (even when he or she was being held). Making the point that household size will affect the nature of early interactions in more global ways than holding and responding to cries, the Munroes reanalyzed Ainsworth's (1967) data on Ganda infant attachment behaviors and showed that the rated level of mother–infant attachment was inversely related to household density.

Much of the significance of the Whiting's approach for assessing the developmental impact of the larger social context on early development depends on the degree to which types of interaction learned in one setting may generalize to other settings with potential interactors of different age/sex/kinship identities. To some extent this generalization will depend on the number of different social settings that are available to the child, the frequency with which the child moves from one setting to the next, and the relative constancy of each setting throughout development. In any case, there is evidence that types of interactive behavior learned in one setting do generalize to other settings. For example, the Whitings found that an average of 26% of the variance in "intimate-dependent" behavior was accounted for by the age/sex/kinship identity of the interactor, as was 25% of the variance in "nurturant" behavior, 25% of the variance in "aggressive" behavior, and 31% of the variance in "sociable" behavior. Probably the best example of this sort of generalization comes, however, from a study by Carol Ember (1973). She found that Oyugis boys in Kenya who filled the role of child nurse for their infant siblings (because of a unique sex ratio; girls are preferred for this role) were also significantly more nurturant to noninfants than other boys who did not have to act as child nurses.

Most of the research conducted by the Whitings and their students and colleagues has been on children older than 3 years, but there is no reason to expect that the wider social context would not affect the behavior of infants as it does these older children. The work of the Munroes just cited suggests, for example, that at least the number of interactors besides mother can affect mother–infant interaction. In most cases it would be difficult to identify all of the social settings that even an infant encounters, let alone the age/sex/kinship identities of his or her companions and caretakers in each one, but it has been shown that by far the major determinants of the number and age/sex/kinship identities of a child's most common interactive partners are the size, type, and composition of his or her residence group (Minturn and Lambert, 1964; Leiderman and Leiderman, 1977; Weisner and Gallimore, 1977; Whiting and Whiting, 1975). Only in industrial Europe and North America does the small, isolated nuclear family predominate, while in the rest of the world the social environment of infancy ordinarily includes a large number and wide variety of siblings, aunts, uncles, grandparents, cousins, and familiar, if not always related, neighbors of all ages who often play a major caretaking role for infants (cf. Weisner and Gallimore, 1977). There is a need for research on how much the behavior patterns that an infant develops in interaction with one caretaker may generalize to interaction with another, but again there is no reason to doubt that they could generalize. If infants develop patterns of behavior in interaction with mother that generalize to others (perhaps for the rest of the infant's life), then presumably if the infant spends much of his or her time with somebody other than mother, the behaviors developed in their interactions can generalize to interaction with mother.

Thus, to reiterate, in studying development as adaptation it is necessary to determine whether the infant's response to a perturbation is successful. A successful response, as discussed above, is one that at least maintains the infant's ability to respond successfully to future perturbations. In determining the success of the infant's response to a perturbation in mother–infant interaction it is necessary to "closely scrutinize" (in Bateson's words) the wider social context in which the perturbation occurs, for the success of the response may be partially a function of the infant's interactions with people other than mother. The infant's response to the perturbation may be successful to the extent that he or she can elicit behaviors from these others which counteract the effects of the perturbed mother-infant interaction. There is, of course, no need to assume any intentionality on the part of the infant or these others who may respond "for" the infant; there *may* be intentionality on their part, but the success of the infant's response through these others may depend only on their simple presence and ordinary patterns of interaction with the infant. To the extent this is the case, these others may represent an alternate pathway to normal development for the infant and they may figure prominently in the analysis of the mechanisms whereby the infant's successful responses are preserved.

SUMMARY

At the most general level my argument in this chapter has been that viewing the process of development as a special case of the process of adaptation may be useful for theory and research in child development. The logic of this argument derives initially from the fact that both processes involve change and continuity over time and from the fact that there is a concept of biological adaptation which is not limited to changes in the genotype from one generation to the next but which includes, begins with, and may depend upon the most immediate behavioral responses to environmental perturbations by individuals—of any age. The utility of viewing development as a manifestation of the process of biological adaptation derives from the powerful evolutionary biological rationale that this concept provides for models of development which predict behavioral plasticity or adaptability in the child. An evolutionary trend toward increased behavioral plasticity and adaptability are predicted by this concept of adaptation, and I argue that the complex and sophisticated environmental tracking systems that it predicts are manifested in human behavior, especially social and cultural behavior. Some of the specific evolutionary mechanisms whereby increased behavioral plasticity and adaptability can be produced are *K*-

selection and its concomitant, neoteny. Both of these evolutionary mechanisms have been operating in hominid phylogeny and I thus argue further that there are good evolutionary biological reasons to expect such behavioral adaptability in humans, especially infants and children.

The specific use made of this view of development as adaptation is in the research strategy that it suggests: a review of the literature on attachment indicates that a likely perturbation in infancy would be disruptions in mother-infant interaction. However, because I expect behavioral flexibility and adaptability in infancy and because of the infant's potential capacity to respond adaptively to perturbations by embarking on an alternate developmental pathway, I suggest that particular attention must be paid not only to the timing of the infant's behavioral response to the perturbation, but also to the larger social context in which the perturbation occurs, for the success of the infant's response may be at least partially a function of interaction with other individuals besides mother. I believe that this approach will be useful in child development research because it is well-suited for exploring the question of why early experience affects later behavior under some circumstances, but not under other circumstances.

2
The Environment of Navajo Infancy

PERTURBATIONS IN THE ENVIRONMENT OF NAVAJO INFANCY

ONE of my main arguments in the preceding chapter was that studying development as adaptation would provide a research strategy especially useful for studying the effects of certain experiences in infancy on later behavior and for determining why such effects might appear under some circumstances but not under others. Another argument was that the first step in such research would be to identify a likely perturbation in the developmental environment of a particular group of infants in order to analyze their responses to the perturbation. The particular group of infants I chose to work with were those of the Navajo people of Arizona because I hypothesized that the cradleboard, as used by the Navajo, could constitute such a developmental perturbation because of the ways it might disrupt mother–infant interaction and thereby the process of attachment as well.

However, I also made the argument that there are good evolutionary biological grounds for expecting developmental plasticity or adaptability in the child and that the response of the child to a perturbation in mother–infant interaction may represent an adaptive alternate developmental pathway and that the adaptability of the infant's response may be at least partially a function of interactions with others, besides mother, in the infant's wider social context. Thus, I argued finally that not only must the infant's response to a particular environmental perturbation be closely observed, special attention must also be directed toward describing the context in which the perturbation and the response occur. The purpose of this chapter is therefore to describe the wider social, cultural, and physical environment in which Navajo infants develop. In the following chapter I will focus on a

41

description of the cradleboard, how it is used by the Navajo, and the reasons why it might—or might not—constitute a perturbation in the environment of Navajo infant development.

THE NAVAJO

A Brief Ethnography of the Navajo

The Navajo, who refer to themselves in the Navajo language as *Diné* ("The People"), and in English as members of the Navajo Nation, are an Athabascan-speaking people who entered the United States from northern Canada about 500 to 600 years ago. Today, with a population of about 150,000 and occupying a reservation of some 18 millions acres in portions of Arizona, New Mexico, and Utah, they are the largest and one of the most successful groups of Native Americans in the United States. Their survival and successful maintenance of a distinct cultural identity has been achieved, however, in the face of severely limited natural resources and a long history of often devastating relations with more powerful neighboring peoples.

The 18 million acres of the Navajo Nation lies entirely on the Colorado Plateau, a geologic formation of immense, but very harsh, beauty. Navajo land is high, ranging between about 3000 and 10,000 feet above sea level, and consists in large part of sand and sandstone and has been subject to eons of erosion which has cut it into a succession of mesas, alluvial sandy plains, and deep canyons. Rainfall is sparse, ranging from an average of only 8 inches per year in the lower elevations up to 22 inches in the smaller, mountainous areas. Most of the land is classed as arid semidesert, and agriculture is limited to dry cultivation and irrigation in a few favored locations around the widely scattered permanent springs and small streams. Although nights are usually cool, even in summer, daytime summer temperatures can reach well into the hundreds while winter temperatures drop well below freezing. The winter also brings severe blizzards which often bring travel on the reservations's many miles of dirt road to a complete halt, as do the spring runoff and summer rains in many areas.

The Navajo entered the Southwest with an economy and social organization that had already long been based on hunting and gathering. There was no political or economic organization above the level of rather loosely organized bands, but there was a common language and an extensive clan system which cross-cut membership in the scattered bands. In spite of intermittent raiding warfare with the already present Pueblo Indians, the Navajo borrowed much of Pueblo culture, including the techniques of agriculture, which the Pueblos had been practicing for centuries. Because of the erratic spatial distribution of adequate soil and water, and especially because of the erratic temporal distribution of adequate rainfall, the adoption of agriculture by the Navajo was never extensive and they continued to fill a hunting-gathering niche. The band-level social organization and mobility common in hunter-gatherer adaptations were not inimicable to agriculture, but agriculture was practiced intermittently, on an opportunistic basis, as another niche to be exploited as seasonal movements and rainfall permitted. However, because sheep and goats can survive and even thrive on the reservation's sparse vegetation and erratically distributed water, when the Spanish introduced these animals (along with the horse) in the mid-1500's, the Navajo were quick to adopt them. The adoption of pastoralism did not, however, entail major changes in Navajo social organization, at least not immediately, because in order for pastoralism to succeed with the reservation's spotty rainfall and poor grazing conditions, flocks must be small and must often be herded long distances to take advantage of better grazing conditions or rare water. Thus, even with the adoption of agriculture and pastoralism, the primary units of Navajo hunter-gatherer social organization did not have to change much and were indeed "preadapted" for farming and herding in an area of erratically disturbed resources.

The smallest unit of Navajo social organization and residence is the nuclear family, but nuclear families are often or usually associated into larger extended family groups, the second unit of social organization. The families in these larger groups are usually united through matrilateral kinship ties and generally form a matrilocal residential cluster with a distinct spatial identity, known in the literature as a "camp." Polygyny, especially sororal polygyny, was more common in the past, but is not unknown today even though it is illegal by Navajo Tribal law as well as Federal law. The third level of Navajo social organization is more difficult to identify and is variable from one area of the reservation to another. Known as an "outfit" or "residential lineage," it is a bilateral kin group that cross-cuts camp and clan membership in one area. It is a cooperative, mutual aid group that owns no property and has no power, becoming apparent only when some task requires more help than can be provided by the members of one camp. The fourth level of Navajo social organization, the "local clan element," refers to all members of the same clan in one area of the reservation. The local clan element, like the outfit, owns no property and has no corporate power, but is simply the functional unit of the fifth level of Navajo social organization, the clan proper. Navajo clans, numbering about 80, are named, matrilineal and exogamous, and while often concentrated in particular areas, may be found anywhere on the reservation. Navajo clans are traditionally linked to certain other clans to form informal phratries which are unnamed and have no apparent function other than the regulation of marriage, for these unnamed phratries are also exogamous, at least in theory. These "linked clans" form the sixth level of Navajo social organization and traditionally there was no higher level of organization unless it was the band itself, but little is known of aboriginal Navajo band organization. Today, however, there are two levels of social organization above the level of linked clans: the "community" and the Navajo Tribal government itself. Navajo communities were originally informal aggregations of families in areas more or less vaguely defined by natural geographic boundaries. With the coming of United States power in 1848, and especially with the formation of the reservation in 1868 and the coming of the railroad in 1881, traders began to set up stores in many parts of the reservation for trading manufactured goods for Navajo wool. Most, if not all, Navajo communities today have at their center a trading post or old Bureau of Indian Affairs (BIA) office building. In many cases, however, the word "community" is misleading, for in many of the smaller and more isolated communities only a handful of families may live within a few miles of the local trading post, while the rest may live up to 15 or 20 miles away. Thus, Navajo communities have a much lower population density than virtually any small community of Anglos.[1] Navajo communities today also provide the first level of tribal organization, each community sending an elected representative to the Navajo Tribal Council at the capitol of the Navajo Nation in Window Rock, Arizona. The tribal council, of course, provides the last level of social organization for the Navajo, but it is distinctly modern in nature, having been formed in the 1920's to carry out negotiations with oil companies for lease rights to reservation land.

Today, while sheepherding is still practiced by most Navajo families, especially in the more isolated areas, few families can survive on the income from sheep alone. Since World War II, and particularly in the past decade or so, there has been a great increase in cash income from welfare and social security payments as well as from wage work on and off the reservation. Navajo silverwork and weaving also continue to provide a small, sporadic income for some. Unemployment is very high (up to 75% in parts of the reservation), however, and most Navajo people are well below official Federal poverty levels. The reservation's sparse settlement, great size, and bad roads have required that an increasing number of families make a major investment in pickup trucks, but most Navajo hogans and houses still have no electricity or running water and, indeed, a constant task is to haul water and firewood to the scattered camps with these trucks. Especially in the more rural areas, even for those families who have a reliable source of cash

---

[1] In Navajo, white Americans are called *bilagáana* (from the Spanish, "Americano") but in English they are called "Anglos."

income, the daily cycle is still largely determined by the demands of the sheep, for if sheep do not often provide an adequate cash income, sheep are still highly valued and can provide a variable subsistence income and cushion against hard times.

In material terms one goal of Navajo life is "the life of material possessions" (Topper and Begaye, 1978) or health, wealth, and security (Hobson, 1954, Ladd, 1957) and for many Navajos the most reliable means to this goal is still through sheepherding. In Navajo sacred (and ethnopsychological) terms, however, the goal of life is hózhǫ́ ("balance, beauty, harmony") (cf. Witherspoon, 1977). One of the routes to hózhǫ́ is through the accumulation of material possessions, but the most common and pervasive route is through the hatáál ("sings") of traditional Navajo religion. Hatáál are held to protect, bless, and cure, and function by protecting, instilling, and restoring the conditions of hózhǫ́. They are led by a hataałii ("singer"), range in length from one to nine nights, and nearly always involve the participation of at least the patient's family and usually a much wider circle of kin. The patient's family must pay the singer's fee and provide food for all others in attendance. These sings are still common throughout the reservation, especially in summer when the 'Ana'í Ndáá' ("Enemy Way") or so-called "Squaw Dance" is usually held, and traditional ceremonialism remains important to the majority of Navajo people.

A Brief History of the Navajo

When the Navajo entered the Southwest they engaged in much peaceful trade and acculturation with the Pueblo Indians, but at the same time, both Navajo and Pueblo mythology abound with references to each other as enemies and it is generally accepted that they were accomplished raiders of Pueblo Indian villages. When the Spaniards entered the Southwest in the middle and late 1500's, bringing horses, sheep, and goats, the material rewards of such raids greatly increased. Early Spanish accounts also abound with references to the Navajo as accomplished and insistent raiders (e.g., Spicer, 1962). While the rewards of raiding increased with the coming of the Spanish, so did the chances of retaliatory raids on the Navajo, and these early Spanish acounts similarly abound with references to attacks on the Navajo. On their own, and allied with the Spanish, the Utes and Paiutes also engaged in raids on the Navajo, and with the coming of the Mexicans in 1821 and the Americans in 1848, the number of enemies of the Navajo continued to grow. Thus, for perhaps as much as 500 years, the Navajo lived with the threat or promise of a raid never very far away.

In addition to this extended period of military insecurity must be the constant insecurities of attempting to wrest a living from a semidesert environment. Wide dispersal in small, mobile bands was the aboriginal Navajo hunter-gatherer pattern of social organization. This pattern was not greatly altered by the adoption of casual agriculture because a complete switch to agriculture was impossible due to the erratic spatial and temporal distribution of water. With growing flocks of sheep stolen from the Pueblos and the Spanish, and later the Mexicans and Americans, the pressures to retain small, mobile bands was at least maintained—sheep need to be continually herded to good grazing and scattered water holes. At the same time, the small, mobile bands provided a good defensive tactic against retaliatory raids by various enemies, and stolen horses helped to implement this tactic. Thus, in addition to some 500 years of military insecurity, there were also the insecurities inherent in balancing the demands of a mixed hunting-gathering-farming-herding-raiding economy.

These 500 years of economic and military insecurity did not end with the coming of the Americans in 1848. In fact, after the United States assumed sovereignty in the Southwest, raiding and warfare with the Navajo escalated to such an extent that the Union effort in the Civil War was affected; Congress ordered Col. Kit Carson to end the "Navajo problem" once and for all by waging a scorched-earth campaign against the Navajo. By keeping the various Navajo bands continually on the move and by burning hogans, destroying fields, and killing or capturing livestock, Carson made it impossible for the Navajo either to resist or to continue running and hiding. In 1864 all but a few hundred Navajos were forced on The Long Walk to prison camp at Ft. Sumner, New Mexico, where, for 4 years, they suffered from disease, malnutrition, persecution, and their first taste of federal Indian policy.

After their release from Ft. Sumner in 1968, when treaties were signed and the Navajo reservation was established, the Navajo entered a period of struggle to restart their economy and to learn to live under the bureaucratic paternalism of the Federal Government. In the following years the Navajo have greatly increased their number and the reservation has actually grown in size. However, from the Navajo point of view, relations with the larger Anglo society, if no longer overtly warlike, have been characteristically confusing, insensitive, and often threatening. Besides adjusting to the highly changeable and contradictory policies emanating from the several branches of the government responsible for Navajo affairs, the Navajo have had to deal with unscrupulous traders, businessmen, and BIA officials, the vagaries of a western capitalist ecomony, and the confusing bureaucracy of a modern welfare state. For over 100 years the Navajo have had their children (often forcibly) removed to BIA and missionary schools where they were punished for speaking Navajo and often allowed home only during the summer.

During the 1930's, the most liberal and respected Commissioner of Indian Affairs, John Collier, turned out to be the man who initiated the still-rankling livestock reduction program, in which thousands of Navajo sheep were slaughtered (the Navajo were paid for the sheep) in an effort to preserve the sadly overgrazed range land of most parts of the reservation. Recently, many Navajos are dismayed by the number of large oil and coal companies that are drilling and strip mining areas of the reservation which they hold especially sacred. Many Navajos are also dismayed by the apparent insensitivity and bungling of Congress which has resulted in the failure to resolve the decades-old territorial dispute with the Hopi tribe. Finally, racial prejudice is not unknown in the Southwest, even today.

This brief history of the Navajo is one-sided, but it is the side that perhaps most Navajos would relate. The reasons for presenting Navajo history in this light will become more apparent in the following section. It will suffice for now to suggest that under the circumstances of most of Navajo history it would be understandable if people tended to be anxious and suspicious of outsiders and strangers.

Navajo Behavior

It is difficult and both humanistically and scientifically dangerous to characterize in any but the most precise and least affect-laden terms possible the "typical" behavior or personal style of even an individual, let alone the individuals of a separate racial or ethnic group. Such characterizations are reported here for heuristic purposes and to later debunk some of their aspects, with full awareness that the days of the modal personality construct are rightly long gone and that the possibility exists that the views expressed by some of the researchers discussed in this section were colored by outdated concepts, methods, and lingering ethnocentrism. These problems notwithstanding, the purpose of this section is to attempt to describe a dimension of the beliefs and behavioral styles of many Navajo adults that have impressed a number of non-Navajo researchers in anthropology, psychology, and psychiatry. These "typical" beliefs and personality and behavioral styles might constitute a significant part of the social and cognitive developmental environment of Navajo infancy. Further, as discussed in detail in the following chapter, some of the behavior patterns that these researchers impute to the Navajo might be predicted from a narrow interpretation of attachment theory and the supposed effects of disrupted early mother–infant interaction.

Taking their accounts out of context may make them appear one-sided and even prejudiced, but it is also true that most non-Navajo researchers have seized upon one dimension of Navajo personality or behavior as especially salient. That dimension is the one of anxiety and depression, or as Kluckhohn put it, "morbid melancholia" and "endemic uneasiness" (1947:85). In their classic monograph, The Navaho (1974 [1946]), Kluckhohn and Dorothea Leighton summarize what they feel are some of the basic "premises of Navaho life and thought." The first premise they list is that "life is very, very dangerous," and they note that while all sensible people appreciate that life does have hazards, ". . . to many whites Navahos seem morbid in the variety of threats from this world and from the world of the supernatural . . ." (1974:303). Among the several tactics for living a life that is "very, very dangerous," Kluckhohn and Leighton list two that are especially relevant here: "be wary of nonrelatives" and "when in a new and dangerous situation, do nothing" (1974:305–306). They elaborate the former by saying that while most people are more wary of strangers and outsiders, among the Navajo this fear is so great that it extends to other Navajos who are not members of the same community or kin group. Evidence for this interpretation resides, they claim, in the fact that many Navajos carry anti-witchcraft medicine to occasions where they might encounter strange Navajos. Elaborating the second tactic, Kluckhohn and Leighton claim that when ritual precautions are ineffective or unavailable, Navajos often do nothing at all. As evidence, they suggest that Navajos have a tendency to "freeze up" and become silent and withdrawn in new and strange situations.

Kluckhohn and the Leightons are repeatedly explicit about high levels of anxiety and depression among the Navajo. In his 1944 monograph, Navajo Witchcraft, Kluckhohn argues that pervasive beliefs in witches and witchcraft are a cultural response to these high levels of anxiety. Similarily, in an analysis of Navajo dreams, he finds the same "emphasis upon anxiety" (1962:363). Alexander and Dorothea Leighton (1942), in an analysis of the sources of Navajo fear, found that in the Navajo view the most common sources of anxiety were disease, accidents, and things that were ch'ịịdii (evil spirits, devils, ghosts, spirits of the dead). The second most common source of anxiety was social relations, including family fights and quarrels and exploitation by others. Together, these two sources of fear were more common than fear stemming from relations with Anglos, the physical environment, Mexicans, or peoples of other tribes. Along similar lines, Leighton and Kluckhohn (1948) suggest that by Anglo standards "Navahos are hypersensitive to shame or ridicule," but also note that for the Navajo, shyness-shame shades into "respect–avoidance" more than it does for Anglos. They go on to say that " . . .while it would be very incorrect to place a one-sided emphasis upon the uneasiness in Navaho psychology, still we must recognize the presence of such trends" (1948:110). The Navajo, according to

Table 2.1. Whiting and Child's (1953) Ratings of Navajo Fear

Type of fear	Navajo rating	Range in all societies
Fear of human beings	7	0–11
Fear of spirits	10	0–11
Fear of ghosts	9	0–11
Fear of animal spirits	3	0–10
Overall fear of others	17	4–21

Leighton and Kluckhohn, are emotionally "volatile," and ". . . the main point is the changeability of Navaho emotions which can run the gamut from bubbling jocularity to despair, from inert apathy to destructive violence, within a quite brief space of time." Moreover, the Navajo are ". . . impulsive rather than spontaneous" (1948:110–111).

Given these views of Navajo anxiety and depression, it is not surprising that Whiting and Child (1953), in their pioneering study of relationships between adult personality and child training variables, rated the Navajo above the median on several measures of fear, for they relied for their ratings on the publications of Kluckhohn and the Leightons. Still, if only to place these reports of anxiety and fear among the Navajo in cross-cultural perspective, it is worth reporting the Whiting and Child ratings for the Navajo (Table 2.1).

While both the quantity and quality of psychiatric epidemiological research among the Navajo is limited, at least two such studies have provided results that are in general agreement with the conclusions of Kluckhohn and the Leightons. Schoenfeld and Miller (1973), for example, in a sample of nearly 400 Navajo psychiatric patients, found that the single most common diagnosis was that of "depressive neurosis." Jewell (1952), in a similar but less extensive study, reported an "unusually high incidence of catatonic schizophrenia" and he speculated that the Navajo may be "predisposed" to this withdrawn form of schizophrenia for cultural reasons.

In addition to these more or less subjective reports of Navajo "uneasiness" and "melancholia," reports based on more objective observations of Navajo nonverbal communication are broadly suggestive of the same general behavior styles. Perhaps that aspect of Navajo nonverbal communication that has most struck Anglo observers is gaze aversion. For example, Edward T. Hall has noted:

> Unlike middle-class whites, the direct open-faced look in the eyes was avoided by Navajos. In fact Navajos froze up when looked at directly. Even when shaking hands they held one in the peripheral field of the eyes, letting the message of the other person's warmth and pleasure at seeing a friend seep through a long-clasped, but delicately held hand. I ultimately learned that to look directly at a Navajo was to display anger (1969:379).

Many Navajo people with whom I have spoken said that they felt shy or embarrassed (*yáhásin*) when they chanced to look another person full in the face. One mother said that she explicitly warned her children not to look others in the eye when they shook hands unless this other person was known. Another person said, "I don't look at their eyes because I am afraid that they will look at me." A man whom I spoke with used the word *yíníshlichíí* ("red stare") to describe mutual gazing with a stranger or person not known well. Asked to elaborate on the meaning of the term *yíníshlichíí*, he said that receiving a direct stare was like "staring at someone with the red eye of a bull about to charge." A girl said that when she first learned to speak English, the Anglo teacher told the class to "look at her right in the face," to see better how the English sounds were formed. The girl still remembered being upset by this and said, "I just couldn't do it." A college-educated Navajo man told me that he developed a technique for interacting with Anglos which helped him when he went away to school: "I still don't look anyone right in the eye. I look at their ear or at their mouth, but not right in the eye."

Gaze aversion is suggestive of shyness or anxiety in face-to-face inter-action (e.g., Chance, 1962; Argyle and Cook, 1976) but there are other indicators as well. Citing the work of Mowrer, herself a Navajo, Basso (1970) states that the social context of silence among the Navajo is "strikingly similar" to that of the Western Apache, for whom he notes that silence when meeting strangers " . . . is directly related to the conviction that the estab-lishment of social relationships is a serious matter that calls for caution, careful judgment, and plenty of time" (1970:218). He also states that " . . . keeping silent in Western Apache culture is a response to uncertainty and unpredictability in social relations" (1970:227). Strangers who im-mediately launch into conversation, are, according to Basso, viewed with "undisguised suspicion." If the strangers are Anglos, Western Apaches sus-pect that the Anglo wants to teach them something, but even if he stranger is another Apache, the suspicion is that he or she "wants something." Court-ship is another context in which silence is common behavior, and Basso reports that the people he spoke with said they kept silent because of their "intense shyness" and "acute self-consiousness."

These vague reports of anxiety, depression, fear, shyness, and reserve have not been well documented, but they have been widespread and are generally consistent. It would be worthwhile to investigate their determi-nants, in spite of the fundamental conceptual and methodological problems that would have to be solved before the components of "uneasiness" and "melancholia" could be defined and measured without mixing etics and emics in a hodgepodge of confusion. Kluckhohn did not feel that he under-stood the sources of Navajo anxiety and depression, but believed in their prevalence among the Navajo to such an extent that he began to question aspects of psychoanalytic theory which had guided much of his research. He begins the conclusion of his major work on Navajo infancy and childhood (1947) with a question:

> . . . how can this picture [of a psychoanalytically "ideal" childhood] be reconciled with the facts on Navaho witchcraft, on the states of morbid melancholia and endemic uneasiness which have been so well documented for adult Navaho? How can the anxiety level be so high among a people where infants are nursed whenever they want to be, where childhood disciplines are so permissive, where there is so much genuine affection for children? If the writings of certain psychoanalysts were literally true (and the whole truth), adult Navahos ought to have calm and beautifully adjusted personalities. However this is most certainly not the case. In spite of the fact that Navaho infants receive a maximum of protection and gratification, they tend to be moody and to worry a great deal when they become adults (1947:85).

Kluckhohn did conclude that frequent ill health in childhood (he conducted his research in the 1930's and 1940's when morbidity on the Navajo reservation was considerably higher than it is today), teasing, rather abrupt weaning, and "delays in response to crying" might contribute to the answers, but he is not emphatic about these conclusions. He closes with an observation that seems especially likely in view of the history of the Navajo discussed in the previous section: "the high degree of tension observed among Navaho adults" may also be traced to the "exceedingly grave pressures" facing Navajo society.

This brief introduction to Navajo cultural ecology, history, and "typical" behavioral styles provides a broad context for the closer look at the environment of Navajo infancy that follows. It would be impossible to explore all the ways that Navajo infancy might be affected by these large categories of variables, but some of the more salient causal pathways will be traced out in some detail below. To foreshadow, it is sufficient to stress here that the adaptations made by the Navajo even hundreds of years ago could affect the modern environment of Navajo infancy. As LeVine (1977) recently argued,

> . . . cultural evolution within human populations also produces standardized strategies of survival for infants and children, strategies reflecting environmental pressures from a more recent past, encoded in customs rather than genes and transmitted socially rather than biologically (1977:16).

COTTONWOOD SPRINGS

The Ecological Setting

Cottonwood Springs is a small and widely dispersed community of about 1000 people in the northwestern part of the Navajo Nation. The social and economic center of the community is the Cottonwood Springs Trading Post, but residents of the community, who define each other as anyone who regularly trades at this store, often live as many as 20 miles away from the trading post, thinly settled (ca. 1.4 persons per square mile) on the 700 square miles of Rainbow Plateau and Paiute Mesa. A distinguishing feature of the community is its isolation: there is one, often impassable, dirt road into Cottonwood Springs which dead ends at the trading post. The nearest neighboring Navajo community is 35 miles away, the nearest paved road is 40 miles away, and the nearest off-reservation town is 100 miles away. Flagstaff, Arizona, the nearest major southwestern city, is 180 miles away.

The major feature of the Cottonwood Springs landscape is *Naatsis'aan*, the mountain behind the trading post that rises abruptly from the 6000-foot-high Rainbow Plateau to a total height of 10,500 feet. Nobody lives on the mountain, but it dominates the horizon, influences the local weather, and plays a significant role in the local ecosystem. *Naatsis'aan* has affected eons of drainage patterns such that Cottonwood Springs is more sharply defined geographically than most Navajo communities; it takes the shape of a triangle and is separated from neighboring Navajo communities on one side by Navajo Canyon, on another by Paiute Canyon, and *Naatis'aan* itself

Fig. 2.1 Cottonwood Springs (from a map by Collier, 1966:15–16).

forms a barrier on the third side. The rough terrain and physical isolation of Cottonwood Springs are major reasons that this area of the Navajo Nation was ever settled: in the 1860's Navajos from the eastern part of the reservation came to the Cottonwood Springs area to escape Kit Carson's roundup and in the latter part of the 1800's more moved in to avoid increasing contact with Anglo settlers in what is now the southern and western parts of the reservation.

Besides having determined, in part, that people should be living at Cottonwood Springs at all, *Naatsis'aan* has greatly influenced local settlement patterns as well. Like most parts of the reservation, Cottonwood Springs receives very little precipitation (12–16 inches per year on the plateau, 16–27 inches on the mountain, and 7–11 inches in the canyons) and has extremely poor, sandy soil. The terrain is mixed soft sand-stone outcroppings, sparse low vegetation, and denser stands of piñon and juniper on the high elevations. Erosion is a constant problem, even from the rare rainfalls, but especially from the spring runoff from the several feet of snow that accumulate on *Naatsis'aan* each winter. Snow begins to fall on the mountain several weeks or even months before the first snow has fallen on the plateau; more important, a winter's snowfall on the mountain usually melts only slowly in the spring because the daily cycle of thawing and freezing extends the runoff over as much as four or five weeks. On the plateau, even in the dead of winter, 3 or 4 feet of snow can melt in only a few days when the storm passes and the skies are clear again. These rapid thaws on the plateau not only wreak havoc on the already bad dirt roads that criss-cross Rainbow Plateau and Paiute Mesa, but also have serious consequences for the next summer's grazing for the sheep and goats which are the basis of Cottonwood Springs' subsistence. The rocky and sandy soil cannot hold water unless it is introduced slowly, and heavy rains and sudden thaws create flash floods that carry away the already scarce topsoil. The slow melt from the mountain, however, while it deepens the washes and canyons that mark off Cottonwood Springs from the surrounding areas and make local travel in a straight line impossible, also allows enough water to soak in slowly or to be collected in low-lying areas so that the water table does not sink below the level of the windmill-powered pumps that are now necessary to water the greatly increased sheep population. The accumulation of snow on *Naatsis'aan* also helps to maintain the two or three natural springs that flow from its flanks, beneath the plateau, emerging at the edge of various canyons to provide water for sheep or small fields of corn, melons, or peaches. The most significant social effect of this particular ecosystem, based on rugged terrain, bad soil, and drought, is the isolation of small groups of people caused by the necessity of dispersing in order to maximally exploit the limited and erratically distributed resources. The impact of this settlement pattern on Navajo infant development will be dealt with in detail in a later section.

The Historical Background

Prior to the permanent settlement of Cottonwood Springs, small bands of Paiute Indians occupied the area, and some Cottonwood Springs residents claimed that many of these Paiutes were made slaves by the early Navajo settlers. Other accounts also suggest that early Paiute-Navajo relations were not always good (Dyk, 1938; Collier, 1966). There has, however, been considerable intermarriage since then, and many of the present Cottonwood Springs Paiute have been incorporated into the Navajo clan system (e.g., the Paiute 'Ashiihi clan is the Paiute branch of the Navajo 'Ashįįhi [Salt] clan). At present, there are probably no more than 100 Paiutes at Cottonwood Springs, and there is little that distinguishes the Navajo and Paiute ways of life. The Paiute have been almost entirely acculturated to the Navajo way of life, although the Paiute language remains (most Paiutes are bilingual in Paiute and Navajo), as do aspects of Paiute kinship and ceremonialism.

The most prominent early settlers of Cottonwood Springs were Hashke'neini ("He Gives Out Anger" or "The Mean One") and Chach'osh ("Chancres"; his other names, referring to the incident which drove him into the isolation of Cottonwood Springs, were "Whiteman Killer" and "Killer of the Red Moustache"). He Gives Out Anger apparently migrated to Cottonwood Springs in the early 1860's to escape U.S. military pressure in the eastern reservation, and Whiteman Killer migrated there in the 1890's to avoid a murder charge in Tuba City, Arizona, where he had been accused of killing a Mormon. He was finally acquitted of this charge on the grounds of justifiable homicide, but the incidents that drove both of these early settlers to Cottonwood Springs, and their very names, are good indicators of Navajo-Anglo relations of the time.

At Cottonwood Springs, contact with outsiders and strangers, Navajo and non-Navajo, has always been limited. There was no road into the area until 1923 when the trading post was opened. Even in 1974 and 1976, after many improvements on the road, it was still bad, and like all local roads, often impassable in winter or after heavy rains. While low in quantity, however, Cottonwood Springs' contact with Anglos has generally been high in quality, and the few Anglos who have been long-term residents have become respected and liked. Until recently, and for nearly 40 years, the trading post was operated by the same Anglo woman, who grew up on the Navajo reservation and was completely fluent in Navajo. In 1936 the BIA built a day school for beginners and first graders near the trading post, and in the 1940's, it became a boarding school. It was run by a highly respected and well-liked Anglo teacher until only a few years ago. In 1942 an Episcopalian missionary added Cottonwood Springs to his circuit around the north-central part of the reservation, and over the years he too has become well-accepted. He was a most passive proselytizer, translating the Episcopalian mass into Navajo, wearing his hair in Navajo style, and firmly believing that there was no fundamental incompatibility between Christianity and traditional Navajo religion. These three Anglos have provided the longest and most consistent, face-to-face contact with Anglo society that most Cottonwood Springs people have had until recently; they all speak at least some Navajo and have acted as sympathetic interpreters and informants, literally and figuratively, for the community concerning the ways of the Anglo world. They have also served as vital buffers between the two cultures (cf. Adams, 1963).

In spite of its isolation and paucity of contact with Anglo society, Cottonwood Springs has, of course, undergone considerable change. Most of this change has occurred, however, not as a result of face-to-face contact with Anglos, but through the more pervasive effects of BIA policies and the larger U.S. economy. Moreover, to a great extent, the changes that have occurred represent Navajo reworking of Anglo concepts and material items into a distinctly Navajo framework. This is more than the simple abandonment of something Navajo for something Anglo, as has happened more often in other Native American tribes where contact was earlier and/or more intense. In a study of culture change at Cottonwood Springs between 1938, when Malcolm Collier did her pioneering research there, and the early 1960's, when they conducted their research, Shepardson and Hammond (1964) concluded that

> Rainbow Plateau retains all of the action systems which met the functional pre-requisites of the traditional society. The alien authority systems in which it parti-cipates provide alternatives and supplements, which served to support, rather than replace, the traditional structure. Persistence, therefore, is more deep-going than change in this little community (1964:1049).

I observed some of the patterns on which they based their conclusion 10 years later: continued widespread use of traditional clothing (by the women) and hairstyle (mostly the women, but many men), forked-stick hogans, arranged marriages, polygyny (but only four cases) mother-in-law avoidance, witchcraft beliefs and accusations, performance of the *kinaaldá* (girl's puberty ceremony), and at least the maintenance of a wide variety of other traditional practices.

Among the larger changes at Cottonwood Springs since Collier's work, and even since Shepardson and Hammond's work, is the increase in the number of children going to school. Education is highly valued among the Navajo, and not just because their children are given, by treaty rights, room and board while away at school. Only a few years ago children from Cottonwood Springs who went to school had to spend months away from home as

far away as Flagstaff, Phoenix, Albuquerque, and even California or Okla-
homa. Many of the parents of the children I worked with at Cottonwood
Springs remember school as a particularly anxious and lonely time, where
they were punished for speaking Navajo, had their heads shaved, and were
given "good English names." Metcalfe (1976) has shown that Navajo
women who spent several years away from home in boarding schools as
girls showed more signs of anxiety and depression, were less optimistic, and
more disdainful of "the old ways" than another group of Navajo women
who had not been away to boarding school, or for as long. Further, the
children of the women who had been away at school for long periods were
themselves also judged to be more anxious or insecure (more whining,
crying, thumbsucking, and attempts to increase proximity to mother).

Such experiences with the BIA education system notwithstanding, schooling remains important to the Navajo, and they are succeeding in getting
more schools built on the reservation, closer to home, where it is possible for
children to come home every weekend. More children are going to school
now, and while Navajo is still the first language of all children at Cottonwood Springs, children as young as 5 years are now also being taught
English as a second language. A daily preschool was established at Cottonwood Springs in the late 1960's, and some children of only 3 and 4 years
begin to learn a few words of English. The main value of education seems to
be learning English. The school dropout rate is still very high, but most
children remain in school long enough to become fluent in English. Of the
people under about 35, perhaps 80% speak English; of the people over 35,
perhaps as few as 20% speak English well. More men than women speak
English, and few of the people living on Paiute Mesa speak English.

One of the values of education (i.e., learning English) is that each family or
camp will then have at least one fully trusted interpreter, again both in the
literal sense and in the sense of translating the meaning of state and federal
policies for the entire family. To some extent, learning English, like many
other aspects of Navajo culture change, is something that many Navajos
may see will better enable them to remain quietly separate from the outside
Anglo world. To be sure, there is and has been contact with the outside
world, but at Cottonwood Springs there is a feeling of isolationism, something that may better be achieved in the 1980's through more familiarity
with English and Anglo society.

The Demographic Structure

Another aspect of change at Cottonwood Springs (and throughout the
reservation) over the past 30 to 40 years and more has been the very great

population increase. In 1971 to 1972 the reservation-wide crude birth rate was estimated at 28 to 34 per 1000 (Kunitz, 1974). Kunitz (1976) has also estimated that the crude birth rate in the U.S. Public Health Service (USPHS) district that includes Cottonwood Springs was an amazing 57.3 per 1000 in 1968 to 1969. In 1938 Collier (1966) estimated Cottonwood Springs' population at 175. In 1962 Shepardson and Hammond (1970) reported that it had risen to 581, and in 1974 to 1976 I estimated that it had risen further to about 1000.

Cottonwood Springs thus reflects the great reservation-wide increase in population. The major reason for this population increase is a recent decline in Navajo infant mortality. As late as 1949 to 1951 infant mortality was 139.4 per 1000, but by 1971 had decreased to 31.5 and is still decreasing (Brenner, Reisinger, and Rogers, 1974; Kunitz, 1976). Kunitz has also shown that the Navajo Nation has a demographic structure very like that seen in developing countries, where infant mortality is decreasing but fertility remains high. One reason for high Navajo fertility, as Kunitz (1974) showed, that is especially true at Cottonwood Springs, is that many Navajo women (as contrasted to Hopi women, for example) continue to bear children well into their forties. Navajo infant mortality has been sharply decreasing due, in large part, to greatly improved medical delivery systems by the USPHS, improved childhood nutrition programs, and continuing health care and supervised nutrition while children are away at school.

The population of the Navajo Nation has also been increasing because the people have wanted it to increase. In spite of the fact that the Navajo reservation can scarcely support its present population (especially by traditional subsistence means), large families have always been desired. Among the reasons for desiring large families is the significant contribution that children of even only 6 or 7 years make in sheepherding, farming, gathering and cutting firewood, and especially, caring for younger siblings. Furthermore, if a family has more children than it can readily provide for, there are always other families with fewer or no children at all, and even today it is not uncommon for a large family to "give" a child to another family, usually closely related, to help them and to provide company and affection. Some children are clearly seen as a form of old-age insurance, especially girls and later or last-born children who provide companionship and domestic help while their older siblings provide economic assistance. Sometimes the grown children of an elderly couple will send one of their own children to live with his or usually her aged parents, thus, in a sense, transferring their obligation to their parents onto their children.

To say that the Navajo simply and unreservedly love and want children may be banal and nonexplanatory, but it is a good description. In addition to the desire to reproduce themselves, Navajo parents may also value children because of the insurance value these children represent. But it may not be just their own insurance they are thinking of; children belong not only to a nuclear family, but also to an extended family and a local clan element. In the past, many children were needed just to counteract the high infant mortality. However, they were also needed, and still are, to provide a pool of individuals who were of potential value to other families in the local kin groups. The Navajo extended family and larger kin groupings serve many functions and can provide an immense amount of social security, but this security must, of course, also be earned. One's own children are one's own, but they are also members of large social groups. As Kluckhohn put it:

> The worst that one may say of another person is "He acts as if he didn't have any relatives." Conversely, the ideal of behavior often innumerated by headmen is "Act as if everybody were related to you (1974:100).

High fertility has meant, and still means, social security for the Navajo. This form of social security is needed in spite of improved economic conditions. Because of improved education and because continued overgrazing of the range has lessened economic opportunity, more children are leaving home when they complete their schooling. However, the social security of one's own or one's close kinsmen's children is still of potential significance. It is also true that in spite of greatly improved USPHS and BIA health and education programs and a variety of federal and state, direct and indirect welfare assistance programs, most Navajos, like most Native Americans, have little faith or trust in government policy. In the past, all too often, programs for the benefit of the Navajo have been to their actual detriment, and there has been a general lack of continuity in Federal policy. Further, the vagaries of the environment and especially of the western capitalist economy simply add to their uncertainty and anxiety. There are few incentives for families to limit the size of their families. Birth control is practiced by only a few younger and better educated families. The mean number of children per mother at Cottonwood Springs is 5.2.

Present-day Cottonwood Springs families are probably larger than they were even only 30–40 years ago because of the much decreased infant mortality rate. Today's families probably also differ from precontact families in having a mean birth interval of only about 2 years. This suggests that one difference in the environment of Navajo infancy today is the greater opportunity for the infant to interact with more siblings (or other coresident children) and a greater demand on mother and other caretakers for their time and attention. To some extent, however, this effect is counteracted by the fact that many more children are now going away to school, so there is a new element of "binge" sociality in interactions with older siblings who come home on weekends and vacations.

The Economic Base

Over the past several years there has been a slow but steady increase in the standard of living at Cottonwood Springs. In 1938 per capita income was estimated at $108.23 (Collier, 1966). In 1960 to 1969 it had risen to $449.94 (Shepardson and Hammond, 1970). I gathered no data on income, but guess that per capita income has approximately doubled since the early 1960's. With inflation and the increase in population taken into account, this estimate is in line with income figures reported by Adams and Ruffing (1977) for the nearby Navajo community of Shonto. Per capita income, however, is not a good measure of value at Cottonwood Springs because the cash and subsistence economies mix intermittently and because of Navajo kinship-based patterns of reciprocity and exchange. For example, while a lamb may bring its owner $30.00 if he or she sells it to the trader, the value of the same lamb is considerably higher if the owner eats it himself and saves the price of store-bought meat. The value of the lamb may be even higher if the owner "invests" it in a large stew to feed guests at a sing, for this is good "kinship behavior" and helps to ensure the later support of his kinsmen.

However measured, the increase in income at Cottonwood Springs has been primarily from welfare and social security benefits and, to a lesser extent, from wages from more numerous but still few jobs at the local trading post, the local missionary-run health clinic, the BIA boarding school, or state highway department. However, while Cottonwood Springs relies more on individual cash income from welfare, social security, and wages than income from traditional sources, it must be emphasized that *subsistence* sheepherding is still well-developed and thriving and that it still dictates the daily activities of most families. The increasing reliability of cash income is, in part, an adaptation to the overgrazing and bad soil that characterize most of the reservation, the increasing Navajo population, and the inability of the larger U.S. economy to provide adequate prices for wool and mutton or to provide sufficient local jobs. Thus, instead of being the sole source of income, sheepherding has become more a new form of insurance and economic flexiblility. Subsistence sheepherding helps to stretch out the monthly checks, provides a potential cushion against hard times, and a flock of sheep may even provide investment capital "on the hoof"—to take advantage of a rise in lamb or wool prices. Of course, sheepherding is a highly valued traditional activity and sheep continue to hold great symbolic significance for many Navajo people.

Agriculture was never extensively developed at Cottonwood Springs, because of the bad soil and severe drought conditions that prevail. At present, it provides only small extra income for a few families. Likewise, Cottonwood

Table 2.2. Percentage of Total Cottonwood Springs Income by Source, 1938 to 1962

Year	Reference	Source	Percentage of total
1938	(Collier, 1966)	Livestock	34.0
		Agriculture	20.0
		Wages	—
		Welfare, social security	— } 46.0
		Crafts	—
1960 to 1962	(Sheparsdon and Hammond, 1970)	Livestock	35.3
		Agriculture	1.9
		Wages	22.6
		Welfare, social security	39.0 } 62.8
		Crafts	1.2

Springs is not a major Navajo arts and crafts center, and only a few families earn extra income from weaving and silversmithing. An indication of the continuing local dependence on livestock (including small numbers of cattle) and the increasing dependence on wage work, welfare, and social security can be seen in Table 2.2 which compares total Cottonwood Springs income by source over a span of only some 20 years.

Equivalent data from Cottonwood Springs today would likely show even more than 62.8% of the total income deriving from wages, crafts, welfare, and social security. Adams and Ruffing (1977) report that in the Shonto area in 1971, fully 85.5% of all income was from paychecks and various forms of welfare and social security checks.

In spite of the improved standard of living at Cottonwood Springs, for the most part there has been little corresponding change in the patterns of family life that determine the immediate environment of infant development. The general conditions of life have been improved through better nutrition and medical care, but most people at Cottonwood Springs are still poor. While the increased cash income is spent more and more on disposable diapers and bottles and formula, daily activities and residence patterns are still structured by sheepherding and the demands of family life much as they have been for many years. Except for a few families who live in the trading post-BIA school complex and a few others who live along a recently installed pipeline that carries spring water down from Naatsis'aan, no families have running water. Until 1975 there was no electricity at Cottonwood Springs except for the diesel-powered generators that supplied the trading post and BIA school. In the same year the Navajo Tribal Utilities Authority extended a power line into the area. However, only those families living within a few yards of this line could afford to pay for the installation of feeder lines to their hogans or houses. The majority of families at Cottonwood Springs must thus continue to haul, for long distances by pickup truck, drinking water and wood for cooking and heating. In fact, for reasons that will become apparent in the following section, that aspect of the improved standard of living and increased cash income which has probably had the greatest effect on the environment of infancy at Cottonwood Springs is the pickup truck.

Residence Patterns

As discussed in the previous chapter, a current theme in much anthropological research on child development is the ways in which mother–infant interaction and children's developing behavioral styles may be systematically influenced by variations in their opportunities for interaction with others besides mother. The case was also made that perhaps the major determinants of these opportunities were the size, type, and composition of the residential groupings characteristic of the child's society and that major influences on these residence patterns were each society's subsistence activities and economic structure. In this section the residence patterns at Cottonwood Springs will be described. I will show how they are influenced by Cottonwood Springs' economic and subsistence patterns, and suggest that some changes in the environment of infancy at Cottonwood Springs may be due in part to the recent greater availability of the pickup truck.

In a classic analysis of Navajo social organization, Aberle (1963) noted that the apparent contradictory quality of published reports on the Navajo was not necessarily due to the ethnographers' fuzzy thinking and sloppy fieldwork. Instead, he argued that this "fuzziness" was due largely to the availability of several acceptable variant courses of action which made for an adaptive flexibility in patterns of social organization. He enumerated four factors which made such social flexibility adaptable and which could be expected to produce different patterns of organization in different parts of the reservation under different conditions. These factors were rapid social change, resource instability, expanding population, and the conflicts between acculturation and kinship organization in a tribally based society. The essence of his argument is that the Navajo are not slaves to tradition, especially as reported by Anglo ethnographers, and that we should expect variation in patterns of Navajo social organization.

One area where the "fuzziness" that Aberle sought to understand has been virtually endemic is that of residence patterns. One problem in this area has been that of the definition of residence types (cf. Witherspoon, 1970) and another has been the dearth of analytical studies which could provide a general model accounting for the great reservation-wide variance in residence patterns in terms of the "acceptable variant courses of action" open to the Navajo. My research at Cottonwood Springs was not devoted to the analysis of residence patterns. However in the course of gathering material relevant to the study of the environment of Navajo infancy, I included detailed residence data on the 38 children in my sample that might be relevant to such a general model of Navajo residence patterns.

My residence data indicate a high absolute rate of neolocal residence at Cottonwood Springs and are suggestive of a dramatic increase in neolocal residence rates since Collier (1966) measured it in 1938 and Shepardson and Hammond (1970) last measured it in 1960 to 1962. The 38 children in my sample lived in 27 separate households (hogans or houses) in 26 separate and distinct residential clusters or camps. Although this sample represents more than 90% of all camps with small children, it represents slightly fewer than one-half of all camps. Nonetheless, of the 27 different households, 14 (52%) were what I classified as nuclear, neolocal family camps. The term "neolocal camp" is commonly used (e.g., Levy, 1962; Reynolds, Lamphere, and Cook, 1967; Shepardson and Hammond, 1970) to refer to an independent, separate nuclear family household that is not "close" (of this, more later) to either husband's or wife's kin. Of the remaining 13 households, six were matrilocal, six were patrilocal, and in one the family was residing with others related by different kinship ties. In contrast, Collier (1966) reported that in 1938 only 13.6% of all households were neolocal camps. Shepardson and Hammond (1970) reported that in the early 1960's this figure had risen only to 15.0%.

There seem to be three reasons why my neolocal camp residence rate may differ so much from that of Collier and Shepardson and Hammond. The first reason is perhaps initially the most obvious, but I do not feel that it is entirely valid: our neolocal residence rate figures may differ so much simply because my small sample is inadequate for generalization to the entire population of camps at Cottonwood Springs. However, as the parents of small children, the adults in my sample should be younger than the other adults at Cottonwood Springs, and according to the developmental cycle of Navajo domestic groups (Reynolds, Lamphere, and Cook, 1976), one would expect these younger adults to be living with one or the other set of their own parents more often than my data indicate they do. In other words, my sample should be biased toward an overrepresentation of extended family camps but shows instead a high rate of neolocal residence. Thus, even if my neolocal residence rate of 52% is inflated, it is not inflated unduly, and is at least highly suggestive of an increase in neolocal residence.

The second problem, that of defining neolocal residence, is less easily resolved. Neolocal residence among the Navajo has always been notoriously difficult to define, but there are two good approximations. First, Collier (1966), Kluckhohn and Leighton (1974), Levy (1962), Reynolds, Lamphere, and Cook (1967), and others have all included spatial criteria in their definitions of the camp. For example, the hogans in an extended family camp are "within earshot" of each other (Collier, 1966:24); "geographical proximity" is the "major criterion for describing and defining the camp" (Levy, 1962:783). Shepardson and Hammond define a neolocal household as one in which both the husband and wife have left their natal homes to set up a new household by themselves; they state too that in their experience the camp "is always a clearly defined territorial entity" (1970:46).

On the other hand, while it seems to be true that in most cases the Navajo camp does have an easily defined territorial identity and the hogans and houses in a camp usually are well "within eashot," this is not invariably the case. As Witherspoon (1970) has argued, an uncritical application of simple spatial criteria may result in residence classification schemes that are quite nonsensical to the people involved. Witherspoon suggests instead that a camp consists of those individuals who have the right to take firewood from the same pile, to draw water from the same barrel, to plant in the same or adjacent agricultural plots, to herd together or on the same customary range land, and to receive rides from each other without cost.[2]

Although he does emphasize matrilineal kinship, matrilocal residence, and the matrifocality of the entire Navajo conceptual system, Witherspoon's definition is nonetheless a functional one. He proposes that the commonly used term "camp" should be replaced by the essence of its function: more or less daily, face-to-face social and economic cooperation among members of the "subsistence residential unit." In his analysis the subsistence residential unit (camp) is a "corporation organized, structured, and integrated by the symbols of motherhood" but it is also "a functional unit for the purposes of residence and subsistence" (1970:60).

In my own definitions of residence types, I used Witherspoon's cooperation criteria, classifying as neolocal those households that consisted of a family (in my Cottonwood Springs sample it was always a nuclear family) living separately and not cooperating on a more or less daily, face-to-face basis in household or subsistence chores with the kin of either husband or wife, even if these kin lived "within earshot." However, not counting three neolocal households in the local trading post-BIA school complex, in only one instance would the "within earshot" criterion have been in some conflict with Witherspoon's cooperation criteria. In this case a nuclear family lived about 150 yards from their nearest neighbor (the wife's father's brother's family), over a rise and out of sight on a separate entrance road.

---

[2] In my own experience at Cottonwood Springs people regularly give rides to each other without expectation of giving or receiving payment.

Each hogan had its own firewood pile, each had its own water barrel, and their sheep were penned separately at night. Nevertheless, I classified this household as part of an extended family camp because not only did the two families regularly visit each other and give each other rides to the trading post, during the day their sheep were herded on the same customary grazing land, even if separately. Thus, with only this one possible exception, the camps I studied at Cottonwood Springs in 1974 to 1976 had a spatial identity as clearly defined as those studied by Shepardson and Hammond in 1960 to 1962.

There is no Navajo basic term equivalent to the word "camp" (Lamphere, 1977; Reynolds, 1979), and to my knowledge there have been no attempts to provide an emic justification of any residence classification system. I did not conduct any such study either, but an informal validation of sorts was provided, by English-speaking Navajos at least, when I asked directions to find various families in the course of my work. When they referred to individual families that I classified as living in extended family camps, they usually located these families with reference to another *person*. For example, "they live at Old Man Graymountain's place," or "they live with those people at Joe and Mary's place." The people so named seemed to correspond to what Reynolds, Lamphere, and Cook (1967) have called the "resource-controller"—the oldest able-bodied male of an extended family camp. In contrast, when they referred to people living in what I classified as neolocal camps, they would usually locate the family with reference to a *physical landmark*. For example, "they live near where that one road comes out on the main road by the second windmill," or "at the BIA school," or "at the end of the first road on the left after you get across the canyon." The point occurred to me that they might as easily have located the extended family camp families with reference to a physical landmark.

Even though I used Witherspoon's cooperation criteria in my definition of the neolocal camp, I am thus confident that my neolocal camp residence rate of 52% is as valid as Shepardson and Hammond's rate of 15.0% for 1960 to 1962. This is not only because of the indirect validation of my system suggested above, but especially because there was only one instance where the "territorial entity" of a camp was not clearly identifiable.

The third reason why my neolocal residence rate figure may differ so much from that of Shepardson and Hammond is that there has in fact been an increase in neolocal residence at Cottonwood Springs since their study in 1960 to 1962. What is the cause and significance of this change? It should be noted first that high rates of neolocal residence among the Navajo are not uncommon and, problems in definition notwithstanding, a number of reports suggest that the common stereotype of the Navajo as matrilocal is at least exaggerated. For example, citing a government survey of the reservation in the 1930's, Aberle (1961) notes that 53% of all households were listed as "independent consumption units," while only 32% were matrilocal, 5% were patrilocal and 10% were mixed. Aberle specifically notes also that these government figures are at "marked variance" with Collier's 1938 Cottonwood Springs neolocal residence rate of 13.6%. On the other hand, Collier (1966) reported that in 1938 in the eastern reservation area of Klagetoh 48% of the families were residing neolocally. In 1964, Reynolds, Lamphere, and Cook (1967) found that 45% of all residence groups in the Rimrock area were nuclear family camps. In the Rough Rock-Black Mountain area in the late 1960's to early 1970's, Witherspoon reported that 30% of the "subsistence residential units" consisted of a single household (1975). Finally, in their survey of Navajo community studies, Henderson and Levy (1975) report that of the 13 communities for which at least some data existed, 10 had a neolocal camp residence rate greater than 30%.

There have been a number of attempts to explain the great reservation-wide variance in local residence patterns, but the most common set of explanations focus on economic-ecological factors: Aberle (1961), Kluckhohn and Leighton (1974), Levy (1962), Ross (1955), and Sasaki (1960) have all argued that variation in Navajo residence patterns is best attributed to specific aspects of local economy or ecology, and many of these authors make the point that neolocal residence rates seem to increase with local reliance on wage work and increased cash income generally. However, as Henderson and Levy (1975) note, there are many exceptions to this generality, and its predictive power is not great. The reason for this, they argue, is that "virtually all of the past research on the Navajo has been descriptive and not analytical" (1975:122). One of the troubles with these descriptive studies, which simply note correlations between social or economic factors and local variations in residence patterns, is that their independent variables are not independent but are "packaged" (Whiting, 1976), that is they are global variables which may have a large number of unknown covariates, making it impossible to analyze alternative causal pathways that show *how* "economic change," for example, actually influences residence patterns in different ways under different circumstances. Two aspects of "economic change" that may be especially relevant for devising a model of Navajo residence patterns are technological change and income disposal, that is, the number and pattern of roads in a community, the distribution of pickup trucks in that community, and how both relate to access to local natural resources and wage-paying jobs.

This is my reasoning. In her recent study of Navajo residence patterns and ideology, Reynolds concluded that ". . . residence is a matter of subsistence economics. It involves access to resources as well as to the manpower for exploiting and processing them" (1979:148). According to Reynold's informants, the most important criterion for locating a camp is proximity to grazing land and/or fields. A corollary of this point is that camps should not be so close to each other that neighboring camps have to share grazing land in their immediate vicinity. Other factors include the terrain of a specific potential camp site, access to water for drinking, and closeness to a major road—to save wear and tear on motor vehicles, provide better opportunities for ride-sharing and hitch-hiking, and to be near school bus routes. To the extent that electric power lines often follow major roads, proximity to these roads also makes installation of home power lines less expensive. Reynolds argues that "the location of a residence site does not determine the kind of use people make of the land. Rather, they think it desirable that the way the people use the land determine residence site. They prefer the geographical location of dwellings to reflect the occupants' subsistence activities" (1979:33). In his discussion of Navajo residence patterns, Downs (1964) makes a similar point. He concluded that the most important criteria for deciding where to locate a camp are distance to firewood, distance to water for the sheep and for domestic use, distance to adequate grazing land, and distance to the local trading post. The determinants of camp location will not be perfectly isomorphic with the determinants of camp composition, that is, residence type, but where the determinants of location are such that camps must be widely dispersed, there should be a tendency toward smaller camps and hence toward neolocal, nuclear family camps. This is the pattern that exists at Cottonwood Springs, and the development of this pattern may have been made possible by the greater availability of the pickup truck.

This is because the pickup truck effectively changes the functional distance between a camp and all of the resources the camp will be exploiting. Depending on the type and spatial distribution of these resources, the availability of the pickup then constitutes an important intervening variable between "economic change" and residence patterns. In the eastern half of the reservation, where there are both more paved roads and better opportunities for wage work, there also seems to be a tendency for clustering of residence sites close to the roads (T. Reynolds, personal communication, 1980). At Cottonwood Springs, on the other hand, where there are very few opportunities for wage work, it is still true that total income from welfare, social security, and wage work has increased and made it possible for more families to purchase pickup trucks. Because of the deteriorating grazing land it has been adaptive to disperse flocks of sheep over the range in smaller and more widely scattered herds; with the greater availability of pickups, it has been *possible* to disperse both sheep and residence groups more widely and in smaller numbers over the range. I gathered no data on the size of sheep herds at Cottonwood Springs, but Adams and Ruffing (1977) report that in the nearby Navajo community of Shonto the population was more widely dispersed in the early 1970's than in 1953 and that while the total number of sheep at Shonto had *increased* from 3525 to 4995, the average herd size had actually *decreased* from 93 to 83 sheep per residence group (1977:72). With more widely distributed residence groups and with smaller herds of sheep, there can be more effective utilization of the already overcrowded and deteriorating grazing lands. Adams and Ruffing report too that not only did residence groups with large herds have difficulty in meeting the peak labor demands of herding as effectively as groups with medium-sized herds, the larger herds did not provide significantly greater income per sheep than medium-sized herds. And, as cash income from all sources goes up, as has been documented for both Shonto (Adams and Ruffing, 1977) and Cottonwood Springs (Shepardson and Hammond, 1970), large herds, which are already a significant ecological and management problem, become less necessary as the sole or even major source of income, and paychecks and welfare and social security checks can be used to purchase and maintain steadily increasing numbers of pickup trucks.

In any case, the pickup truck is a completely well-established part of Navajo life and has become a necessity on the reservation today. With a pickup, camps may be well-dispersed, located perhaps only on the basis of water and grazing for the sheep, since firewood and drinking water can be readily hauled by truck. Although it is ultimately a losing proposition, even water for the sheep can be hauled by truck during an emergency, as happened for a few weeks at Cottonwood Springs during a severe drought. Also, with a truck, families can make more frequent trips to distantly located agricultural plots, or to still more distantly located areas of the reservation where there may be a particularly rich piñon nut harvest. Without a truck, and with larger herds of sheep, it was not practical in the past to move the entire herd very far away to take advantage of good grazing. Now, with a truck, and smaller herds, short-term summer and/or winter sheep camps can be maintained near better grazing that might be as far as 30 miles from a family's main camp. Finally, possessing a truck, or having access to one, also enables families to bring their children home from school on weekends and holidays, something that is not only enjoyable for all, but that can be of significant economic impact, for example, during labor-intensive lambing or roundup time. Although Cottonwood Springs is not a major arts and crafts center, silverwork and rugs bring better prices when sold closer to off-reservation tourist centers like Flagstaff. The pickup, like many other expensive property items (e.g., jewelry), is also a form of insurance: when a woman at Cottonwood Springs needed a sing prior to entering a hospital for a major operation, her family promptly sold the pickup to finance the sing and pay the singer's fee.

While the role of the pickup truck in modern Navajo life seems self-evident, to my knowledge Downs (1964) is the only ethnographer of the Navajo to publish the number of pickups in his study area. He estimated that in the Piñon area in the early 1960's between only one-third and one-half of the people either owned or had access to a truck. At Cottonwood Springs in 1974 to 1976 this figure was closer to 90%, since virtually every camp had a pickup (0.67 pickups per household). Given the very great use that the Navajo make of the pickup, along with local variation in income, opportunities for wage work, number and condition of roads, and local ecology and terrain, it seems likely that at least some of the variance in Navajo residence patterns can be attributed to the way that the pickup influences residence choice by altering "access to resources as well as to the manpower for exploiting and processing them" (Reynolds, 1979:148). Thus, not only is the pickup truck a ubiquitous feature of the everyday environment of most Navajo infants, it may also be an important intervening variable between large-scale economic and ecological factors and the size and type of the social groups in which the infant spends most of his or her time and which provide the infant with the very opportunity for interaction with others of different age, sex, and kinship identities (see also Chisholm, 1981a).

Life in the Camp

The nature of the camp determines the social universe of the Navajo child more than any other social structural variable. The precise kinship structure of the camp probably makes little difference to the child (and it is not clear that it makes much difference to adults), but the differences in numbers and age/sex/kinship identity of coresidents may. The essence of the camp for the child is familiarity. Navajo Iroquoian kinship terminology reflects this familiarity as well as anything: mother and mother's sisters (and all women of their generation in the same clan) are merged (shimá: "mother"; shimá yázhí: "little mother" or "mother's sister") as are father and father's brothers (shizhe'e: "father" or "father's brother") and siblings and parallel (but not cross) cousins. In a unilineally organized camp the identity of cousins with siblings is more than simple customary terminology, for all children in the camp, of all ages, form a ready-made play group, and in terms of familiarity, there is no difference between "siblings" and "cousins." The infants and younger children in an extended family camp have a great number and wide variety of caretakers among their older sibling-cousins and mother-aunts; the older children have, as an everyday occurrence, playmates of both sexes and a potentially wide age range. The children in an isolated nuclear family camp have only thier mother, father, and true siblings as either caretakers or playmates.

The immediate vicinity of the hogans, houses, and (summer) brush shelters that make up a camp is a familiar playground with a wealth of natural toys. The number of store-bought toys available varies from none at all to as many as any Anglo family might have, but older children especially (whom the toddlers ordinarily follow about) seem to prefer running in and out of each other's hogans, around the sheep corral, the firewood pile, the wrecked trucks (kept for spare parts), and old wagons. Playing with water is about the only thing that is forbidden. Even playing with the sheep is permissible as long as it is done gently. There are always plenty of dogs and cats about and it does not matter much how roughly they may be played with. Sand, small insects, sticks, stones, and rubbish are the toys of most toddlers. Inside the hogans and houses, even the ones that have a bit of furniture, most household objects are readily at the hand of even very small children. Perhaps more important, inside the hogan (but less so in houses with more than one room) people are also readily available, and family size and birth-spacing being what they are there is usually a number of potential interactors even in the evenings and at night when (in an extended family camp) the other children go back to their own nuclear family hogans. Infants up to a year or so, on or off the cradleboard, usually sleep next to their mothers; if the mother sleeps on a bed instead of sheepskins on the floor, her infant may sleep on the floor next to her. Whether on beds or sheepskins, siblings (of the same sex only after 2 or 3 years) sleep together.

The timing of everyday events is extremely flexible. The sheep and the sun determine when most things happen, but even within their dictates meals are prepared whenever people are hungry, infants are nursed or given a bottle when they demand it, people of all ages take naps when they are sleepy, and there are no set bedtimes. Indeed, at least some children wake in the night and play quietly; in gathering information on the sleep habits of children in my sample, it appeared that the Navajo concept *nila* ("it's up to you") applied even to infants of only a few months, and unless they were ill or noisy, night waking was not a cause for comment.

In the hogan and within the boundaries of the camp, then, everything is social, familiar, unscheduled, and indulged for children. Outside the camp, however, all is less familiar, and most important, less social, less indulged, and while still not rigidly scheduled, may be more so than at home. The nearest neighbor is likely to be a minimum of a mile away, but usually much more. For the smallest children, however, even a few hundred feet beyond the edge of camp is a psychic boundary of some force: in over 1100 spot observations (see Chapter 4) on children from only a few days to 3 years old,

I recorded only five occasions when a child was outside this boundary (loosely defined as more than 100 feet away from an imaginary circle around all the hogans in a camp) and in all but one of these cases the child was with an older sibling or adult.

Although the pickup truck has increased casual visiting, such visits are irregularly spaced and, almost by definition, involve people who are already at least slightly familiar to even a child of only a few months. The only time that strangers are ordinarily seen by infants is at the Cottonwood Springs Trading Post. Older children see strangers at sings, but infants are not usually taken to sings. Furthermore, even when complete strangers are met (unless they are Anglos), in the polite and quiet Navajo way of interaction with strangers, these people will usually simply ignore the child. On the other hand, if an adult knows a child, even an infant, he will usually greet the child with a handshake just as he would another adult.

For children under the age of about three, when (and if) they start going to the local preschool, perhaps as much as 99% of all social interaction with anybody occurs in the camp with familiar people. Strangers are seen, but not interacted with, and are seen at irregular intervals, away from home. Some of the more isolated Cottonwood Springs children never see a stranger until they are 3 or even 5 years old, when they start at the local BIA school.

The environment of Navajo infancy will be considered more closely in the next chapter, where a description of patterns of cradleboard use and aspects of the behavior of newborn Navajo infants will be described. This chapter, however, has provided the broad context in which cradleboard use and the behavior of newborn Navajo infants must be seen, for, as anthropologists never tire of pointing out, even the most minute and apparently discrete item of any people's customs or behavior is invariably deeply "embedded" in the total fabric of their culture.

3
The Cradleboard

HAVING provided a broad description of the environment of Navajo infancy in the previous chapter, this chapter will focus on a narrow but potentially pivotal part of this environment—the cradleboard and its use. My purpose in this chapter is to discuss the theoretical and empirical work relating to cradleboard use in order to show why it might be expected to disrupt mother–infant interaction, why it might therefore qualify as a perturbation in the environment of Navajo infancy, and why focusing on the response of the infant to cradleboard use would be an appropriate topic for studying development as adaptation. The first parts of the chapter will thus provide a rationale for the specific hypotheses advanced in the last part of the chapter.

THE CRADLEBOARD AND SWADDLING IN CROSS-CULTURAL PERSPECTIVE

In spite of their widespread historical and spatial distribution in both the New and the Old World, the cradleboard and swaddling (its functional equivalent in many respects) have inspired many misconceptions, stereotypes, and simplistic theories, but virtually no empirical research useful for cross-cultural comparison or the analysis of patterns of use and possible effects in terms of current theory in child development. The purely psychoanalytic hypotheses seem to be interesting speculations at best, offering little hope of ever being testable. The ethnographic material is more suggestive and useful, but for the most part ethnographers simply report that the cradleboard is used, provide little useful detail, or are themselves of a psychoanalytic bent. The best material, from the standpoint of attachment theory and developmental ethology, has come from pediatricians and physiological developmental psychologists. Combining the data, insights, and speculations of psychiatrists, ethnographers, and experimental human physiologists, however, it becomes clear that the cradleboard and swaddling could have a significant impact on the interaction of the Navajo mother and child.

For the purposes of this chapter, unless otherwise noted, the cradleboards and patterns of cradleboard use observed at Cottonwood Springs can be considered broadly representative of the entire reservation. With respect to the potential effect of the cradleboard on the infant's physiology and interaction with others, they can also be considered broadly representative not only of most Native American societies but even of all societies where the cradleboard (and to a lesser extent, swaddling) is, or was, a major feature of infant care.

This is not small number of societies. From Barry and Paxson's (1971) cross-cultural codes on infancy and early childhood, it can be seen that of the 139 societies for which information is fully available, 20.9% use " . . . a cradleboard or other mechanism for restricting movement of the limbs as well as the body" for at least "much of the time" during the first 9 months of life (1971:468). When the category defined as "Body movement is limited by swaddling, heavy blankets, or a small cradle" is added to the "pure" cradleboard figure, a surprising 51.8% of all societies reported were found to practice some form of infant restraint. Cradleboard use and swaddling are not as rare as many think; when numbers of infants are counted, the concern for infantile freedom from restraint is the major concern, but when numbers of societies are totaled, this is of minor concern.

North America, Europe, and nontropical Asia are heavily represented as societies for which data are available. However, the cradleboard and swaddling are not uncommon in other culture areas. J. Whiting (1971), using another cross-cultural sample, found that 40 of 48 societies in the tropics (between latitudes 20°N and 20°S) were reported to have "close and frequent contact" between mother and infant whereas 29 of 37 societies above 20°N and below 20°S "used heavy swaddling or the cradleboard." In a recent (1981) extension of this work, Whiting has found that mean temperature of the coldest month of the year is a better predictor of cradleboard use than latitude. Where the temperature is less than 10°C (50°F), approximately 66% of societies use the cradleboard, but when this temperature is above 10°C only about 8% use the cradleboard. This worldwide distribution is not merely a function of simple borrowing between cultures, for Whiting was also able to show that in the major culture areas of the world, temperature accounts for more of the variance in use of the cradleboard than does language family. To some extent then, there is a clear association between climate and cradleboarding or swaddling, and this association helps to account for the concentration of these practices in North America, Eastern Europe, and nontropical Asia. This association also suggests one of the functions of cradleboarding and swaddling, although there is certainly more to it than simple temperature regulation. It is not immediately clear, for example, why mean temperature in the coldest month of the year should be so closely correlated with a practice that occurs year-round. Richards (Chisholm and Richards, 1978) has suggested that a better correlation might be obtained when humidity is considered along with temperature. In many societies where the cradleboard is used (e.g., the Navajo) summer temperatures are as high as in many tropical locations, but humidity remains very low. It is possible that tropical peoples avoid the cradleboard and swaddling not so much because of the temperature per se, but because the high humidity might promote bacterial and fungal infections under the swaddling or cradleboard binding material. This seems especially possible when it is considered that one of the functions of the cradleboard (among the Navajo at least) is to actually *retain* urine and feces, just as a diaper does (see below).

THE CRADLEBOARD AND ITS USE

There is, to be sure, considerable variation in the designs and patterns of use of cradleboards, not only throughout the world (e.g., Bloch, 1966; Lipton, Steinschneider, and Richmond, 1965; Sofue, 1957; Whiting, 1981) but also among Native North Americans generally (e.g., Dennis, 1940a, 1940b; Mason, 1886), and even among the Navajo (e.g., Bailey, 1950; Kluckhohn, 1947; Kluckhohn et al., 1971; Leighton and Kluckhohn, 1948; Roberts, 1951). Nonetheless, the essence of cradleboard design and use that is relevant to its effect on mother–infant interaction can be exemplified with reference to Cottonwood Springs.

The Navajo cradleboard ('awééts'áál; literally "baby diaper," which gives an immediate clue to one of its functions) consists of three parts: a back of one or two boards totaling about 10 by 36 to 40 inches, a hinged (with leather thong or string) footboard about 10 by 5 inches, and a hoop arching over the head and face of an infant lying on the board. The infant is placed on the board in the following manner: first, bedding material of some sort is placed on the back as a mattress. A blanket is then spread over the bedding material and the infant is placed supine on the blanket. Neonates and infants of only a few months, especially if the weather is hot, may wear only a diaper; older infants and toddlers, especially if the weather is cold, ordinarily wear more clothes (but never shoes). Young infants often have a folded cloth placed between their legs; this prevents the infant from rubbing his or her legs together when bound up in the cradleboard. The rationale for this is to further immobilize the infant and to prevent chaffing and irritation of the inner surfaces of the infant's legs.

After the child is positioned on the cradleboard the edge of the blanket on which he is lying is brought tightly around his body, passing under each armpit and bringing a layer of the blanket between his arms and his trunk. The other edge of the blanket is then passed tightly over both arms, which have been extended at the infant's sides, and tucked underneath the baby. The blanket is similarly tucked in tightly under the infant's legs and feet.

Thus with the child partially immobilized and held in place by whoever is placing the child on the cradleboard, the lacing of the cradleboard begins. Ordinarily, but not always, this begins at the top, since if the infant resists being put on the cradleboard (which is common) it is better to first immobilize his arms. The buckskin or cloth covering of the cradleboard is attached to the sides of the cradleboard back, and meets in the center over the baby's stomach where loops or eyelets are placed for the lacing thongs. The two halves of the cradleboard cover are then laced tightly their whole length. When the child's feet are reached, often after a bout of retucking if the infant resists, the footboard is brought up perpendicular to the back of the cradleboard, against the child's feet, and it too is tightly laced in position.

The result—which can take as little as 2 or 3 minutes with a quiet baby and experienced mother—is an almost completely immobilized infant, covered to his chin in the tightly bound swaddling material. The infant is usually unable to touch himself anywhere, except for perhaps rubbing his fingers together. The child in the cradleboard can freely move his head, but all other movements are limited except for isometriclike movements against the binding. Sometimes the "mattress" on which the child is lying extends up underneath the head, sometimes it does not. Some Cottonwood Springs mothers told me that having only a short mattress, with the infant's head resting a bit lower than his trunk against the back of the cradleboard, made for "a long neck," which some people, they said, consider to be an attractive feature. Some mothers also told me that they thought occipital flattening was attractive; others said the opposite. Some old women told me that "in the old days" not only was the infant's body tightly bound to the cradleboard, but often so also was his head, using a band of material attached to the sides of the cradleboard besides the child's head.

The hoop arching over the infant's head, usually interpreted by Anglos as protection should the cradleboard fall, also has the more important day-to-day function of holding a cloth or blanket which can be lowered over the baby without touching his face and interfering with his breathing. The cloth draped over the infant in this manner keeps direct sun off the infant's face, as well as wind, insects, and blowing sand; it also cuts off the infant's view of whatever may be going on around him.

Kluckhohn (1947; Kluckhohn and Leighton, 1974) reports that the Navajo infant does not go on the cradleboard until his third or fourth week. At Cottonwood Springs, however, all but one of the children who used the cradleboard went on it within the first week of life—usually on the day they returned from the hospital (where more than 95% of all Navajo children are now born), aged three or four days. Rabin and his colleagues (1965), in their study of the relationship between cradleboard use and congenital hip disease among the Navajo, reported that 40% of the children in their Many Farms sample went on the cradleboard in their first week, 19% in the second, 11% in the third, and the remaining 30% in the fourth week. Kluckhohn (Leighton and Kluckhohn, 1948) says the child goes on a "temporary cradle" within a few hours after birth. Although I never saw one used, Cottonwood Springs mothers said that some newborns were swaddled in a tightly bound sheepskin, wool-side in, for a few days or weeks until they "graduated" to a regular cradleboard.

Throughout his work, Kluckhohn implies that use of the cradleboard by the Navajo was essentially universal. While the incidence of cradleboard use was undoubtedly higher in his day than is the case today, it is important to realize that cradleboard use is not, and presumably never was, a cultural universal. At Black Mesa, a very conservative area of the reservation, Aberle (personal communication, 1974) reports that "almost nobody" used the cradleboard anymore. At Cottonwood Springs, on the other hand, also a very conservative area, more than 90% of all infants in 1974 to 1976 were on the cradleboard for at least a few months, and in the rather acculturated area of Many Farms, Rabin et al. (1965) reported that 85% of the children used the cradleboard. There seems to be no simple correlation between amount of cradleboard use and level of acculturation.

Kluckhohn (1947) reports that the average age at which the cradleboard is no longer used at all is 11.6 months, with a range of 8 to 15.5 months (sample size and standard deviation are not reported). Bailey (1950) reports that the cradleboard is used "for about a year"; some of her informants, like some of mine, said that in the past the cradleboard was used for as long as 3 years. Rabin et al. (1965) say that by 10 months, 40% of the children have stopped using the cradleboard and that by 12 months 70% have stopped; the remaining 30% using the cradleboard at night only up to 24 months. Mothers' reports on months of cradleboard use for those children in my sample who had ceased using the cradleboard are given below in Table 3.1.

Finally ceasing to use the cradleboard is by no means a clear-cut event; it is usually a gradual process, taking place over several weeks or months. The child ordinarily begins to use it less and less during the day, then at night, but with occasional relapses when he or she "just wants to use it again." This gradual tailing-off is shown graphically in Fig. 3.1.

Almost without exception the end of a child's cradleboard career is, as

Table 3.1. Months of Cradleboard Use among Cottonwood Springs Infants

	$\bar{X}$	SD	Range	n
Boys	10.79	3.95	2–21	11
Girls	9.72	4.42	1–18	10

many mothers said, "*bila*" ("it's up to him"). The reason, they said, that a child "decides" not to use the cradleboard anymore is that it becomes less comfortable as the child grows bigger ("he just didn't like it anymore because he got too big"). A small percentage of children end their cradleboard careers during a bout of sickness, with diarrhea being the most common precipitating factor. The constantly wet and soiled diapers caused irritation, according to some mothers, so their children "just wanted to be left out" so that they could "kick and move about" and let the air reach their irritated parts. One mother whose child had ended his career on the cradleboard this way said that the baby found her constant removal of him from the cradleboard, diaper changing, and tying back on the board irritating; she did not say that *she* found this irritating, but it is easy to imagine it would be. The one case in which a mother herself seemed to be taking all the responsibility for ending her child's cradleboard career was the one mother who said it was bad to keep infants (hers was 4 months old) on the cradleboard in very hot weather.

As will become more clear later, the most significant aspect of cradleboard use is almost definitely not simply the total number of months that a child uses the cradleboard, but the number of hours per day—and even more significantly, what is happening during these hours. Unfortunately, as Kluckhohn also found, it has proved difficult to obtain precise data on the

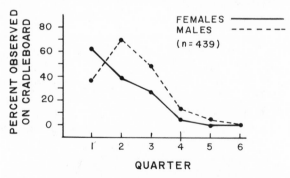

Fig. 3.1 Cradleboard use by quarters.

Table 3.2. Estimates of Daily Cradleboard Use in Hours

Age of infant	Kluckhohn (1947)	Cottonwood Springs
0–3	22	15–18
3–6	20	12–15
6–9	18	9–12
9–12	15	6–9

number of hours per day each child is on the cradleboard. From data on spot observations (see Chapter 4), however, and from more casual observations and interviews, I feel that previous estimates of hours per day on the cradleboard are too high. Dennis (1940a), for example, says that Hopi infants (ages unspecified) may be on the cradleboard for as much as 23 out of every 24 hours. There is no evidence that the Navajo infant spends anywhere near this much time on the cradleboard, except just possibly a few infants under the age of about 3 months. My impressions are also that Kluckhohn's (1947) estimates of cradleboard use are slightly high; I list his estimates in Table 3.2 along with my estimates from Cottonwood Springs.

It should also be stressed here that not only is the child asleep for most (perhaps 85%) of the time that he or she is on the cradleboard, but that there is also a very great variation in the number of hours per day on the cradleboard when the child is awake, and an even greater variation in the activities of others surrounding the child when the child is both on and off the cradleboard while awake. While the cradleboard may have been used more each day in the past than it is today, I doubt that is was used much more. The usual argument that the Navajo used the cradleboard because they were so nomadic just does not hold up. While a newborn infant, in fact, might have spent 23 hours a day on the cradleboard during a seasonal trek to better grazing areas, patterns of use today strongly suggest that as soon as a camp was established the infant would revert to a more normal 15–18 hours a day.

In a total of 26 months at Cottonwood Springs I only once saw a Navajo mother carrying her infant in a cradleboard strapped to her back in the classical and stereotypical, but extremely rare, "papoose" carry. Older Navajo people that I spoke with, when pushed, admitted that just maybe infants were carried this way more "in the old days," but to them it was something of an ethnic joke that Anglos have this curious imge of Navajo women with babies strapped to their backs. The one occasion of this carry that I saw was during lambing time in the early spring, a period when caring for the sheep becomes particularly labor-intensive. The infant was just over

4 months old and was breastfeeding, all able-bodied adults and older children were in the sheep corral, and all the younger children in the camp were
being cared for in one hogan by an aged grandmother. When I asked the
woman why she was carrying her baby that way she said, with some surprise
at the obviousness of it all, "so I can feed him." She added later that the
other children played with him "too much," so she did not want to leave
him with the other children in the hogan between feedings.

The cradleboard has a great many functions, only one of which is related
to infant transport, and this function was probably never the main reason for
its use or existence; it certainly is not today. Very simply, the cradleboard is
a baby-tending, or baby-sitting device. In Blurton Jones's (1972a) terms, it is
for caching more than for carrying. The cradleboard is ordinarily carried in
the arms and only from the hogan as far as the pickup truck. In the pickup
itself, however, the cradleboard serves as a handy and safe cache for the
infant, just as it did in the past when hanging from a saddle.

Another function of the cradleboard, at least in the past, was quite literally
as a diaper. The Navajo 'awééts' áál translates exactly as "baby (his)
diaper," and before cloth and disposable plastic diapers became common,
the bark of the desert cliffrose was shredded up and placed under the child
and between his or her legs on the cradleboard; by limiting the child's
movements, the swaddling effect of the cradleboard served to hold the
absorbent bark in place. The cliffrose plant itself is also called 'awééts'áál in
Navajo.

Yet another function of the cradleboard is that of the subtle regulation of
the infant's state (level of physiological arousal or responsiveness). Because
the cradleboard has a rigid back it is possible to alter the angle of the
cradleboard by propping it up against the wall of the hogan, a piece of
furniture, or a tree. Most cradleboards have a V-shaped notch in the top of
the board itself, making it possible to securely wedge the cradleboard
against whatever it is leaning on. Only rarely is the cradleboard hung anywhere off the ground. As will be discussed in more detail later, the angle of
the cradleboard has an effect on the infant's state. Data from 167 spot
observations (see Chapter 4) of children on the cradleboard showed that if
the child was in a waking state, the cradleboard was much more likely (p
$< .001$) to be propped upright; if the infant was in either of two sleep states,
the cradleboard was more likely to be laid flat on the ground or a bed. (Note,
however, that these correlations say nothing about the intentions of the
person who placed the infant in the upright or flat position.) When in the
upright position the cradleboard infant is at eye level with those around him,
at least in those houses and hogans with no furniture. Whether at eye level
or not, however, the cradleboard infant can simply see a great deal more of
his or her surroundings when in the upright position.

After the child is about 3 months old, his arms are sometimes not bound into the cradleboard next to his body, but are left free, with the swaddling extending up only to his armpits. This practice is limited almost exclusively to waking babies, and if one sees a child sleeping with his arms free, the chances are good that he only just feel asleep. Sometimes a toy, or any object that interests the baby, will be tied to the lacing of the cradleboard so he can play with it when his arms are free; the child can always reach the object and caretakers do not continually have to fetch dropped toys for the baby. Almost all cradleboards have a few beads, feathers, bits of turquoise, or a length of yarn attached to the hoop of the cradleboard directly in front of, but slightly above, the child's face. When his arms are free, this too can sometimes be reached for or batted at; when his arms are not free, the child can still watch it as it moves in the breeze or as he himself may jiggle it with his isometriclike movements under the swaddling material. To the extent that the infant may control, or learn to control, the movement of these beads, yarn, and so on, he may also increase the amount of response-contingent stimulation that he receives while on the cradleboard (cf. Watson, 1972).

Some mothers said that they found it uncomfortable to nurse their infants while they were on the cradleboard and so removed the baby for each feeding. Many others, however, did not report such problems and were observed to easily nurse their children without removing them from the cradleboard. The cradleboard hoop, in addition to holding up a cloth or blanket with all of its functions, can also help with feeding small infants: once or twice I observed harried mothers tying a baby bottle to the hoop, or simply propping one against the hoop, so that the baby could suck on the bottle unattended.

PREVIOUS STUDIES OF THE CRADLEBOARD

The Culture and Personality School

Virtually all anthropological and psychological attention to the cradle-board and swaddling, at least until recently, has been concerned with aspects of motor and personality development, two topics where now-outdated theory predicted that the effects of infant restraint would be most clearly seen. In the case of personality development, with the exception of Kluckhohn and Dennis and J. Whiting's recent work, all anthropological and psychological consideration of the cradleboard and swaddling has been guided by the attempts to explain adult personality characteristics in terms of Freudian concepts. The "swaddling hypothesis" of Gorer (1949) and Gorer and Rickman (1949) is the prime example. According to this hypothesis, the restraint of swaddling (and the cradleboard) causes an adult personality structure that inclines people to alternate meek submission to ambivalently regarded authority with explosive excess in the expression of emotion. Adult Russians and Eastern Europeans who were swaddled, according to Gorer, learned that passivity and restraint are necessary to secure milk, love and freedom, which can then only be enjoyed in excessive outbursts of emotion, which are ambivalent nonetheless, for the mother is both the cause of "imprisonment" and the release from it. Erikson (1963) was an enthusiastic supporter of this view, relating Oglala Sioux "stoicism" and its "opposite," outbursts of violence in war and in the Sun Dance, to Oglala use of the cradleboard (see also Petit, 1946).

Ruth Benedict (1949) and Margaret Mead (1954; Mead and Metreaux, 1953) took the position that swaddling is not so much a *cause* of adult personality as an *expression* of the adult personality and culturally deter-mined values and beliefs which are communicated to the infant. Benedict, for instance, notes differences in the adult personalities of Russians and Poles, in spite of the fact that they both swaddle their infants. The reason for the difference lies in the beliefs and values surrounding adult's *reasons* for swaddling and not the swaddling itself. Benedict and Mead are thus less strictly Freudian than Gorer and Rickman, arguing that the effects of swaddling by themselves do not necessarily have lifelong effects but that the complex of beliefs and values surrounding the practice of swaddling may.

The theoretical underpinnings of J. Whiting's recent (1971, 1981) cross-cultural research on carrying practices are in some ways similar to those of the old culture and personality approach, with the important exceptions that Whiting actually provides quantified measures of his variables and uses a far-reaching model for psychocultural research (J. Whiting, 1973) that goes beyond the question of the effects of early experience on adult personality. Whiting's model attempts to show how environmental and historical factors may influence infant care practices, how infant care practices may influence adult personality, and how adult personality may influence the projective-expressive systems of a society. Thus far, Whiting has concentrated on the first link, that between the environment (temperature) and infant care prac-tices (how infants are carried), and has left as open the question of how different infant carrying practices may affect adult personality and pro-jective-expressive systems, although he does offer some tentative examples of possible causal links. He notes, for example, that belief in high gods and guardian spirits is characteristic of cultures using cradleboards (1971), and B. Whiting (1978) has suggested that cradle cultures are more likely to produce adults experiencing high conflict over dependency motivations. In sum, however, Whiting states that the evidence for long-term effects of different infant carrying practices on adult personality "are not yet in." He notes that cradleboards and swaddling seem to have no lasting effect on motor and cognitive development, perhaps because of "catching up" in later childhood, but he also suggests that "styles of social interaction and early learned defenses against emotional conflict are much more resistant to change" (1981:176) and that hypotheses about these effects would be the most promising to develop and test.

Kluckhohn, as is well known, was heavily influenced by psychoanalytic theory, and his descriptions and analyses of Navajo childhood are replete with Freudian concepts and insights. In addition, however, Kluckhohn was not only cautious and aware of the immense variety of social-cultural and biological-genetic (1946:178) factors that could at least be influencing personality—throughout the life cycle—he was also aware of "the need for an adequate quantitative basis for generalizations" (1946:178). It is perhaps for these reasons that Kluckhohn says of Gorer " . . . he is guilty of loose statements, unwarranted assumptions, dubious analogies, and factual errors . . ." but then goes on to say that " . . . he seems in many significant respects to have been right . . . perhaps even for the wrong reasons" (1955:217). Perhaps for these reasons Kluckhohn dared not, or could not, attribute any characteristics of adult Navajo personality to the effects of the cradleboard per se. Kluckhohn clearly approved of the cradleboard—in the context of the total Navajo social-cultural and physical environments, but he says nothing about long-term effects.

Theoretical considerations quite aside, the "swaddling hypothesis" is weak on definitions, observations, and measurement. Adherents of the "swaddling hypothesis," like many non-Native American middle-class parents in favor of "freedom" for their infants, have neglected to consider, among other things, that swaddling the infant and using the cradleboard are not simple "either-or" propositions but that both follow a parametric distribution within societies and especially for individuals over time. Most important, they failed to see that this distribution of use is partially a function of the *infant's* behavior and that the infant is not simply a passive recipient of stimuli but can affect the actions of others—including whether or not he or she is swaddled or placed on the cradleboard.

Biological and Physiological Studies

Lacking the theoretical paradigm to focus his attention and especially the methodology to quantify his observations in a satisfying way, Kluckhohn was appropriately cautious about possible cradleboard effects. However, since the "swaddling hypothesis" and Kluckhohn's original description of

Navajo childhood, there have been a handful of studies by pediatricians and physiologically oriented developmental psychologists that are immediately relevant to these issues, and theory, methods, and quantified data begin to come together.

Among the first of these new studies of cradleboard effects was one by Rabin and his colleagues (1965) on the epidemiology of congenital hip disease among the Navajo. High rates of congenital hip disease (dysplasia and dislocation) had been reported for the Navajo; they also found "an exceedingly high prevalence." They suggest that "multigenetic" factors may predispose the Navajo to this condition, but they also found that the incidence of congenital hip disease was lower in the children in their sample than in the adults. This led them to search for changes in the environment which might have retarded the development of the disease in today's children. They concluded that prior to the introduction of diapers on the reservation, when only the shredded bark of the cliffrose was used, the binding of the cradleboard and consequent immobility of the infant's legs in a constant adducted position may have exacerbated the dislocation or at least helped to maintain it. They were able to establish, however, that the children in their sample had used the cradleboard as infants and that they had also used cloth or disposable diapers. They then suggested that the cradleboard and the diaper may have acted synergistically to actually *treat* hip dislocation: the diaper forces the infant's legs slightly apart in a slightly abducted position, and the cradleboard binding holds them there, constituting a condition close to the accepted orthopedic procedures for correction of congenital hip disease.

As mentioned above, much of the early anthropological and developmental interest in the cradleboard was related to its possible effects on motor development. Anglos who are asked about cradleboard use usually say that it retards motor development and offer this as a reason why they would not use it for their own children. In spite of the apparent logic of the premise, however, there is no evidence that the cradleboard or swaddling has any effect on motor development. Dennis (1940a), for example, in a study of Hopi children on the cradleboard, found that motor development appeared quite normal and that milestones like the age of walking occurred at the same time for those who had and had not used the cradleboard. Kluckhohn (1947; Kluckhohn and Leighton, 1974) also failed to find any cradleboard effects on motor development. Hudson (1966) suggests that inasmuch as the cradleboard bindings do not entirely prohibit all movements, but in fact make such small movements isometric in nature, then the infant's isometric-like movements under the cradleboard bindings may serve to counteract the fact that the infant is unable to practice crawling and walking.

Whatever the reason, the cradleboard and swaddling do not seem to affect motor development. One reason must certainly be that most infants are not on the cradleboard long enough for it to have any such effects. Not only are Navajo infants not on the cradleboard as many hours each day as had been earlier thought, but most of the time they are on the cradleboard they are asleep and thus are not missing out on time to practice crawling and walking. Even if a child were on the cradleboard for as much "23 out of every 24 hours," however, what happens in that 1 hour a day of "freedom" might be very important, as Zelazo et al. (1972) and Super (1976) have suggested. The thrust of their arguments are that cases of precocious or retarded motor development are cases of gene–environment interaction in which the particular environment is likely to be the efficient cause of the precocity or retardation. Following Zelazo's experimental data, Super showed that so-called "African infant precocity" in motor development was primarily a function of the infant's being able to practice motor skills and even being explicitly taught them. Even only minutes a day of specific teaching might balance out the effects of 23 hours a day of (near) immobility. In casual conversation with a few sets of parents at Cottonwood Springs toward the end of my fieldwork there, I asked if children were ever taught to walk. Answered in the affirmative, I then asked why parents would try to teach their children how to walk and was told by two sets of parents that "it helps them to walk sooner." In any case, the 21 Cottonwood Springs children on whom I have mother's recollections took their first unaided steps at a mean age of 13.7 months. There was no relationship between the age at which each began to walk and the length of time he or she was in the cradleboard.

Next to advances in the concepts and methods of attachment theory and developmental ethology, the most important recent work relating to the environment of the cradleboard and its effects on the infant come from studies of the physiological effects of the cradleboard and swaddling. The most significant of this work is that of Lipton, Steinschneider and Richmond (1965). In an extensive review of historical and cross-cultural data on the cradleboard and swaddling, they attribute much of the pediatric, psychological, and lay resistance to the cradleboard and swaddling to J. B. Watson's (1919) view that there was a "negative reaction to restraint in early infancy." Noting that experimental studies of motor restraint in animals showed no ill effects, and indeed showed a general lowering of the animal's arousal level, they proceeded to carry out experiments with human infants. With the infants in each of three experimental conditions (fully swaddled, swaddled only up to the armpits, and unswaddled), they recorded a variety of vital signs before, during, and after swaddling and the presentation of various experimental stimuli. They found that infants who were swaddled slept more, had reduced levels of motor activity, fewer startles, and lower heart rate variability than nonswaddled infants. They found no decrease in the capacity to respond to stimulation (excepting, of course, large muscle movements) but only a decrease in the frequency of response to stimulation. In all cases the "arms-free" condition was more similar to the completely swaddled condition, except for startles, which were similar to the un-swaddled condition. As will turn out to be especially significant later, they noted that when first swaddled most infants struggled and protested for a few minutes, but that these infants also "gave up" long before simple muscle fatigue could have set in. They also noted that older infants and those with less experience in being swaddled struggled more than infants used to the experimental swaddling procedure.

They conclude that this general lowering of arousal and irritable responsiveness is a function primarily of motor restraint, which results in decreased afferent proprioceptive stimulation to the central reticular formation of the brain stem. Lipton and his colleagues thus argue that the essence of swaddling, and of the cradleboard, is motor restraint, but that this restraint operates at a physiological level and not a motor developmental or psychodynamic level. They dispute claims that swaddling affects motor development but they are simply silent on the question of personality development.

There is, however, more to the cradleboard and swaddling than motor restraint. Brackbill (1973) has shown that continuous stimulations of a wide variety also have the effect of lowering arousal level, and that these effects have some stability over time—several hours at least. These effects are also ontogenetic phenomena, more powerful in infant animals than in adults. Brackbill found that the continuously presented stimuli of "white noise," a constant light, constant temperature—and swaddling (constant tactile stimulation)—all reduced heart rate variability, respiratory irregularity, motor activity, and state. She feels that the constant tactile-proprioceptive stimulation of the swaddling material is just as important as the motor restraint. Giacoman (1971) notes similar results but adds that swaddling did not reduce levels of visual alertness or responsiveness.

As briefly mentioned above, if the Navajo infant is awake and on the cradleboard, the cradleboard is more likely to be upright, propped against the wall. Greenberg et al. (1960) and Harper (1972) have presented data on the neurophysiology of posture in infants that is particularly relevant to this aspect of cradleboard use. They have suggested that a near-vertical posture quiets the infant and enhances visual alertness through stimulation of the reticular activating system by the vestibular system. In one of her studies, Korner (Korner and Thoman, 1972) makes a similar observation. In an earlier study (Korner and Grobstein, 1966) she reports that picking an infant up lowers its arousal level but increases visual alertness, also suggesting that upright posture is implicated. Recently, Korner and her colleagues (1976) have singled out vestibular stimulation per se as the crucial factor in soothing and alerting, and not upright posture per se (although Harper's neuroendocrine reasoning still seems plausible). Korner and her colleagues (Gregg, Haffner, and Korner, 1976) also show that vestibular stimulation (whole-body movements such as those associated with rocking, bouncing, swinging, and being picked up) are better soothers and alerters than tactile stimulation or sucking alone. White and Castle (1964) have shown that extra handling and rocking tends to increase visual alertness in institutionalized infants, and similar results were reported by Ottinger et al. (1968). Freedman et al. (1966) report that extravestibular stimulation of one premature infant twin resulted in a greater weight gain for him than for his brother. Pederson and Ter Vrugt (1973) and Scarr-Salapatek and Williams (1973) all make generally similar observations for humans while Denenberg (1969), Levine (1969), Mason (1968) and Scott (1971) do so for a number of different species. Summarizing many of these studies, Prescott (1970a, 1970b, 1973) presents a wide-ranging theory of the role of "somatosensory deprivation" in the etiology of several abnormal social and emotional behavior patterns. The importance of physical contact per se, then, stressed so much in all of Harlow's work and much of Bowlby's, may be very slightly misleading, as Gregg, Haffner, and Korner (1976) point out: it may be that because physical contact and tactile stimulation are so much a part of vestibular stimulation in the human (and primate) environment of evolutionary adaptedness that one was mistaken for the other.

What this means for the cradleboard infant is difficult to say, for it has not been established how much vestibular (or tactile) stimulation is necessary, when it is necessary, or if all infants in all environments need the same amount. It has also not been established that all infants in all environments respond in the same way or to the same degree to the motor restraint that lowered the arousal level of the infants in the studies by Lipton and his colleagues. It is even possible, for example, that when the infant's level of arousal is habitually low, he or she may "need" less vestibular stimulation than more irritable or aroused infants. In short, while the physiological data has shown that swaddling (and the swaddling effect of the cradleboard) does have a measurable impact on experimental infants—and this is a significant advance over psychoanalytic approaches which imputed unmeasurable effects on the basis of theory only—neither the physiological nor the psychoanalytic approaches have actually observed the infants of a cradle or swaddling culture in their natural, every-day environments. There is certainly more to the life of a cradleboard infant than arousal level, vestibular stimulation, and unmeasurable psychodynamics; nor does recent research support the notion that the infant is the passive recipient of the environmental input that the physiological and psychoanalytic positions argue is so determining. It may be that how and when the stimulation is received, and the fact that the infant influences both how and when, are just as important as the nature of the stimulation itself.

Freedman's Biocultural Theory

For a number of years Daniel Freedman of the University of Chicago has made the point that not only does the infant have a significant effect on the behavior of its caregivers, infants of various populations may also differ in their behavior for genetic reasons. Thus, genetic factors may be implicated in population differences in the behavior of caregivers through their effect on the behavior of infants. Working originally with dogs, Freedman (1958) documented consistent behavioral differences in the puppies of several breeds and argued that these breed differences in behavior reflected gene pool differences. Moving on to investigate the possibility of similar geno-typically determined behavioral differences in human infants, Freedman and Keller (1963) showed that the behavior of newborn identical twins was significantly more similar than that of fraternal newborn twins. Using an earlier form (Freedman and Brazelton, 1971) of the Brazelton Neonatal Behavioral Assessment Scale (Brazelton, 1973), he then showed that there were significant racial/ethnic differences in the behavior of newborn African, Chinese, Japanese, Caucasian, Aboriginal Australian, and Navajo infants of only a few hours old (Freedman and Freedman, 1969; Freedman, 1971, 1973, 1974a, 1974b). Throughout this work, Freedman argues that these racial/ethnic differences are caused by gene pool differences and that the gene pool differences exist because of gene drift.

Freedman's work on the behavior of newborn Navajo infants takes the experimental physiological work of Lipton, Steinschneider, and Richmond an important step further, for the essence of Freedman's results are that Navajo infants have a lower level of arousal and are less irritable at birth. Comparing data on Chinese, Japanese, Caucasian, and Navajo newborns, Freedman found that the Chinese, Japanese, and Navajo infants clustered together and differed as a group from the Caucasian infants, more drama-tically on the test items which measured " . . . temperament, which seemed to tap excitability/imperturbability" (1971:220). The Navajo infants and their gene pool relatives, the Chinese and Japanese infants, differed from the Caucasian infants in being less irritable, slower to reach a crying state, less labile in state, better at self-quieting, and more easily consoled if they did become excited. He reports other differences as well, but this overall "irri-tability" factor is particularly relevant to cradleboard use and its possible effects on the child's physiology and on mother–infant interaction.

Freedman does not believe that the Navajo cradleboard can somehow "train infants towards subdued behavior"; he argues that " . . . if one observes actual cradleboarding practices, it becomes clear that this cannot be the case. Among the Navajo, if a baby indicates he wants out, he is readily untied and released, and the board is never used as a miniature jail" (1974b). Instead, Freedman turns the theme of the swaddling hypothesis on its head and argues that it is not the cradleboard that causes "subdued behavior," but that "subdued behavior" causes the cradleboard. In other words, nature, in the form of genotypical differences in neonatal behavior, selects the cultural practice of the cradleboard when the biological "template" includes nonirritable infants. Freedman continues then to cite a number of studies which are represented as showing the long-term effect of this quieter, genetically based temperament on Navajo and Chinese and Japanese child rearing, art, religion, and ethics.

Freedman's data on the behavior of newborn Navajo infants is of vital concern for anybody interested in child development and the relations among genotype, phenotype, and environment. His observation that Navajo newborns are quieter and less irritable than Anglo newborns at birth is of singular importance, as is his suggestion that the cultural childrearing practices of a group are at least in part an adaptation to the kinds of infants they have. As will be seen, however, Freedman, like the psychoanalysts and physiologists and the culture and personality school, failed to actually observe and to measure the process of interaction itself. He did not describe how the cradleboard is used and how it fits into the wider social, cultural, and physical environment of Navajo infancy. Thus, Freedman cannot say how the behavior of the infant, even if it is genetically determined, interacts with use of the cradleboard, patterns of mother–infant interaction, and the particular course of development that originally low levels of irritability may take. Nor (as I will discuss more fully in a later chapter) can he assume that population differences in behavior which happen to correlate with known genetic markers are themselves a product of the genetic differences. Finally, following Hebb (1953), Freedman takes the position that "all behavior is 100% acquired and 100% inherited" (1974:144). The effects of the cradleboard are patently not 100% acquired and 100% inherited and such an assumption of gene-environment interaction can never show how any given phenotype might arise from any given gene-environment interaction.

THE HYPOTHESES: DOES THE CRADLEBOARD AFFECT NAVAJO CHILD DEVELOPMENT?

From the discussions in the preceding sections of this chapter it has become apparent that the cradleboard can have an effect on the behavior of infants. From the discussions in the first chapter on the effects of the infant's behavior on the behavior of its caregivers, it also becomes apparent that the cradleboard might affect the behavior of the infant's caregivers through its effects on the infant. Thus, one of the general hypotheses that guided the work I present here is that the cradleboard would affect Navajo child development because of the effect it has on Navajo infant behavior and patterns of mother–infant interaction.

I hypothesized that the cradleboard would affect Navajo mother–infant interaction for the following reasons. First, a number of channels of communication are denied the cradleboard infant; he or she cannot express all the so-called "attachment" behaviors or simply the full range of behaviors otherwise possible because of the physical restraint of the cradleboard. The child on a cradleboard, for example, cannot approach or follow his or her mother. Second, the infant on the cradleboard cannot receive the full impact of behaviors directed toward him or her by others. For example, the child on a cradleboard is denied a portion of his mother's body warmth and skin-to-skin contact; because of the size and weight of the cradleboard he may be picked up less often and/or held for shorter periods of time; and because he cannot locomote, or reach to another, he is less likely to be interacted with as a result of his initiative toward somebody else. Third, at the same time, because of the decreased level of arousal caused by the swaddling effect of the cradleboard, the cradleboard baby may be less motivated to respond to a variety of stimuli, animate or inanimate. Because the cradleboard child's response threshold is raised by the swaddling effect of the cradleboard he or she may find the wider social and physical environments less interesting and may thus be less inclined to explore this environment (even if only visually because of the motor restraint of the cradleboard). Finally, because of the cradleboard child's decreased ability to respond motorically and his or her decreased motivation to respond to or initiate social interaction, others around the cradleboard baby might also find him or her less "interesting," less responsive. I thus predicted that when on the cradleboard a Navajo infant would have fewer and shorter bouts of social interaction with his or her mother than when off the cradleboard, and that when on the cradleboard the interactions that did occur would be less mutually responsive than when off.

There was no a priori reason for believing that the effect of the cradleboard on the infant's level of arousal and responsiveness would, by itself, constitute a perturbation for the infant. From a consideration of attachment theory, however (see Chapter 1), it appeared that there might be good reason for believing that the effect of this lowered arousal level and diminished responsiveness on mother–infant interaction could constitute a perturbation for the infant. Most generally, as Ainsworth and her colleagues put it,

". . . socialization results from reciprocal mother–infant responsiveness" (1974:118). As discussed in the first chapter, low maternal responsiveness has been consistently implicated in less-than-optimum patterns of attachment; mothers in Ainsworth's various studies who were rated as low, insensitive, or inconsistent in their responsiveness more often had infants who were judged "anxious/avoidant" or "anxious/resistant" in their attachment. Those infants whose mothers were most insensitive and most unresponsive were

> . . . extremely passive and easily distressed both at home and in the strange environment. Infants in this subgroup experienced no consistent feedback to their signals and were given little opportunity to explore and gain feedback by learning to control inanimate objects. Consequently, they were strikingly passive and tended to engage in excessive autoerotic behavior. They were highly distressed in the strange situation and could not cope with the opportunity to explore nor with excessive stresses. Upon reunion with mother, they showed fairly strong attachment behavior, limited somewhat by their pervasive passivity, but . . . they also displayed angry contact-resisting behaviors . . . they react to stress with heightened ambivalence to the mother . . . they attack the mother angrily in a futile expression of their distress (Ainsworth, Bell, and Stayton, 1971:48–49).

Further, the infants who showed most fear of strangers in Ainsworth's strange situation tests had mothers who were judged to be the most "highly insensitive."

An unresponsive infant does not invariably mean an unresponsive mother, but the thrust of most research on the effect of the infant on its caregiver suggests that such an infant is more likely to have such a mother. This is because the unresponsive infant provides his or her mother with less (and less immediate) feedback and is thus more likely to eventually become a less interesting social partner to mother. The opposite, of course, is also true: an unresponsive mother does not invariably mean an unresponsive infant, but is simply more likely to do so. However, the point, as Ainsworth and her colleagues continually stress, is not laying the "blame" on mother or infant, but on examining the effects of *mutual* responsiveness or unresponsiveness on the development of the child.

In short, the predicted effects of the cradleboard are similar to those conditions that many attachment theorists suggest give rise to "avoidant" or "resistant" attachment, and it is for this reason that I hypothesized that the cradleboard might constitute a perturbation for the developing Navajo infant. For reasons that I will discuss immediately below, however, I did not design my research to test the hypothesis that cradleboard use was related to "avoidant" or "resistant" attachment, in spite of the possible reasons for doing so. One reason is the experimental physiological evidence showing that the cradleboard lowers infants' levels of arousal and responsiveness, but this reason is not entirely sufficient because of the fact that infants' levels of arousal and responsiveness are not the only factors determining the nature of their attachment. The other reason is even less satisfactory, but might appeal to those particularly zealous adherents of the belief that early experience must affect later behavior—who see a possible connection between mutually unresponsive interaction in infancy, "avoidant" or "resistant" attachment, and the themes of "endemic uneasiness" and "morbid melancholia" in Navajo adults (see above). This syndrome of anxiety and depression is impressionistically consistent with many of Bowlby's characterizations of adults who have been "anxiously" attached as infants. But Navajo adults are not Navajo children and this sort of hypothesis, like several old culture and personality hypotheses, is in fact untestable. Further, even if one accepts these anecdotal and impressionistic reports of "endemic uneasiness" and "morbid melancholia," there is every reason to believe, as Kluckhohn suspected, that they are the results of Navajo history and the "exceedingly grave pressures facing the Navajo society."

The most general reason, however, for not phrasing the hypothesis about cradleboard effects in terms of attachment stems from the view of development as adaptation advanced in Chapter 1. In this view a crucial property of normal development, like adaptation, is the ability to make successful responses to environmental perturbations. An evolutionary view of child development suggests that there would have been great selection for the behaviors underlying a strong and secure attachment between mother and infant, but this same evolutionary view also suggests that adaptability—the ability to make successful responses to environmental perturbations—may have been selected for just as strongly. Indeed, it is possible that the more crucial secure attachment became during hominoid evolution, the more selection there might have been for the ability to form secure attachments under a variety of conditions and through a variety of pathways. The theoretical approach to child development outlined in Chapter 1 provides an evolutionary biological rationale for expecting this sort of adaptability or flexibility in development.

Thus, expecting developmental plasticity, I did not extend my hypotheses about the effects of the cradleboard on Navajo mother-infant interaction to include any predictions about the effects of shorter, fewer, and less mutually responsive interactions between mother and infant on the nature of their attachment. Even though shorter, fewer, and less mutually responsive interactions between mother and infant have been generally implicated in "avoidant" and "resistant" attachment, and even though Navajo adults are often said to display behavioral patterns that are not inconsistent with some of the supposed long-term effects of disturbed attachment in infancy, there is no evidence that Navajo infants are anxiously attached to their mother in any way. In fact, the complete lack of evidence for anxious attachment in

Navajo infants is itself suggestive of developmental plasticity, for the experimental evidence showing how the cradleboard can affect infant behavior appears solid and these effects appear to be major antecedents of anxious attachment. The question therefore becomes, "if the cradleboard has the effects on mother–infant interaction that are predicted, why don't these effects lead to anxious attachment?"

Viewing the process of development as one of adaptation suggests a strategy for studying this question. The expectation of developmental plasticity means that in studies of the effects of early experience on later behavior one cannot leave the choice of the dependent variables simply to high theoretical expectations. Instead, one must focus attention on the response of children to perturbations and analyze the efficacy of these responses in alleviating any stress associated with the perturbation. At the very least, one must observe the immediate response of a child to a perturbation in order to rule out the possibility that his or her immediate response is a short-term effect that may prevent it from having any long-term effects. Such a strategy will also be necessary for describing possible developmental pathways and the phenomenon of canalization, for the child's response to the perturbation may also be his or her first step along such an alternate pathway. In analyzing the efficacy of the child's response to a perturbation it is necessary to consider the possibility that the efficacy of the child's response depends not only on the presence of other individuals, but also on the child's ability to communicate the existence of his or her perturbation to these others and on their ability to respond for the child. The child's mother, of course, is likely to be the primary agent for ensuring the success of the child's response, but it is necessary to also consider the fact that mothers and infants do not exist in social vacuums and that not only may others besides mother respond for the child, the mother may herself also be the source of the child's perturbation, and her interaction with her child may also be affected in systematic ways by the number and age/sex/kinship identities of others in the developmental environment of the child.

In sum, with the evolutionary view of development advanced in Chapter 1, I expected adaptability or plasticity in the Navajo infant's response to the hypothesized perturbing effects of the cradleboard on mother–infant interaction. At the same time, because of this expectation of developmental plasticity, I focused my attention on those responses to the cradleboard that might prevent it from having any long-term effects.

4

The Research

ANTHROPOLOGY AND ETHOLOGY IN CHILD DEVELOPMENT RESEARCH

THE descriptive, observational, and recording techniques that I used to quantify patterns of Navajo mother-infant interaction were those of the young discipline human ethology. Clyde Kluckhohn, the first to conduct child development research with the Navajo, would have approved, I believe, of the use of these techniques, for he felt "the need for an adequate quantitative basis for generalizations" in his own research (1946:178). My reasons were the same: when small items of objectively observable behavior are recorded as the units of analysis, observer bias and interpretation are greatly reduced. The raw data that emerge from ethological observation are relatively pure etic description, relatively free of unstated and often unknown emic impressions and projections. Emic research, of course, does not need to be defended, but when emic data are unknowingly and unsystematically mixed with etic data, the result is a mare's nest of confusion. The goal of the ethological method is simply to consciously strive for as high a degree of etic "purity" as possible. Further, because the unit of analysis is so small, objectively observable, and capable of easy description, numbers emerge in a meaningful way with clear referents in the natural world. This makes it possible to more rigorously test hypotheses that arise from the data themselves during analysis. This is one of the advantages of the ethological approach: by rigorously applying a quantitative natural history approach to a wide range of behaviors, induction is both possible and fruitful.

The common criticism (e.g., Cooper et al., 1974) that ethologists are naive in their claims to be using an inductive approach, is simply wrong. The classic hypothetico-deductive approach of psychology certainly exists in ethology, in a manner as strong and often more useful. Ethologists *do* have hypotheses. Perhaps the reason they are so often accused of not having hypotheses is that they traditionally place little emphasis on their specific working hypotheses and often do not explicitly state the general hypothesis on which the discipline rests: that the causes of behavior are many and complex and must be sought in their natural environments (cf. Blurton Jones, 1972b; Tinbergen, 1951, 1963). For this reason, while employing a hypothetico-deductive approach, ethologists minimize their preconceptions and their commitment to any specific working hypothesis by casting a wide research net, thereby maximizing their chances of both disproving the specific hypothesis and at the same time benefiting from their wide research net by being better enabled to generate *new* hypotheses from their data (cf. Richer, 1974). In this sense ethology and much of anthropology are alike, and both differ from much of psychology, especially experimental psychology.

The use of classical ethological techniques by anthropologists conducting cross-cultural research on child development is in its infancy. Many more anthropologists conducting such research have used variations of the research techniques developed by John and Beatrice Whiting and their students and colleagues in the Six Cultures studies (Whiting et al., 1966; Whiting and Whiting, 1975). Briefly, the Whitings employ a time-event sampling technique in which interactive behaviors are classified as: seeks help, seeks attention, seeks dominance, suggests responsibly, offers support, offers help, acts sociably, touches, reprimands, assaults sociably, assaults, and symbolic aggression (Whiting and Whiting, 1975:57). Like any observation technique, this one presents advantages and disadvantages. Among other things, observing with a short time sample means that it is impossible to examine the social and environmental correlates of such things as length of interaction, which may often last for long periods of time. The small number of events sampled (12) means that information will be lost and the relatively subjective nature of the event definitions requires a certain degree of intuitive decision making by the observer, especially when a behavior might reasonably be classified into more than one category (e.g., when is a touch a "touch," or "acts sociably," or "offers help," or "offers support?").

On the other hand, the advantage of this sort of observation technique is just where its more objective ethological alternate technique is weakest: in the realm of "meaning." The items in an ethologist's behavior catalogue are derived from observation and defined in terms of observable behavior. These catalogues thus do not include items that are subjective, inferential, or even partially defined in terms of motiviation (cf. Blurton Jones, and Woodson, 1979). However, because the acts observed in the Whitings' approach are derived from previous cross-cultural research and a specific theory of social interaction (e.g., Whiting and Child, 1953; Sears, Maccoby, and Levin, 1957), this approach yields data that can be readily interpreted in terms of widely held psychological constructs initially unavailable to the ethologist. This does not mean that ethology is theoretically impoverished. It means only that ethology more sharply separates methods and theory. There is no reason why ethologically described behavior patterns cannot be analyzed in terms of any particular social-behavioral theory. One problem, of course, is the difficult one of demonstrating just what the relationship between cognition and behavior may be. Before this can accomplished, ethologists argue, we must at least have good descriptions of behavior. In the meantime, when the different approaches yield similar findings, we may conclude that the finding is especially robust.

All of the research reported here focused on Navajo infants in interaction with their mothers. My reasons for focusing on *mother*-infant interaction were several. First, for reasons outlined in the previous chapters, mothers are likely to be the primary agents through whom infants respond to their environmental perturbations. In this sense, throughout human evolution mothers, more than fathers, have been the predominant source of environmental feedback on whom infants base their own behavior and through whom infants adapt in the most fundamental sense by learning that there is a relationship between their own behavior and their environment. Whatever difference it may make to mothers, fathers, and society, there seems to be no good evidence that shows that *mother*–infant interaction is more significant to the infant than interaction, per se, with any sensitive, responsive person. That females give birth and lactate is due to fundamental genetic and evolutionary factors relating to reproductive strategies, parental investment strategies, and kin selection, but parturition and lactation probably have relatively little to do with the infant's ability or motivation to interact with anyone. That mothers and females care for and interact with infants and children more than fathers and males is a result of the interaction of genetically determined sex differences and the social-cultural views and uses of those sex differences, and is probably little influenced by the nature of infants.

Thus, my decision to focus on mother–infant interaction is appropriate in the sense that I focus on an *interaction*, and more appropriate in the sense that it is a statistically significant interaction, that is, Navajo mothers care for and interact with their infants far more than any other single age/sex/kinship category. Further, in order to standardize my observations—partly to see if there *were* any differences between the interactive behaviors of mothers and others—I had to focus specifically on mothers because not all children in the sample had fathers, grandparents, aunts, uncles, or siblings. In all of the work reported here each child's mother was present and there *could* have been an interaction, but all interactions the infant had with anybody were recorded. No attempt was made to control for the number or identity of others present (unless there were several strangers in the hogan), as variations in the social environment were a primary independent variable hypothesized to affect patterns of mother-infant interaction.

The hypotheses that guided the research were presented in Chapter 3. For the sake of simplicity they are rephrased here as four general questions about how hypothetical independent variables might relate, directly or indirectly, to the dependent variables of mother–infant interaction. These four questions are: does the cradleboard affect Navajo mother–infant interaction? Are there differences between infants at birth that affect mother–infant interaction? Are there individual differences in the environment of mother–infant interaction that affect their interaction in the same or different way as the cradleboard? And last, what affects the amount and timing of cradleboard use?

A wide variety of aspects of mother–infant interaction constitute the dependent variables in each of the first three of these questions, but since one of the goals of this study was to examine some of the mechanisms whereby the infant might successfully respond to the hypothetical perturbation of the cradleboard, the fourth question (what affects the amount and timing of cradleboard use?) is phrased as the reciprocal of the first three. The cradleboard is hypothesized as an immediate, proximal cause of variation in patterns of mother–infant interaction, but the patterns of cradleboard use themselves may be affected in systematic and perhaps adaptive ways by the very nature of mother–infant (or infant–other) interaction while the child is on the cradleboard. An obvious but not banal example of a factor that affects the amount and timing of cradleboard use, and thus patterns of mother–infant interaction, is the Navajo concept of the cradleboard as a child-care device. At least one of the reasons that the Navajo use the cradleboard is that they simply have the tradition of cradleboard use.

While the subtitle of this book is "An Ethological Study of Child Development," I nevertheless make use of some of the methods of such disparate disciplines as social anthropology, developmental psychology, and pediatrics; clearly, no one discipline commands all the methods necessary for adequately describing all the variables affecting infant behavior in any given culture. The observation techniques of human ethology provided quantified measures of the mother–infant interactive behavior dependent variables while the observation categories of social anthropology provided the more qualitative descriptions of the social and physical environments in which these interactions took place. Participant observation and both formal questionnaires and informal, open-ended interviews provided most of the material on each child's developmental history and family background as well as on the daily routines of child care. In addition to these observation techniques, however, two formal testing procedures were also utilized: the

Brazelton Neonatal Behavioral Assessment Scale (Brazelton, 1973) and a technique for measuring the development of children's fear of strangers. These and all other research methods will be described in detail in a later section of this chapter.

Throughout all phases of this research, the primary focus was on the main sample, the 38 children at Cottonwood Springs between the ages of a few days and nearly 3 years whose parents consented to take part in the research project. After I had been at Cottonwood Springs only a few weeks, however, I drove to Flagstaff, Arizona to meet some friends who were coming to Cottonwood Springs for a period of consultation. At dinner that evening in a Flagstaff restaurant we happened to notice an Anglo couple at the next table who had their 4-month-old daughter with them—on a Navajo cradleboard. We immediately struck up a conversation with this couple, and suffice it here to say that through this couple and their friends I was eventually able to include into my study a subsample of 11 Anglo infants—six of whom were using, or had used, a Navajo or Apache-style cradleboard and another five who never had. While the numbers (and, as it turned out, the amount of cradleboard use) were small, the possibility of a Navajo/Anglo by cradle-board/no cradleboard research design was too good to pass up. Moreover, observations of the two very different populations at the same time made it easier to see both similarities and differences in behavior and environment by preventing me from becoming too "jaded," or habituated to particularly frequently occurring sequences or items of behavior that were more common to one group than the other. Research in two cultures simultaneously also demonstrated the important fact that the definitions of the behaviors in my behavior observation catalogue were applicable cross-culturally. While the frequencies and durations and patterns of mother–infant interactive behavior differed between the two cultural groups, only one behavior item was truly culture-specific; the Navajo *point with lips*.

THE SAMPLES

Cottonwood Springs

A total of 38 Cottonwood Springs children between the ages of less than a week and 3 years were included in my research. Included in this number is one Paiute Indian child. Data on this child were included because pre-liminary analysis supported my impression that there were no differences from Navajo scores on any measure. These 38 children came from 27 different families in 26 separate camps. A comparison of these children and their families by residence type will be presented later in this section, and a comparison of the 38 Navajo children and their families to the 11 Anglo children and their families will be presented at the end of the next section. Here some general characteristics of the Navajo sample and the procedures whereby families were recruited for participation in the research will be described.

While I was fortunate in many instances, I was nevertheless frustrated by the sampling problems that bedevil most cross-cultural research in child development. On the one hand, because my sample consists of over 90% of all Cottonwood Springs families with small children, I might claim a near-perfect sample. On the other hand, the number of individuals in the entire population is small to begin with, and in comparison to the number of variables under study, the number of children of any given age is often very small. Thus, in order to have sufficient numbers of individual children in each potential age or sex comparison group I was forced to use quite broad age cohorts in the analysis. Realizing that this would be the case, only one criterion was used for rejecting children from the sample: that of health. In the end, only one child had to be excluded from the study. He had a difficult birth and suffered from afebrile convulsions during the first few months of life. As a consequence he received large doses of pheno-barbital to control the convulsions. All other children in the sample were physically normal and healthy in all respects (not counting normal minor colds or gastrointestinal problems; not counted as unhealthy or seriously abnormal were two cases of polydactyly, which has a high incidence in Native North American populations anyway [Bingle and Niswander, 1975]).

In fact, the sample was self-selected by virtue of the parents' decisions to take part in the study. Only three of 32 families approached chose not to take part in the study from the beginning, and of these three, one had the only set of twins in the community. That this family chose not to take part is perhaps not surprising. Twins are often identified with the Hero Twins of Navajo mythology (cf. Reichard, 1950) and are thus regarded as "special." They are sometimes believed to need more protection from a variety of potential dangers (Bailey, 1950; Levy, 1964), including strangers.

The purposes and methods were explained to the community as a whole at a local chapter meeting through a member of the community who often served as interpreter for the chapter. In attempting to justify this research to the community, I included the point that whereas most pediatricians serving the Navajo were Anglo, and whereas most of them had had little experience with healthy and normal Navajo infants, I wanted to write something that would help these doctors know better what was normal for Navajo children.

By way of example I pointed out that most Anglo doctors usually considered thumb-sucking normal among Anglo children and that they would probably not therefore think it remarkable in a Navajo child. But I knew, and the community knew, that it is rare indeed to see a Navajo child sucking its thumb—a trait that many Navajo people think is unique to Anglo children.

Except for the handful of women who spoke English fluently, each mother was approached for the first time with the help of one of the three female Navajo interpreters who worked with me during the 20 months of the study. Each family was paid an "informants fee" for each interview session and for each observation session. Perhaps in part because of this "informant's fee" the dropout rate was very low; of 29 families with which I started, only 2 dropped out. I was able to determine that in one of these families the mother and the father (who was always away during the day) thought it a bit suspicious that I, an Anglo male, should be "driving around alone" all over the community visiting Navajo women and their babies. As I had suspected though, this turned out to have nothing to do with my interest in infants and children but with what this one set of parents thought might be my interest in Navajo women. Happily, they were the only ones who seemed to feel that way.

Only three of the women in the sample were employed. Two had full-time jobs in the local clinic and BIA boarding school and the other had an erratic and part-time schedule at another job. Only one of the fathers had a full-time job, working at the local trading post. All the other fathers were either occupied all day with sheepherding, farming, and other camp activities, or worked full time, but intermittently, on a Navajo tribal or state welfare or job-training project. Three of the women in the sample were either divorced or widowed and not living with a man, but only one of these women was living neolocally and there were adult male relatives living in the camps of the other two.

As a means of describing some of the more detailed specifics of the Navajo infants and their families, and at the same time, providing a more detailed account of how residence patterns may affect the environment of infancy, Table 4.1 lists some of the background characteristics of each family by family or camp type. Because none of the differences between patrilocal and matrilocal extended family camps were significant, these types have been grouped (along with one family living in another type of extended family) into an "extended family camp" category and contrasted with those families living in a "nuclear family camp."

At a glance, Table 4.1 suggests that nuclear family camp couples are older, less well-educated, have more children, live in more crowded houses or hogans, and are closer both to the trading post and to their neighbors than are the extended family camp couples. That age and education are roughly

Table 4.1. Navajo Family Characteristics by Residence Type[a]

	Extended family camp families n = 13			Nuclear family camp families n = 14			
	X̄	SD	n	X̄	SD	n	(p <)[b]
Age[c] of father	31.4	10.3	13	40.8	11.5	14	.05
Age of mother	30.7	8.3	13	32.2	5.8	14	
Size of mother's family	7.8	4.5	13	8.3	3.5	12	
Mother's birth order	5.2	3.4	13	5.3	3.6	13	
Father's schooling (years)	7.1	4.9	11	4.5	4.5	13	
Mother's schooling (years)	4.7	3.8	13	3.9	4.9	14	
Mother's age at marriage	18.9	2.6	11	21.1	4.3	12	
Number of children	4.4	2.6	13	5.9	3.1	14	
Birth interval (weeks)	128.9	61.79	13 (34 births)	102.0	50.2	14 (55 births)	.05
Camp population[d]	15.0	4.2	13	7.9	3.1	14	.001
Household population	6.9	2.3	13	7.9	3.1	14	
Number of rooms[e]	1.5	1.1	13	2.4	1.7	14	
Pickup trucks per household	.77			.57		(x², n.s.)	
Miles to trading post	10.2	5.5	13	7.5	7.8	14	
Miles to nearest neighbor[f]	1.3	1.3	13	.4	.3	14	.05

[a] All figures are for the house or hogan in which the family lived for most of the time during 1974–1976. Few nuclear families moved at all. Many more extended families had summer and/or winter sheep camps where they lived for a few weeks or months, but their main camp was readily identifiable in all cases.

[b] Two-tailed t-tests except where noted.

[c] All ages were determined from birth records and reckoned on the last day of the field study (March 8, 1976).

[d] Defined according to Witherspoon's (1970) criteria (see above, page 63).

[e] A hogan = one room; a house = one or more rooms.

[f] The nearest neighbor outside of camp.

100

inversely correlated is not surprising, or is it surprising that older couples have more children or even that they are living neolocally, in nuclear family camps. This probably reflects the normal developmental cycle in which the larger, older nuclear family couples have split off from the natal camp of husband or wife some time ago when the sheep herd and/or camp size grew beyond a comfortable level.

What might not be entirely consistent with the traditional developmental cycle of Navajo domestic groups, and what leads me to suspect that the traditional extended family camp is under some pressure at Cottonwood Springs, are the significant differences noted in Table 4.1 between the two residence types in distance to nearest neighbor and birth interval. First, as mentioned, the range at Cottonwood Springs is still overgrazed and of poor quality and cash income from livestock and farming has decreased while income from nontraditional sources has greatly increased. Second, as Aberle (1962) and Levy and Kunitz (1974) have argued, Navajo society was not, and still is not, as completely classless as is commonly believed. Some camps are better situated than others for grazing, water, firewood, farming, or access to jobs, and some families have members who are better educated and can more readily obtain jobs than others. In a nuclear family camp the oldest people are the parents, and averaging no more than about 40 years of age, they are too young to receive old age social security or pension checks; in most extended family camps there are older people who have retired and who can contribute such monthly checks to the family budgets. The facts that the extended family camps are farther from the trading post, and especially that they are farther from their nearest neighbors, are consistent with the hypothesis that they have more available grazing land. That the youngest parents in my sample generally live in these apparently favored extended family camps is a priori evidence that for them, at least, the traditional developmental cycle is still working and is still an efficient way to manage and exploit resources.

I do not know how many couples in the nuclear family camp sample started married life in the camp of either set of their parents, but my data show that the women were older when they got married and that the nuclear family camp husbands are significantly older than the extended family camp husbands. This might be evidence that wherever they started married life it was perhaps more difficult for them to accumulate the sheep, grazing land, or other property necessary to establish a family.

Finally, that these nuclear family couples are living significantly closer to their neighbors (the mean is lowered, however, by three nuclear families living in the trading post–BIA school complex) leads me to suspect that the great increase in neolocal, nuclear family residence at Cottonwood Springs has resulted in large part from the attempt of hard-pressed extended family camps (those that are nearer to the trading post and nearer to their neighbors) to provide for their newly wed sons and daughters by allowing them to share the large camp's customary grazing land even if they cannot herd all their sheep together or share in all of the daily activities of household maintenance—both of which are still characteristic of the more distant and isolated extended family camps. The nuclear family camps in my sample that herd sheep at all do so separately, even if they live only one half mile or so from their parents. The mean of 1.3 miles between neighboring extended family camps is slightly misleading, given the approximately 1.4 persons per square mile at Cottonwood Springs. The reason for this is that there tend to be groups of two or three otherwise widely separated independent camps in those areas where grazing is good; while camps within these areas average only 1.3 miles apart, it is usually 10 or more miles to the next such favored area and another camp or two.

The significantly shorter birth interval in nuclear family couples was an unexpected finding. One possible interpretation is that inasmuch as nuclear family couples are older and less well-educated, they might also be expected to be more "traditional" in their attitudes toward birth control. Although my data on this point are sketchy at best, of the 12 women known (from medical records) to be using birth control pills, only one was a nuclear family woman. However, regardless of how much nuclear family couples use birth control, the simple fact that they are older than extended family couples probably accounts for the 1.5 more children in the average nuclear family. On the other hand, even though they are older, the nuclear family couples married an average of 2.2 years later than the extended family couples. It is difficult to say what affect this age difference at marriage would have on birth interval or family size, but it represents quite a change from traditional practices, where girls married within a year or so of menarche and boys at 17 or 18 (Leighton and Kluckhohn, 1948). The greater age at marriage of nuclear family couples is probably a reflection of their somewhat less secure economic position and is thus probably a correlate of their shorter birth interval and not a cause of it.

Another interpretation of the residency type difference in birth interval was suggested by another unexpected finding: nuclear family mothers breast-feed their infants for a significantly shorter period than do extended family mothers. Table 4.2 summarizes these residence-type differences in nursing. Data is presented only for those mothers who had ceased breast-feeding by the time field research was completed.

The reason for the greater birth interval among extended family couples may be related to their longer period of breast-feeding. Because lactation is known to at least partially suppress ovulation (Crosignani and Robyn, 1977), the factors that reduce breast-feeding or the frequency/duration of breast-feeding bouts (Konner and Worthman, 1980) might also help reduce the birth interval. One of these factors could be relatively less close emotional

Table 4.2. Navajo Residence Type Differences in Length of Breast-feeding

Factor	Nuclear family mothers	Extended family mothers
$\bar{X}$	4.14 months	13.75 months
SD	4.10	11.57
(n)	9	8
Range	1 week–9 months	1–36 months
Number who never breast-fed	4	4
	$t = 2.23$	
	$p < .05$	

support provided the nuclear family mother because she does not live with her own or her husband's family (cf. Raphael, 1974). A more likely, but related, explanation might be the practical difficulties of breast-feeding frequently and/or for long periods where there are not only more small children who need care, but fewer older children and adults to provide assistance. In the Cottonwood Springs extended family camps there were significantly more people around the mother, including 1.6 more infants (aged 0–3 years), another 2.9 potential child caretakers/playmates (aged 3–12 years), and another 3.6 teenaged or adult caretakers. Excluding the 1.6 infants besides her own (for whom she would have to help care for to some extent), the extended family camp mother has an additional 6.5 people over the age of three who may not only help her with her own children but also free her for more exclusive time with her children by relieving her of some of her other camp duties.

Some of the implications of these residence-type differences in birth interval and length of breast-feeding will be dealt with in later chapters, but some obvious ones to mention here are the effects of birth spacing on IQ reported by Zajonc (1975), the effects of "mother's helpers" on the amount and quality of interaction that mothers can have with their children (Weisner and Gallimore, 1977), the effects of different numbers and age/sex/kinship identities of caretakers and playmates on child socialization (B. Whiting, 1980), and the effects of residence type on physical growth reported by Cravioto et al. (1969). They found that 1-month-old infants living in nuclear families in a Mexican peasant community tended to be equally distributed in the upper and lower neonatal weight gain quartiles. In contrast, 15 of the 16 infants living in extended families had weight gains during the first month that placed them in the highest quartile ($p < .01$). Their conclusion, which agrees well with the data reported here and the general conclusions of the Whitings, Weisner, and Gallimore, and others, is that because mothers and mother substitutes were more available to the extended family children, this initial advantage was carried through at least the first month and was re-flected in greater weight gain. Cravioto and his colleagues took pains to demonstrate that this greater weight gain for the extended family children was not a function of socioeconomic class: there was no difference between the household types in per capita income.

Flagstaff, Arizona

Flagstaff, Arizona, 180 miles away from Cottonwood Springs (usually a 4-hour drive) is in close proximity to the Navajo reservation, and is the governmental, commercial, and educational center of northern Arizona. It has a population of about 30,000 and is one of the more heterogeneous cities of its size in the United States. It is at the junction of the major east-west route across the southern United States and the major north-south route in Arizona. Because of its location—close to the Grand Canyon, a number of national monuments, and archaeological sites, and in the midst of great natural beauty—it is a major tourist center. Many residents derive their income directly from tourism. The many nearby American Indian reservations are also tourist attractions. Flagstaff is also a major world marketing center for the weaving and silverwork of the Navajo, Hopi, and other tribes.

The town has a highly transient population, not only because of the tourists but also because of a large student population at Northern Arizona University. Being the only large city in northern Arizona, Flagstaff is also a favorite weekend shopping and holiday spot for people from the many nearby reservations. The Navajo reservation, by tribal law, is dry, and Flag-staff's main street has three or four "Indian bars" where many Anglo pre-judices are reinforced on Friday and Saturday nights; in other bars around town the stereotypical Friday and Saturday night drinking behavior of real American cowboys just "off the range" can also be reinforced.

In town there are sizable permanent numbers of educated middle-class Anglos, blue collar and clerical workers, cowboys, Blacks, Native Americans of several tribes, students, and a large number of Chinese-Americans who settled there after working on the railroad that created the town in the 1870's. In spite of the fact that Coconino County, in which it is located, is one of the largest and most sparsely settled counties in the United States, Flagstaff itself is actually crowded and land is at a premium because so much of the surrounding countryside is federally owned national park or national forest or is owned by various Native American tribes. The popu-lation density of Flagstaff is thus much greater than the 1.4 persons per square mile at Cottonwood Springs.

In many respects the 11 Anglo families in the Flagstaff sample were nothing at all like a representative sample of any "typical" urban middle-class Anglo population. Indeed, I think the fact that they could be so characterized would please them, and the fact that they might be pleased with this characterization by exclusion itself suggests an initial description of the group (and not a random collection of individual families). Their selection was entirely *nonrandom.* The only basis for selecting them was that half had used, or were still using, the cradleboard, and the half that did suggested names of friends who were not, and never had used, the cradleboard. Because cradleboard use among Anglos is so uncommon, having located perhaps all the Anglo cradleboard users in Flagstaff, I was at a loss to decide with whom they should be compared. By selecting mothers and infants from within one more-or-less clearly defined circle of friends I thought I might let their friendship itself help me to control for some of the infant-care practices and attitudes that might be expected to covary with cradleboard use.

Consequently, this small sample is quite homogeneous on a number of scales. At the most general level they were actively striving to avoid any typical urban middle-class way of life and were seeking and experimenting with alternatives to the lives that most of their parents seem to have led. Aspects of these alternatives included abiding concerns for the ecology, minority group relations and equal opportunities, self-sufficency and individuality, freedom of self-exploration and expression through drugs, nontraditional religions and philosophies, and, for some, communal living and natural foods. For many of this circle, a model alternative was seen in what was believed to be the more natural and satisfying cultures of Native North Americans, especially the Navajo, and it was this that provided the initial idea of cradleboard use for some and made it perhaps more acceptable to the others.

When asked why they had decided to use the cradleboard in the first place, the six mothers who had used it all said they got the idea from Anglo or Navajo friends who had used it and recommended it as either a handy baby-transport device (not for carrying on the back, but in cars, shopping baskets, etc.) or as a means of keeping infants "mellow" or quiet and relaxed. Those who had never used the cradleboard either never thought of using it or had decided that it was too confining and that small infants must be left free to kick and squirm.

Three boys and three girls used the cradleboard, and three boys and two girls did not. One of the three boys whom I counted as not using the cradleboard was in fact put on the cradleboard for a few days when he was 18 months old. Surprisingly, he liked it, but because it was a borrowed cradleboard, his mother did not continue using it. One of the boys used the cradleboard for 6 months, one for 4 months, and the other was still using it (at 6 months) when I left the field. One of the girls used the cradleboard for 8.5 months, one for 6 months, and the other was still using it (at 4 months) when I completed my work in Flagstaff. Unlike the Navajo, the Anglo children rarely used the cradleboard for sleeping at night, although it was often used for naps during the day. The Anglo mothers used it regularly for traveling around town and for longer trips away from home, and felt that it significantly improved their children's ability to withstand the stresses of travel. The Anglo mothers also seemed to be more conscious of the state-reducing function of the cradleboard for, on a number of occasions, when their children became fretful, they remarked on his or her ill-temper and said things like, "well, this will take care of you," or "let's see if you feel the same way after I do this." The Navajo mothers were much more matter-of-fact about putting their children on the cradleboard. One of the Anglo mothers, however, apparently unwittingly, summarized one of the attitudes toward cradleboard use common to both the Anglo and Navajo mothers: I had just arrived for an observation and asked where her son was. She answered that he was asleep outside. Surprised that she would let her child take a nap outside by himself, I asked if he was all alone. She replied, "Alone? No, he's on the cradleboard."

Four of the Anglo mothers were employed, but none worked full time; those who were unemployed chose not to work. One was a part-time student and six had no regular jobs outside the home. Reflecting the fact that this sample was an entirely nonrandom circle of friends, no fewer than five of the ten fathers were artists or craftspeople specializing in Navajo- and Hopi-style silverwork. One of these men was also a farrier. Two of the fathers had full-time jobs in small businesses and three were students. There are fewer "fathers" than mothers in the sample because two of the mothers had never married. One of these women was living with a man whom I counted as the infant's "functional" father, however. The other woman was sharing a house with another couple and their children.

One family lived in a large commune at the edge of town and another family moved into this commune during the course of the study. Except for these two, and the woman who shared a house with one other couple, all the families lived in isolated nuclear family units which were nonetheless always close to neighbors.

Although none of the families were wealthy, most were probably not far from the lower middle-class income level for people of their age. Two or three, however, were poor and needed the "informant's" fee I paid in Flagstaff as well as at Cottonwood Springs. On the other hand, even the poorest Flagstaff family had a radio, television, record player, and often quite a range of other electrical appliances as well. Most also had cars.

Some further specific characteristics of the Anglo sample are presented in

Table 4.3. Summary Characteristics of the Navajo and Anglo Families

Characteristic	Navajo			Anglo			
	X̄	S.D.	n^a	X̄	S.D.	n	$(p <)^b$
Age of father	36.8	11.7	27	26.1	3.0	10	.001
Age of mother	31.5	7.2	27	25.9	3.7	11	.001
Size of mother's family	8.0	3.8	26	3.9	1.9	9	.001
Mother's birth order	5.2	3.4	25	2.0	.9	9	.001
Father's schooling (years)	5.7	4.7	24	14.7	1.7	9	.001
Mother's schooling (years)	4.3	4.4	27	13.9	1.9	11	.001
Mother's age at marriage (years)	20.0	3.5	23	22.2	3.1	9	.01
Number of children	5.2	2.9	27	1.1	.4	11	.001
Birth interval (weeks)	112.4	56.6	27	(All but two first born)			
People in household	7.4	2.9	27	5.6	4.7	11	n.s.
Number of rooms per household	2.0	1.5	27	5.6	2.4	11	.001
Cars/pickups per household	.7			.6			
Miles to nearest neighbor	.8	.8	27	(All < 100 feet)			
The Children							
Cradleboard use (months)	10.3	4.2	21	5.9	1.2	4	.001
Age at walking (months)	13.7	1.9	21	13.6	2.7	6	n.s.
Length of breast-feeding (months)	8.7	9.6	17	13.7	5.0	9	.10
Range	1 week–36 months			2–18 months			
Number who never breast-fed	8			0			
Birth order	5.2	2.9	38	1.2	.4	11	.001
Number of males/females	20/18			6/5			

a Missing data are excluded.
b Two-tailed t-test.

107

Table 4.3; similar group data on the Navajo sample are also presented for comparison.

While hardly an exhaustive list of all measures on which the two samples could differ, Table 4.3 nonetheless gives a clear picture of the difficulties involved in making rigorously controlled cross-cultural comparisons. Even in this very small list, ten of the differences are highly significant, although there are only 11 Anglo subjects. For this reason I will often have to speak of general Navajo–Anglo "cultural" differences because the samples could not be matched perfectly on all background variables. Given the serendipitous nature of the research with the Anglo sample, however, I feel that these general statements are justified and worthwhile if caution is exercised. For example, the fact that all but two Anglo children were first born whereas only five Navajo children were first born could constitute a strictly demographic basis for some apparent group differences in mother–infant interaction that might otherwise appear to be "cultural" in nature. On the other hand, of course, however it may be conceptualized, birth order is an important aspect of the environment of infancy and mother–infant interaction and the mean birth order for all Anglos is somewhat lower than it is for all Navajos.

THE METHODS

The Ethological Observation of Mother-Infant Interaction

In classical ethology the first stage in field research is a period of simply "watching and seeing" what it is that the subject of observation does. This period is necessary to establish the rigorous set of definitions for each behavior finally chosen for the data-gathering obsevations in which hypotheses will be tested (some of which may arise in this initial pilot observation phase). It is this careful definition of a large number of behavior items and the strict adherence to their definitions that gives ethology its methodological power. With a large number of careful definitions based on the most discrete, minute, and objectively observable behaviors one is better able to disprove an hypothesis by making explicit from the beginning what it is that one is measuring. During a year of study with Dr. N. G. Blurton Jones at the Institute of Child Health of the University of London I familiarized myself with his established observation techniques and behavior definitions (e.g., Blurton Jones, 1972c) and carried out this first stage of my research by observing the mother and infants in his studies. A similar "watch and see" pilot project was carried out after my arrival at Cottonwood Springs to ensure that I was aware of any possible differences in items of behavior shown by Navajo mothers and infants. (There was only one: Navajo adults often point at objects with their lips. But this behavior was not common or of any special interest in the context of mother–infant interactions.)

The catalogue of behavior definitions finally used in my research was a collaborative effort on the part of Dr. N. G. Blurton Jones, Dr. F. Hall, Dr. R. H. Woodson, and myself. This behavior catalogue (Blurton Jones et al., n.d.; see also Blurton Jones and Woodson, 1979) was entirely a joint project for the reason that each of us was about to embark on a study of mother–infant interaction and through collaboration at this initial crucial level not only could we use precisely the same behavioral definitions, thereby increasing the comparability of our results, but we also felt that besides benefiting from each other's experience and interest, the very process of arriving at these definitions, in spite of (or because of) hours and even days of discussion about just one behavioral item, constituted the most valid form of interobserver reliability that we could achieve.

The problem of interobserver reliability is certainly much discussed, especially in psychology, but in ethology there is often a suspicion that this issue is something of a red herring that sometimes prevents people from proceeding with the job. At the outset interobserver reliability rates were established that averaged .80 on the behavior items that occurred in the test observation. It should be added, however, that validity and replicability of results were more important concerns than reliability.

In many respects the issue of reliability is one of "damned if you do, damned if you don't." Cooper and his colleagues (1974), for example, argue that the lack of reliability necessarily implies the lack of validity. This is not so. The lack of reliability implies only that one of the observers saw a particular behavior that the other did not. This may mean that one observer is more experienced or competent, but it says nothing at all about the validity of the observation. If the experienced human ethologist sees an eyebrow flash that even 100 inexperienced observers missed, does this make his observation invalid? Too great a concern for interobserver reliability may lead to a stultifying, expensive, and lowest common denominator, "majority rule" approach to science, which is surely unscientific.

On the other hand, high interobserver reliability scores are also sometimes said to mean only that the observers share the same biases. It is true that reliability scores are higher within groups that train together than between such groups, but shared biases do not imply the lack of validity any more than they imply its presence. The whole point of training is to share something, but whether this something is called a "bias" or is used as evidence for validity is to miss the real point that careful definition of the most discrete, minute, and objectively observable behaviors is the first step

toward validity and productive results. Our primary concern throughout the
preparation of our behavior catalogue was to be as explicit about our definitions as possible so that our results could be replicated. This, we felt, was
what the "scientific method" was all about. Not only is it simply difficult
and time-consuming to establish high degrees of interobserver reliability,
reliability by itself means very little and is often emphasized where the units
of observation are more intuitive and subjective. We felt too that the replication of results was a better indication of good science than the nit-picking
replication of methods, perhaps even more so if the methods were not
exactly the same, which can probably never be the case anyway.

With the approximately 150 items in the behavior catalogue memorized,
along with a shorthand code for each one, actually making and recording
observations of mother–infant interaction in the field was straightforward. I
used specially prepared data sheets on which 12 lines representing 15
seconds each had been printed. During the observation I wore in my ear an
inconspicuous small speaker connected to a battery-powered timer in my
shirt pocket; each 15 seconds a click would sound (audible only to me) and I
would begin recording the shorthand behavior codes on the next line of the
data sheet. The accuracy of the timer was checked before every observation,
and the batteries replaced if needed.

Observations at each age point totaled 1 hour divided into a 20- or
40-minute observation one day and the remaining 40 or 20 minutes on any
other day up to 1 week later. The decision to record for 20- and 40-minute
periods was arbitrary; I simply started observing for 40 minutes instead of 30
minutes in an effort to maximize the return on each opportunity for observation rather than counting on a problematic second observation within a
week. In fact, I was nearly always able to return within a week and could just
as easily have made two 30-minute observations. Having started with 20-
and 40-minute observations, I simply continued. The two observations at
each point, of course, were an attempt to average out the possible effects of
"good days" and "bad days" on both mother and infant.

I recorded mother–infant interactions for such relatively long periods in
order to simply give them more time to interact and to thus give myself a
better chance of recording an adequate sample of their longer interactions. I
also recorded for these long periods in order to give them the opportunity to
adjust to my presence at the start of each observation. Although I have no
independent evidence to support my impressions, I nonetheless feel that in
fact my presence and my observation had little or no effect on the mothers
and especially on the infants. I spoke enough Navajo for simple courtesies to
be exchanged and to establish if it were acceptable for me to make an
observation at that time, but otherwise my limited command of the Navajo
language meant that most mothers (and older children) could not talk to me.

Furthermore, Navajo etiquette calls for silence and the polite ignoring of strangers (cf. Basso, 1970), as well as gaze aversion from them. I spoke enough Navajo to know that I was sometimes the subject of conversation while I was observing, but my very strong impressions are that within only one or two visits to each family my purpose and methods were established firmly enough so that I was no longer such a novelty to mother or child that I had an effect on their interaction. In none of the observations on infants discussed here did any child do more than simply look at me. Observations on children over 1 year old, not reported here, included many more behaviors directed by the child toward me (e.g., *approach, proffer, talk, smile*), but in all cases I refused to interact with the child in as gentle and pleasant a way as I could.

After arriving at the home of the child to be observed and making spot observations and administering the fear of strangers test (see below) I established that it was convenient for me to make an extended observation and then engaged the child's mother and other adults and older children in small talk (as best I could). If no one in the family spoke English I would still go through this initial "warm-up" period, practicing my Navajo and attempting to create a relaxed atmosphere. During the 10–15 minutes that I thus spent before actually commencing the observation I noted a series of "background" environmental features (time of day, temperature and weather conditions, the number and age/sex/kinship/ identities of others present, etc.). During this time I also determined as best I could whether or not the child might be ill. When the child was very obviously not feeling well (because of a cold, diarrhea, etc.) I would relate this to the mother and say that I would come back another day. If there was unusual activity in the house or hogan (more than two or three non residents present, for example), I would observe that since they had visitors, or since they were busy, I would not bother them now, but would come back later. Finally, if all conditions for observation were met, I would sit, usually on the floor, about 10 to 15 feet from the child, and prepare to start. Actually beginning to record behavior was determined by a simple rule-of-thumb: since I was interested in mother–infant interaction, and since this interest stemmed in large part from Bowlby's work on attachment, I began recording whenever the mother and child were within 30 feet of each other outside, or in the same room inside, and when either one of them directed an "attachment" behavior to the other. For these purposes an "attachment" behavior did not include any visual behaviors by themselves, but only *approach, leave, cry, talk, vocalization,* and any touching episode or caretaking (feeding, nursing, dressing, etc.). These criteria for starting an observation are summarized in Table 4.4.

As the mothers and their families had been told when I first explained my work to them, my attention throughout each observation was focused on the

Table 4.4. Criteria for Starting an Observation

---

1. Child always at home
2. Child always awake (Brazelton scale states 3–6)
3. Child not obviously ill
4. Mother in same room with child if inside; within 30 feet if both are outside
5. Daylight hours only and only normal daily household activities going on
6. The direction of an "attachment" behavior (except simple, isolated visual behaviors) by mother to child or child to mother

---

child. Naturally, every effort was made to record all mother (and other) behaviors directed toward the child, but because my focus was on the child it was probably not possible to always see all behaviors directed to the child, especially when the mother and others were more than about 10 feet from the child. There may thus be a slight bias in my data that shows children *initiating* interactions when in fact they were *responding* to the initiations of others that I did not see. This is a problem in naturalistic observation that may be impossible to solve, but it can be controlled for to some extent in data analysis and in any case probably involves only visual behavior, facial expressions, and other entirely nonvocal, nonverbal behaviors directed by others to the infant from some distance—a relatively small sampling error overall.

In addition to the 150 or so items in the behavior catalogue, I also recorded a number of what I called "environmental conditions." These environmental conditions included relatively long-lasting and more global features of the social-physical environment of mother–infant interaction that might only with difficulty be reconstructed from the analysis of the individual behavior items. For example, it might be difficult to know that the mother was placing her child on the cradleboard just from the analysis of the discrete behavior items in the behavior catalogue. These environmental conditions are not more subjective than the individual behavior item definitions, but are much less discrete and occur over longer periods of time. Recording a new environmental condition (e.g., "on lap") slightly altered the way in which I recorded some of the 150 discrete items of behavior. For example, *mother adjust (her own) position* was not recorded unless the infant was being held on the mother's lap (and might thus be influenced by the mother's movements). Or, in a bout of diaper changing, the presumably more-or-less standardized and routine touching of the infant by the mother was not recorded (i.e., mother's touches on the baby's trunk in the direct act of diapering were not recorded; if the mother touched, say, the baby's face while diapering, that was recorded). These environmental conditions included 14 ways that a child could be on the cradleboard or in other ways confined or restrained (or none at all), 15 sorts of caretaking activities (or none at all), 12 distance-from-mother categories (six indoors and six outdoors; this set of environmental conditions had no null category).

Each potential interactor with the child, even including any sheep, goats, cats, or dogs (who were lumped in an "animal" category), was represented by a unique code. Sex was noted with the biological symbols X and Y, age was estimated roughly and simply written next to the sex symbol, and *non-coresidence* (in the camp, not the household) was noted with a circle around the sex-age symbols. In keeping with Navajo residence patterns, father's kin were relatively rare. In practice, after only a month or so, I knew the precise age and kinship status of more than 95% of all subjects who ever appeared, and I used a simpler ad hoc coding system to speed the recording of data. For data analysis, however, the limits of my computer program forced me to lump subjects in 26 age/sex/kinship categories.

An observation ended when either 20 or 40 minutes had passed, or when the infant had his or her eyes closed, with only small body movements, *and* if there were no other baby *or* mother behaviors for a full minute. Surprisingly few observations ended in this way, and if I had already gathered more than one-half of the intended data, I considered such shortened observations as complete nonetheless.

The observations at each age point were scheduled 8 to 10 weeks apart, but due to road and weather conditions, lack of communication, and the frequent visiting that most families carried out with friends and relatives all over Cottonwood Springs and the reservation, it was impossible to adhere to this schedule all the times. This was another reason for deciding to use rather broad age cohorts in the data analysis.

Throughout the observations, my focus was always on the child—and I always followed the child wherever he or she went, even if outside and alone. I placed no constraints whatsoever on the activities of mother, child, or others during the observations. Aside from sleeping, any activity was considered appropriate for observation. Never, for example, did I suggest that the child be placed on or taken off the cradleboard.

The Brazelton Neonatal Behavioral Assessment Scale

In an attempt to replicate Freedman's findings that newborn Navajo infants were generally quieter and less irritable than newborn Anglo infants, and in order to establish baselines for individual differences in behavior at birth which could then be related backward in time to prenatal and perinatal factors, and forward to subsequent patterns of mother–infant interaction and behavioral development, I administered the Brazelton Neonatal Behavioral Assessment Scale (NBAS) (Brazelton, 1973) to all the newborns in my sample and to additional Navajo and Anglo newborns not included in my primary samples.

In studying the behavior of the human neonate, developmental psychologists and ethologists have increasingly made use of the NBAS. A number of other neonatal examination protocols are in existence, but most assess the infant's behavior from a more strictly clinical neurological standpoint that is less immediately relevant to the natural social environment of normal infants. Characterized as "the most comprehensive assessment yet devised for the examination of the newborn infant" (Sameroff, 1978), the NBAS is an appropriate instrument for ethological studies of neonatal behavior because it provides a means of reliably quantifying those behaviors of newborn infants to which caretakers are most likely to be responsive (e.g. the infant's own level of social responsiveness, levels of irritability, alertness, motor maturity). The NBAS is thus useful for studying both the effects of the infant on its social environment and the effects of pre- and perinatal events and conditions on the infant's potential for adaptive social development.

The NBAS has been used for a number of different purposes. Horowitz and her colleagues (1973), for example, showed that maternal pain-killing medication during labor affected the newborn's behavior up to a month later, generally by decreasing the infant's responsiveness while increasing its readiness to startle and show tremulousness. Aleksandrowicz and Aleksandrowicz (1974), Yang et al. (1976), and other have shown similar results, although Brazelton himself has questioned whether the NBAS is really sensitive enough to reliably pick up drug effects on neonatal behavior (Brazelton et al., 1976b). Howrowitz et al. (1973) and Bakow et al. (1973), among others, have demonstrated continuities between NBAS items and infant behaviors up to 4 months later. Hall and Pawlby (1981) have also shown that infants scoring highest on the NBAS items assessing alertness also look and smile more at their mothers up to 4 months later. Osofsky (1976; Osofsky and Danzger, 1974) has reported that infants who were more alert at birth had mothers who showed more sensitivity and responsiveness a few days later. Finally, besides Freedman (Freedman and Freedman, 1969; Freedman, 1971, 1974a, 1974b), several other researchers have demonstrated significant racial or ethnic group differences in neonatal behavior. Brazelton, Koslowski, and Tronick (1976a), for example, found Zambian newborns scored lower on activity and attentiveness, but higher on irritability, than an Anglo-American comparison group. Coll, Seposki, and Lester (1981), comparing Puerto Rican, Black, and Anglo-American newborns found that the

Puerto Rican infants showed more alertness and better orientation skills than infants of the other two groups. They suggest that at least part of the group differences may be due to population differences in the effects of biomedical factors on infant behavior. Woodson and de Costa Woodson (Chisholm, Woodson, and da Costa Woodson, 1978) reported significant population differences in the behavior of newborn Chinese, Malay, and Tamil Indian infants in Malaysia, and I recently replicated Freedman's earlier finding of significant Aboriginal-Caucasian population differences in newborn behavior (Chisholm, 1981b). In short, the NBAS has proved its worth as an instrument for documenting both individual and group differences in neonatal behavior. [See Super, 1981 and Lester and Brazelton (1982) for excellent review articles on the cross-cultural use of the NBAS.]

The problems of reliability assessment notwithstanding, in many of the NBAS studies that report significant group differences the question of individual versus group differences becomes methodologically and theoretically vital. The problem here is at least twofold: first, significant group differences in neonatal behavior may be observed because of simple group differences in the distribution of factors causing individual differences. When these factors are not known or controlled there may be a temptation to assume that unexplained residual variation between the groups constitutes evidence for constitutional or group differences. This is a logical mistake that gives constitutional or genetic factors the status of the null hypothesis, and confuses the *untested* genetic "explanation," with the weaker claim of "not yet disproved." Second, even when genetic factors are implicated in aspects of neonatal behavior, their effect may well vary from group to group because such genetic influences are not likely to be static and may develop along complex epigenetic pathways which do not exclude significant environmental input—and not just from birth but from conception (cf. Blurton Jones, Woodson, and Chisholm, 1979).

The NBAS consists of 20 items which score neonatal reflexes on 0 to 3 scales and 27 items which score neonatal behavior on 1 to 9 scales. An adequate conceptual description of the NBAS and what it actually assesses can be achieved here with reference to four "a priori profiles" that Brazelton and his colleagues (Als, 1978) feel underlie infants' performance during the examination procedure. These clinically and neurologically intuitive profiles, I should stress here, played no part in the way I administered the NBAS or analyzed my NBAS data; they are presented here only for conceptual, heuristic reasons (Table 4.5).

Because infant state (state of consciousness or state or arousal) is such a determining factor in infant behavior (see, for example, Moss, 1967; Lewis, 1972, Brazelton, 1978) and because a major dimension of both individual and group differences in newborn behavior is along the lines of state and

Table 4.5. A Priori Clustering of Infant Behaviors on the NBAS

Cluster 1.	*Interactive processes.* This cluster of items on the NBAS assesses the infant's ability to respond to social stimulation and includes specific items measuring aspects of alertness, responsiveness, and how the infant responds to handling by the examiner in certain situations.
Cluster 2.	*Motoric processes.* This cluster includes all of the reflex items as well as other behavioral items that provide a more specific picture of the infant's motor maturity, muscle tone, and coordination.
Cluster 3.	*State control.* The infant's ability to control his or her own level of arousal is assessed by the items in this cluster. The specific test items measure the infant's capacity to habituate to various stimuli, the amount of irritability shown by the infant, the rapidity with which the infant reaches a crying state during the examination, the lability with which the infant changes state during examination, the infant's capacity to quiet him or herself, the infant's capacity to be quieted or consoled by the examiner, and more.
Cluster 4.	*Physiological responses.* The three items in this cluster, although clearly related to items in the three previous clusters, also stand on their own by more directly reflecting the infant's basic neurophysiological development and/or functioning at the time of the exam. The three items are tremulousness, amount of startle, and lability of skin color.

Source: Adapted from Als (1978).

state control (e.g., Freedman, 1974b; Strauss and Rourke, 1978), a more detailed description of the measurement of infant state is appropriate here. In my administration of the NBAS, and in all other situations (e.g., spot observations), I used the Brazelton scale state definitions that are listed in Table 4.6. The child must show the behavior associated with each state definition for at least 15 seconds before it is recorded as having achieved that state.

Brazelton (1973) reports that even when examiners have had no previous experience with infants they can be trained to interobserver reliability levels of .85 or better within a short time. After an intensive period of training in the administration and scoring of the NBAS with Dr. Brazelton and his associates at the Children's Hospital Medical Center in Boston, I achieved an interobserver reliability rate < .90; after 2 years of field research I returned to Boston and my postresearch reliability was still .91.

Table 4.6. Brazelton Scale State Definitions

State 1.	Deep sleep; no rapid eye movement (REM); no body movements.
State 2.	Light sleep; eyes closed but REMs may be present; startles and body movements and smiling or grimacing may occur.
State 3.	Drowsy or semidozing; eyes may be open or closed; body movements are slow and smooth; startles are rare.
State 4.	Quiet and alert; little motor activity, but eyes are open and bright, and the child is alert and attentive.
State 5.	Alertness is variable; eyes are open but attentiveness is low; more motor activity, more vigorous movements; child's face may pucker as if to cry; fretting and whining may occur.
State 6.	Intense crying; long, rhythmical crying.

Source: From Brazelton (1973)

Because the birth process and maternal medication during labor and delivery may affect the behavior of the infant up to several days later, I attempted to administer the NBAS twice—once during the infant's first 3 days of life, and again during days 4–10. More than 95% of all Navajo women deliver in one of the several USPHS Indian Health Service hospitals on, or near, the Navajo reservation (Brenner et al., 1974). At Cottonwood Springs during 1974 to 1976 all pregnant women gave birth at the Tuba City, Arizona Indian Health Service Hospital. Difficulties of transportation and communication at Cottonwood Springs, and especially between Cottonwood Springs and Tuba City meant that it was impossible to control for infants' age more precisely than this.

Whenever a Cottonwood Springs mother gave birth I traveled to Tuba City as quickly as possible after hearing the news. All NBAS examinations administered to infants up to 3 days old were conducted in the same quiet and dimly lit room in Tuba City Hospital. I asked the mother of each child that I examined to be present during the examination. This is not customary in NBAS research, but because I knew that the mothers and other family members would be present during the second NBAS examination in each child's home, I attempted to at least partially standardize the two examination environments by including the mother in the first. In addition, this helped to establish rapport with some of the mothers and gave me the opportunity to learn something of the way they handled newborn infants and to learn about the temperamental differences they sometimes observed between the infant I was examining and his or her older siblings. After completing the examinations, which averaged about 25 minutes, I copied the medical records of infant and mother, including all information on the mother's pregnancy and any of her previous pregnancies. Whenever I made a visit to Tuba City Hospital to examine a Cottonwood Springs infant I also examined any other Navajo infants in the nursery. Since the normal lying-in period at Tuba City Hospital was only 2 days, the nursery ordinarily held only one or two other infants under 3 days old, but in the course of the research I was able to administer the NBAS to 23 Navajo infants under 3 days old.

A total of 18 Cottonwood Springs infants were examined in their homes between the ages of 4 and 10 days. While considerably different from the examination conditions in Tuba City Hospital, the 18 different sets of conditions I encountered in the various hogans and houses at Cottonwood Springs were by no means unacceptable. In spite of the fact that the child's mother was present during both examinations, and in spite of my attempts to control noise and light levels, the presence of variable numbers of other family members during the second examination, as well as some considerable temperature differences, meant that the analyses of any possible individual differences in development from the first examination to the second would be suspect, for as deVries and Super (1978) point out, the context of the NBAS examination can have significant effects on the behavior of the infant.

The possibility of examining individual differences in development between the first and second NBAS examination was further reduced by the fact that of the 18 examinations of infants aged 4–10 days, only eight were on infants I had previously examined on days 1–3. This was because of the problems of travel and communication which made it difficult to always reach Tuba City Hospital before the mother and infant were discharged. Furthermore, not all of the Cottonwood Springs mothers returned there after leaving the hospital, but stayed with other relatives closer to medical care in other parts of the reservation for as much as 1 month before returning home. Because of these difficulties in locating mothers and infants, even within just the first 10 days of life, and because of the small population of newborns to begin with, I made no attempt to select mothers or infants on any basis. Even the fact that the sex ratio in my NBAS sample is 50:50 is a fortunate coincidence. However, the 41 NBAS examinations reported here do not include those on any infants who were not judged clinically normal at birth.

Fear of Strangers Testing

Until the age of about 8 months, most normal children seem to be largely indiscriminant in their responses to strange and familiar others. After about 8 months, however, the majority of children begin to show more or less fear of strangers. While the age of onset of fear of strangers has been reported as early as 4 months and as late as 14 months, and while there is a great range of individual differences in manifestations of fear, there is a sufficiently strong central tendency in the timing of its appearance to justify the common name "8 month's anxiety."

The development of this fear is a topic that has received much attention, and aspects of its development have been related to virtually every subfield within developmental psychology. For example, the infant's fear of strangers has been related to (1) "anxious" attachment (Ainsworth, Bell, and Stayton, 1971; Ainsworth and Wittig, 1969; Bretherton and Ainsworth, 1974; Spitz, 1965); (2) aspects of the child's immediate environment (Bretherton and Ainsworth, 1974; Bronson, 1972; Morgon and Ricciuiti, 1969; Sroufe, Waters, and Matas, 1974); (3) aspects of the child's previous experiences with strangers (Konner, 1972; Schaffer and Emerson, 1964; Rheingold, 1961; Ross, 1975); (4) the child's developing cognitive capacities (Bronson, 1972; Kagan, 1974; Schaffer, 1974); and (5) the interaction of all these factors in the context of the ontogenesis of phylogenetically determined response capacities, including a possible developmental motivational conflict between attachment and exploration and including the possibility of "sensitive periods" and the phenomenon of imprinting (Bronson, 1972; Bischof, 1975b; Hoffman, 1974).

My purpose in assessing each child's fear of strangers was to provide more objective developmental data on the commonly but casually reported "fear" or "shyness" of older Navajo children. I also hoped to relate data on individual differences in the expression and development of fears of strangers to children's experiences with the cradleboard and to variations in their early experiences with different numbers of others and with others of certain age/sex/kinship identities. As mentioned, Ainsworth and her colleagues found more fear of strangers in their "anxiously" attached group (see above) and if the cradleboard contributed to such "anxious" attachment, children who used the cradleboard most might be expected to show more fear of strangers. At the same time, however, the child's fear of strangers might as easily be affected by more pervasive patterns of early interactions with others in his or her larger social environment. One of the objects of testing fear of strangers was thus to see which of these two possible determinants was the best predictor of individual differences.

My techniques for measuring fear of strangers follow closely those developed by Konner (1972). There is a plethora of definitions of fear and an equal number of techniques for measuring it. I chose to use Konner's methods because they recorded a variety of behavior items, they seemed most naturalistic, and because they seemed least intrusive. I made each fear of strangers observation on each child in both samples (Navajo and Anglo) within a minute or two of arriving at the child's home for a regular two-monthly observation of mother–infant interaction. On arriving at the home, I always greeted the child's mother or other adults first, then any older children, and finally the child to be observed. It is common and polite practice for a visitor to a Navajo family to greet everyone present with a handshake, even very small infants, and it was thus possible for me to combine normal polite behavior with a standardized approach and greeting of each child.

In my approach of each child I looked, but did not fixedly stare, at the child. Throughout the entire fear of strangers test I attempted to modulate my behavior so as to maximize the child's "friendliness" score. I did this by approaching slowly, saying the child's name, speaking both Navajo and English, often averting my gaze, smiling, and extending both arms slowly toward the child as I drew closer. The last step in the procedure was to pick the child up and hold him or her at my shoulder for a minute or so. If at any time during this process the child cried or fretted I stopped my approach and concluded the test. If the child locomoted away from me without showing other signs of distress, I followed and continued the test until he or she allowed me to pick him or her up or until he or she cried. I did not stop the test if a child only showed a *pucker face* (the characteristic facial expression of crying, but without the actual cry), but would proceed more slowly, averting my gaze frequently, smiling more, and so on. A smaller number of older children held out a hand or arm to restrain my approach or attempt to pick them up, and this too terminated the test, but simple turning away when I attempted to pick them up did not, or did hiding behind mother or another person.

I used an event-sampling recording technique and after the test was completed I simply noted all behaviors from my checklist that had occurred. Most of these behaviors were ones also recorded by Konner, but I added a few that he had not recorded. These behaviors are listed in Table 4.7 along with the scoring weights attached to each to roughly indicate the a priori degree of "fearfulness" or "friendliness" associated with each. In data analysis these individual behavior scores were simply summed algebraically to give a summary score.

The criteria I used for deciding whether a fear of strangers test should be started were similar to the criteria I used for starting a regular session of observation of mother–infant interaction (see above). However, in order to proceed with a fear of strangers test, the child had to be in state 4 (awake, alert, not crying, not actively moving about) and there could be no mother–infant interaction going on that involved any caretaking (e.g., nursing, feeding, changing). Finally, no non-coresidents (i.e., potential other strangers) could be in the vicinity of the child when I conducted the test. If

Table 4.7. Fear of Strangers Behavior and Scoring Checklist

−3	Laugh
	Touch stranger or initiate handshake
	Arms up to stranger
−2	Smile
	Nonfret vocalization
	Shake hands with stranger when instructed to do so by mother or other
	Approach stranger
−1	Stare at stranger for more than 10 seconds
	Restrain stranger's approach or attempt to pick child up
	Proffer or show object to stranger
0	Hand at mouth
+1	Gaze avert within first two seconds
	Look at mother
	Withdraw from stranger
	Pucker face
	Hide eyes
+2	Approach mother
	Touch mother
	Fret
+3	Cling to mother or mother's clothing
	Get on mother or attempt to get on mother (e.g., arms up to mother)
	Cry

Source: Adapted from Konner (1972).

these criteria were not met within a minute or so of my arrival, when I was ready to start approaching the child, I would not administer the test. Because of these attempts at standardization, and because of the common problem of not finding families at home when I wanted to make observations, it was not possible to administer the fear of strangers test every 2 months to each child as planned, and there are gaps of 4 and even 6 months in some individual records. In the end I administered the fear of strangers test 175 times to Navajo children between the ages of 1 month and nearly 3 years, and 52 times to the 11 Flagstaff Anglo children.

Spot Observations

An extremely useful adjunct to highly focused ethological observation, and, for that matter, to interviewing and participant observation, is what has come to be called the spot observation (e.g., Denham, 1974; Draper, 1975; Konner, 1972; Rogoff, 1978). Spot observation yields immense amounts of data for very little effort and the data are quickly and easily analyzed. Its greatest strengths, however, are in the ways that it provides a means of checking and objectifying one's impressions and of apprehending patterns that are too subtle for the "naked eye" in much the same way that fast-motion film allows us to watch a plant growing.

Spot observation is essentially a time-sampling observation technique in which the focus of observation is on the subject in his or her larger social and physical environment and not specifically or only on the subject's behavior. I used spot observations to provide a more general overview of each child's activities and the immediate social-physical environment of these activities than was at all possible in the much more highly focused ethological observations of mother–infant interaction. As soon as a child was taken into the study I began to make spot observations on that child whenever and wherever I saw that child in the subsequent course of the project. The only exceptions were at a handful of formal gatherings of large numbers of people (e.g., sings, parties at the local preschool, etc.) which I chose to attend in the role of guest instead of formal observer. I also did not make two observations on the same child in the same place (i.e., either at home or at the trading post) on the same day. Observations made during hours of darkness are greatly underrepresented, but I did make some. No attempt was made to observe all children at the same times during the day, and no attempt was made to obtain exactly the same number of observations on each child.

In each spot observation I recorded time of day, location of the child (inside or outside; at home or away from home), distance to mother and to all others present, the age/sex/kinship identity of others present, the child's activity and state, whether or not the child was on the cradleboard, and more.

Altogether I made 1307 spot observations, 1164 at Cottonwood Springs and 143 in Flagstaff on the Anglo children.

Interviewing

In addition to observing mothers and children I also carried out two formal interviews with each mother and more extensive but casual and open-ended discussions with several other women who spoke English and who became major informants. Except for the women whose English was good (some of whom were mothers of children in my sample) I used one of three female interpreters for the more structured, formal interviews.

The results of these interviews, like the results of the spot observations, are scattered throughout this book in various tables and general discussions, for the primary purpose of interviewing was to gather background data on each mother, her family routine, developmental milestones of her child, social contacts of her family and her child in particular, life history, and more specific data on her family's kinship, demographic, and residence structure.

The Strategy of Data Analysis

In the following chapters I present analyses of the data gathered by each of the methods described in this chapter (except for the spot observation and interview data which are scattered throughout). While one of my first tasks in data analysis was to describe and analyze the effects of the cradleboard on mother–infant interaction, an equally important task was to also determine whether or not aspects of the infant's behavior and/or aspects of the environment in which the cradleboard was used might actually prevent it from having long-term effects. Because one aspect of the environment of cradleboard use may include individual differences in infants' temperament or level of responsiveness that they bring to the cradleboard, I therefore begin my data analysis in the following chapter with a statistical description and analysis of individual and group (Navajo and Anglo) differences in neonatal behavior. I then proceed with a similar treatment of individual and group differences in Navajo and Anglo children's fear of strangers because the significant group differences that appeared were better explained in terms of group differences in the distribution of larger social environmental factors causing individual differences in fear of strangers than in terms of any measurement of cradleboard use. This chapter thus provides a sort of foreshadowing of the two chapters on the effects of the cradleboard that follow it. The first cradleboard chapter focuses only on the immediate effects of the cradleboard on mother–infant interaction, and shows that the predicted effects are indeed present. The second cradleboard chapter, however, shows that these immediate effects do not last, and that the significant Navajo-Anglo differences in patterns of mother–infant interaction are better explained in terms of the larger social environmental factors that best explained group differences in fear of strangers than in terms of the immediate effects of the cradleboard.

To an extent, each of the following chapters builds upon the analyses and conclusions of the chapter preceding it, but many of the results of each set of methods discussed in this chapter are not brought together until the final, synoptic chapter. In integrating and summarizing the results of each set of the various methods described in this chapter, the final chapter also provides a justification not only for ethological methods but also for the use of a variety of methods all focused on the same set of problems: by recording a large number (ca. 150) of discrete, minute, and objectively observable behavior items, one maximizes one's chances of both disproving any specific hypothesis, and at the same time benefits from such a wide research net by being better enabled to generate new hypotheses; by employing more than one set of methods to tackle a particular problem, one generates at least two *independent* sets of statistics that can be directed to the problem.

5

The Behavior of Navajo and Anglo Newborn Infants

MY original purpose in administering the Brazelton Neonatal Behavioral Assessment Scale (NBAS) to Navajo infants was to determine whether or not individual differences in behavior at birth might be related to individual differences in reactions to the cradleboard or to the development of individual differences in patterns of mother–infant interaction later on. With the addition of the Anglo comparison group, however, it became possible to attempt to replicate Freedman's finding of greater quietness and lesser irritability in Navajo newborns than in Anglo newborns. This opportunity to describe and analyze group differences in neonatal behavior was especially fortunate because, as it turned out, I was not able to obtain a large sample of infants on whom I had obtained both NBAS data and data describing their reactions to the cradleboard and patterns of mother–infant interaction at a later age. Some of the relationships between neonatal behavior and patterns of later mother–infant interaction (tentative though they are) will be described in a later chapter; this chapter will concentrate on describing and analyzing Navajo-Anglo group differences in newborn behavior.

In this chapter the word "Anglo" does not refer only to American whites, but includes ten English infants. From my early experience with Anglo–American infants in Boston during my training in administering the NBAS, as soon as I had examined only a few Navajo newborns my initial impression was that Freedman was correct about the Navajo–Anglo differences in neonatal quietness and irritability. In order to more rigorously document these differences, I arranged to examine an additional ten English newborns with the NBAS when I returned to London for data analysis, thereby increasing my "Anglo" comparison group significantly over the only five white American newborns born in Flagstaff during my short visits to that town.

THE ANALYSIS OF BRAZELTON SCALE DATA:
METHODS AND RATIONALE

The Navajo and Anglo (English and American whites) samples were divided into two age groups because even within the first several days of life recovery from maternal medication and the process of delivery itself can affect newborn behavior. The first age group (days 1–3) included 10 Anglo infants and 23 Navajo infants; the second age group (days 4–10) included 15 Anglo infants and 18 Navajo infants. All infants in both samples in the first age group were examined in the hospitals where they were born. Two-thirds of all infants in the second age group were also examined in the hospitals where they were born. The place of examination had no relationship to infants' scores in the NBAS in any case (cf. deVries and Super, 1978), possibly because the examination rooms in each of the hospitals were the same in terms of temperature, light, noise, and so on. Of the 15 Anglo infants in the second age group, two-thirds had also been examined in the first age group; of the 18 Navajo infants in the second age group, 10 had also been examined in the first age group. The sex ratio in both age groups was close to 50:50.

All of the ten English mothers received some pain-killing medication, tranquilizers, and/or induction medication during labor or delivery, but none of the five Flagstaff Anglo mothers, two of whom had home births, had any medication of any kind during labor or delivery. Of the 33 Navajo mothers, all of whom delivered in the Tuba City, Arizona IHS Hospital, half (51.5%) had no medication. In terms of maternal medication, then, the two samples are broadly comparable; actual analyses showed that the presence or absence of maternal medication was unrelated to the NBAS items on which Navajo and Anglo newborn infants differed most significantly.

The women in both samples had normal and uneventful pregnancies. Three Navajo women had one blood pressure reading each that was greater than the 140/90 mmHg that is accepted as the definition of hypertension. The subsequent blood pressure readings on each of these women were normotensive (less than 140/90 mmHg), and none were treated for hypertension. All women in both samples had normal vaginal deliveries and all infants in both samples were judged clinically normal by pediatric staff in the respective hospitals. The two Flagstaff mothers who delivered at home reported that as far as they were concerned their labors and deliveries were entirely normal; the midwife attending both women corroborated their views. The major variables describing Navajo and Anglo pregnancy, labor, and delivery are summarized in Table 5.1.

The first step in analysis of the neonatal behavioral data was to determine whether or not significant Navajo–Anglo group differences would appear in

Table 5.1. Characteristics of Navajo and Anglo Pregnancy, Labor, and Delivery

Variables	Navajo			Anglo			$p <$[a]
	$\bar{X}$	SD	n	$\bar{X}$	SD	n	
Maternal age	28.9	8.0	33	22.6	3.4	15	.01
Parity	4.3	3.6	33	1.1	.4	15	.01
Duration first stage of labor (minutes)	673.4	536.5	33	453.0	204.9	13	
Duration second stage of labor (minutes)	18.2	16.2	33	35.1	28.9	13	
Birth weight (gm)	3327.8	451.0	33	3171.3	507.3	13	
APGAR[b]							
1–Minute	8.6	1.3	33	7.8	1.3	13	
5–Minute	9.6	.9	33	(not available)			
No. males/females	18/15			8/7			
No. mothers medicated/not medicated	16/17			10/5			
No. mothers induced and/or augmented/ not induced and/or augmented	14/19			10/5			

[a] All tests of significance are two-tailed chi-square or t-tests.
[b] The APGAR score is a numerical (0–10) expression of an infant's condition at 1 and 5 minutes after birth and is based on heart rate, respiratory effort, muscle tone, reflex irritability, and color.

my sample as they had in Freedman's. A series of t-tests (two-tailed) showed that indeed the group difference was apparent in my sample and that again the Navajo newborns were quieter and less irritable than the Anglo newborns, both on days 1–3 and 4–10. Table 5.2 illustrates, for both age groups, the similarities and differences in Navajo and Anglo newborn behavior revealed by the NBAS.

These independent data support the validity of Freedman's characterization of newborn Navajo infants as quieter and less irritable than newborn Anglo infants. Freedman's characterization, however, was based only on an item-by-item comparison of group means, while an analysis of the ways that the individual items on which the groups differ form clusters might have provided an additional validity index. While newborn infants display a wide range of individual differences in behavior, it has been consistently shown, for example, that a major dimension of these differences is along the lines of "irritability," "temperament," "arousal," "reactivity," or "lability of states." This dimension, which I will call irritability, has an intuitive validity. Als (1978) and Strauss and Rourke (1978) have shown that it has a statistical validity as well. In factor analyses of NBAS data sets, an irritability factor has always accounted for a high percentage of sample variance. To determine whether the observed Navajo–Anglo group differences in newborn behavior

Table 5.2. Navajo and Anglo Brazelton Scale Scores

| | Days 1–3 | | | | | Days 4–10 | | | | | |
| | Navajo (n = 23) | | Anglo (n = 10) | | | Navajo (n = 18) | | Anglo (n = 15) | | | |
Brazelton scale item	X̄	SD	X̄	SD	$p <$[a]	X̄	SD	X̄	SD	$p <$[a]
Response decrement										
To light	7.8	1.3	6.3	2.0	.05	8.6	.7	7.5	1.4	.05
To rattle	8.3	1.1	7.9	1.6		7.8	1.6	7.5	1.7	
To bell	9.1	.6	9.3	1.2		8.5	1.0	8.1	2.0	
Orientation										
Inanimate visual	4.5	1.3	5.3	1.2		5.9	1.1	5.1	1.4	
Inanimate auditory	5.4	.9	6.3	.5	.001	6.2	1.1	5.6	1.0	
Animate visual	5.0	1.7	5.3	1.0		6.2	1.1	5.8	1.8	
Animate auditory	5.5	1.2	6.1	.6		6.1	.9	5.7	1.3	
Animate visual and auditory	5.5	1.6	6.2	1.4		6.4	1.1	6.1	1.5	
Alertness	5.0	2.0	5.2	1.8		6.3	1.5	5.5	1.6	
General tonus	5.5	.7	5.7	1.2		5.7	.9	6.3	.5	.02
Motor maturity	5.0	1.5	4.8	1.5		6.1	1.1	5.7	1.3	
Pull-to-sit	5.3	1.8	6.2	1.7		5.1	1.3	6.0	1.5	
Cuddliness	5.2	1.4	5.1	.8		5.2	2.0	4.9	1.0	
Defensive movements	5.9	1.7	5.3	1.9		6.9	1.1	5.7	1.3	
Consolability	7.0	1.7	6.6	2.2		8.1	2.0	6.6	1.6	.001
Peak of excitement	5.4	1.1	6.3	1.1	.05	4.9	1.3	6.9	1.0	.001
Rapidity of buildup	3.4	1.8	5.4	1.9	.01	2.3	1.7	4.9	1.6	.001
Irritability	4.1	1.8	5.7	1.9	.05	3.4	1.8	5.8	1.2	.001
Activity	4.7	1.0	5.2	1.0		5.2	.9	5.5	.7	
Tremulousness	3.6	1.7	5.3	2.2	.05	2.4	1.3	3.3	1.8	.01
Startle	3.2	1.1	4.9	2.5		2.4	1.0	4.4	2.1	
Lability										
Of skin color	5.4	1.4	5.1	1.5		4.4	1.6	5.2	1.3	
Of states	2.7	.8	6.0	1.7	.001	2.3	1.0	4.7	2.1	
Self-quieting activity	6.9	1.3	4.6	2.1	.01	7.0	1.8	4.7	1.8	.001
Hand-mouth facility	7.5	2.0	5.9	1.5	.02	6.4	2.0	5.3	2.8	.001
Smiles	.5	1.0	.0	.0		1.3	1.3	.6	1.6	

[a] All tests of significance are two-tailed t-tests.

128

Table 5.3. Principal Components Analyses of Navajo Brazelton Scale Data

Days 1–3			
Component No. 1 (Variance explained = 25.8%)		Component No. 2 (Variance explained = 20.3%)	
Consolability	−.66	Response decrement to light	.66
Peak of excitement	.82	Orientation	
Rapidity of buildup	.80	Inanimate visual	.74
Irritability	.78	Inanimate auditory	.73
Lability		Animate visual	.61
Of skin color	.75	Animate auditory	.65
Of states	.89	Animate visual and auditory	.65
Self-quieting activity	−.68	Alertness	.77
		Activity	.79

Days 4–10			
Component No. 1 (Variance explained = 35.5%)		Component No. 2 (Variance explained = 21.4%)	
Response decrement		Orientation	
To light	.86	Inanimate auditory	.72
To rattle	.95	Animate auditory	.72
To bell	.81	Animate visual and auditory	.60
Orientation inanimate visual	.77	Alertness	.65
Consolability	−.66	General tonus	.71
Peak of excitement	.84	Startle	.69
Rapidity of buildup	.66	Lability of states[a]	−.69
Irritability	.78	Hand-mouth facility	−.69
Activity	.90	Smiles	.65
Lability of skin color	.68		
Lability of states[a]	.63		
Self-quieting activity	−.83		

[a] Lability of states is listed twice because it loaded almost equally on the first and second principle components.

clustered along a known dimension of individual differences. I subjected the Navajo NBAS scores to a principal components analysis. Principal components analysis was used because it performs the fewest transformations on the original correlation matrix. The Anglo NBAS scores were not analyzed this way because of the small size of the Anglo sample. Indeed, the size of the Navajo sample is also smaller than it should be for a principal components analysis, but is more nearly adequate and the results obtained are consistent with those of Strauss and Rourke: for both Navajo age groups, the first principal component was an irritability component or factor that was defined by most of the NBAS items comprising the intuitive state control cluster (see above) and on which Navajo and Anglo infants differed most. Table 5.3 lists the first two components for the Navajo NBAS scores on days 1–3 and 4–10.

On both days 1–3 and 4–10 the first component, accounting for the highest percentage of total sample variance, was characterized by high loadings by the NBAS items reflecting infant state, state control, and irritability. It is also on these items that the Navajo–Anglo group differences are most significant and most consistent across age groups. In sum, through the first 10 days of life, Navajo infants were less likely to cry or fret than Anglo infants, slower to reach a crying state, less likely to respond to aversive stimuli with a cry, more easily consoled if they did cry, and less likely to show numerous or rapid changes from one state to another. The small differences between Freedman's data and mine (e.g., I found no difference in Navajo and Anglo *defensive movements*) do not detract from the clear overall conclusion that Navajo infants are quieter and less irritable than Anglo infants. Moreover, these group differences achieve a greater conceptual validity in these data than they do in Freedman's because of the use of principal components analysis which demonstrates that the Navajo–Anglo differences are not scattered randomly throughout the items of the NBAS but are concentrated in what is commonly interpreted as an "irritability" dimension or factor by many researchers.

PRENATAL INFLUENCES ON NAVAJO–ANGLO GROUP DIFFERENCES IN NEWBORN BEHAVIOR

While it was not my original goal to investigate the antecedents of these Navajo–Anglo group differences in newborn behavior, and while my data are not sufficient for definitive statistical analyses, I feel that it is possible to go beyond Freedman's explanations of these differences. Freedman claims that in his studies of neonatal differences in behavior infants were matched "on every potentially important covariable" (1976:37). Finding group differences even after exerting such controls, he concluded that Navajo–Anglo differences in newborn behavior are the result of Caucasian–Asian gene pool differences, and suggests that the gene pool differences are the result of random genetic drift. Freedman thus commits the logical error of confusing the *untested* genetic "explanation" with the weak claim of "not yet disproved" (cf. Blurton Jones, Woodson, and Chisholm, 1979).

In an initial exploration of the influences of "potentially important covariables" on Navajo neonatal irritability I averaged each child's NBAS score on the items best defining the irritability component (*peak of excite-*

Table 5.4. Correlates of Navajo Neonatal Irritability

Variable	Correlation with neonatal irritability		
	r	n	p <
Maternal age	.30	33	.04
Parity	.30	33	.04
Problems in previous pregnancies[a]	.37	33	.02
Second trimester MAP	.67	16	.003
< 24 hours MAP	.35	22	.065
Duration first stage of labor	−.50	33	.01

[a] Problems in previous pregnancies were recorded in each mother's prenatal medical files by hospital or clinic staff and include their notes of the mothers' reports of such conditions as edema, nausea, vaginal discharge or bleeding, headaches, abortions, miscarriages, obesity, alcoholism, insufficient weight gain, and more. Because there were so many types of problems but so few reported for each woman (< 1 per mother), they were simply summed.

ment, rapidity of buildup, irritability, and lability of states) and related this average irritability index to a large number of variables concerning the environment of the test itself, the condition of the child at birth, aspects of the labor and delivery process, qualities of the mother reflecting her reproductive status, and finally, to the mother's blood pressure during pregnancy. The correlations between these variables and the average irritability index that were most significant ($p < .07$) are presented in Table 5.4.

The decision to investigate the possible relationship between maternal blood pressure during pregnancy and newborn irritability was based on the work of Barnes (1975), who demonstrated significant long-term sequelae in children of poor birth status, whose mothers were more likely to have had at least one blood pressure reading during pregnancy that was at or above the accepted definition of hypertension. Maternal pregnancy blood pressure scores were obtained from hospital and clinic medical records after the last NBAS examination of each infant. These blood pressure readings are represented here as mean arterial pressure (MAP) for each trimester of pregnancy (except the first, where there were too few for consideration) and the last 24 hours before delivery, using the formula (Burton, 1965):

$$MAP = (2 \times diastolic + systolic)/3$$

The majority of blood pressure readings from the last 24 hours before delivery were in fact taken during the first stage of labor.

Table 5.4 suggests that at best it is premature to argue that gene pool differences can explain the Navajo–Anglo group differences in neonatal irritability. At worst, such an argument says nothing about the epigenetic mechanisms whereby these differences may develop and is a nonexplanatory begging of the question that actually prevents research into the nature of these mechanisms. What emerges from Table 5.4 is the possibility that the prenatal environment of the Navajo child may influence the degree of irritability he or she manifests at birth. While the small sample sizes and missing data on some variables make it impossible to use the multivariate statistical analyses that would be needed to sort out the effects of these and all other potentially important covariables, we can nonetheless begin to narrow the search for some of these epigenetic mechanisms by focusing on how the variables listed in Table 5.4 might affect fetal development.

All of the pre- and perinatal variables that are correlated with Navajo neonatal irritability are highly intercorrelated (as Table 5.5 shows), and all reflect aspects of the mothers' reproductive condition or functioning. Table 5.5 shows that older mothers have had more children and more problems in previous pregnancies (most likely simply because they are older and have had more time to accumulate such problems). It also shows that those who have had more children tend to have higher blood pressure during the second trimester of pregnancy and shorter first-stage labors and that those with higher second trimester blood pressure also tend to have higher blood pressure during the 24 hours prior to delivery and again, shorter first-stage labors.

Table 5.5. Intercorrelations of Navajo Pre- and Perinatal Variables Related to Neonatal Irritability

	Maternal age	Parity	Problems previous pregnancies	MAP–2	MAP–24	Duration first stage labor
Maternal age	—	.80[e]	.47[d]	.29	.22	−.19
Parity		—	.55[e]	.47[c]	.09	−.40[c]
Problems in previous pregnancies			—	.48[c]	.35	−.36[c]
MAP–2[a]				—	.87[e]	−.37[c]
MAP–24[b]					—	−.12

[a] MAP–2, MAP during the second trimester of pregnancy.
[b] MAP–24, MAP during the last 24 hours prior to delivery.
[c] $= p < .05$.
[d] $= p < .01$.
[e] $= p < .001$.

One interpretation of these intercorrelated predictors of irritability in Navajo newborns is that the prenatal environment of the Navajo infants was less than optimum, possibly because of the relative depletion of uterine function due to age and high parity. This prenatal environmental difference by itself could be a primary cause of the group differences in neonatal irritability and cannot yet be ruled out, but "depletion" is a relative term and there is no evidence that the Navajo mothers or newborn infants were undernourished in any obvious way. In fact, the Navajo infants were slightly heavier and had slightly higher APGAR scores than did the Anglo infants. In addition, none of the prenatal or neonatal clinical records gave any indication of possible mal- or undernourishment *in utero*, or did any of the Navajo infants, either in their appearance or in their performance on the NBAS.

There is, however, a more subtle kind of depletion that could affect the behavior of newborn infants: a relative depletion of placental function due to elevated blood pressure. Anything that affects placental function might also affect fetal development and neonatal behavior because the placenta is such a vital organ of the fetus. It serves as a protective barrier between maternal and fetal circulatory systems, transports both oxygen and nutritive substance from the mother's blood to the fetus, removes wastes from the fetal circulation, and synthesizes fetal hormones. Hypertension is known to be associated with both irritability and relative growth retardation in newborn infants (Myerscough, 1974). Hypertension is also known to reduce uteroplacental blood flow to as little as one-third of the 600 ml/min typical of normotensive women in the last 2 weeks of pregnancy (Browne and Veall, 1953). Browne and Veall (1953) have also shown that the placentas of pregnant hypertensive women are smaller than those of normotensive women. While none of the Navajo or Anglo women were clinically hypertensive during their pregnancies, Woodson, da Costa Woodson, and I (Chisholm, Woodson, and da Costa Woodson, 1978) have suggested that since blood pressure follows a normal distribution and since the 140/90 mmHg cutoff for the diagnosis of hypertension is relatively arbitrary, the mechanisms producing irritability in the children of hypertensive mothers might also be operating, even if in a reduced way, in normotensive mothers. As Fig. 5.1 shows, normal Navajo maternal blood pressure during pregnancy is certainly highly correlated with neonatal irritability.

The mechanism whereby elevated but still normal maternal blood pressure during pregnancy might lead to increased neonatal irritability are not known, but a likely candidate is through the effects of placental dysfunction on the developing fetal neuroendocrine system. Dobbing (1974), for example, has shown that the developing fetal brain is highly sensitive to growth restrictions, especially so during the latter parts of pregnancy when it is growing most rapidly. Another possibility is through the effects of maternal

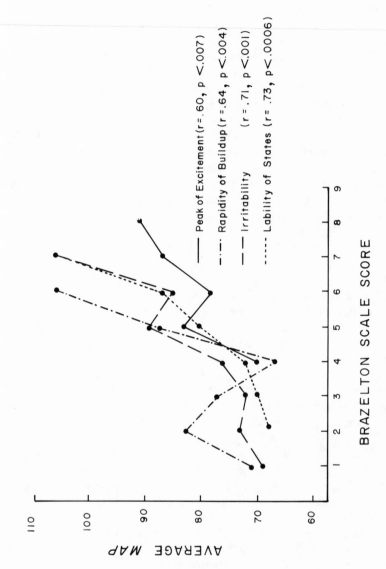

Fig. 5.1. Navajo second trimester MAP and neonatal (days one to three) irritability.

Table 5.6. Navajo and English MAP during Pregnancy

| | MAP | | | |
| | Navajo (n = 16) | | English (n = 10) | |
	$\bar{X}$	SD	$\bar{X}$	SD
Second trimester	80.5	12.9	81.2	6.9
Third trimester	84.0	12.5	86.4	7.9
< 24 hours	97.0	14.6	91.3	9.0

catecholamines, many of which will pass through the placenta, on the organization of the fetal neuroendocrine system (cf. Money and Ehrhardt, 1968). The etiology of hypertension, let alone "elevated" blood pressure, is not well understood, but it is known that, among other factors, psychosocial stress can play a role (S. Levine, 1971; Kaplan, 1978). As part of the human stress response, catecholamines are released into the bloodstream; in addition to their action at specific target organ sites, these catecholamines also have a general vasoconstrictive action which raises blood pressure.

Blood pressure is also known to increase both with body weight, age, and altitude. It is thus interesting to note that the Navajo women who weigh no more than the English women, but who are older and live at 6000 feet, have a slightly lower blood pressure during the second and third trimesters than that of the English women in the sample, all of whom were significantly younger and living at sea level. The pregnancy blood pressure of the English mothers is compared to that of the Navajo mothers in Table 5.6 (the Flagstaff Anglo sample is not included because prenatal blood pressure data were available for only three women).

The fact that the Navajo women have higher blood pressure just prior to delivery is unexplained, but could be a function of their anxiety about having to travel up to 100 miles to the hospital over bad roads, often at short notice and in bad weather. It could also be partially a function of the uneasiness of the Navajo about hospitals and Western medicine in general.

DISCUSSION AND CONCLUSION

Without larger samples it is impossible to perform the more penetrating statistical analyses that could better determine the independent and interactive effects of maternal pregnancy blood pressure on newborn irritability, but the results reported here are consistent with more recent studies which have investigated the role of pregnancy blood pressure in neonatal irritability in more detail with larger samples. For example, Woodson and da Costa Woodson (Chisholm, Woodson, and da Costa Woodson, 1978), studying Malay, Chinese, and Tamil newborns in Malaysia, have also reported a strong positive correlation between normal maternal blood pressure during labor and newborn irritability (no blood pressure data from earlier in pregnancy were available). Recently, with a large sample of English mothers and infants, Woodson and his colleagues (1979) have reported that an immediate precursor of neonatal irritability was lower intrapartum fetal heart rate. Lower intrapartum fetal heart rate was associated with lower APGAR scores, relative (for gestational age) fetal growth retardation, and either oxytocin induction/augmentation of labor, or elevated maternal blood pressure during labor. In turn, relative fetal growth retardation was associated with greater increases in maternal blood pressure from early to mid-pregnancy.

Korner and her colleagues (1980) have also recently replicated the association between normal maternal blood pressure during pregnancy and newborn irritability. Using an automatic electronic activity monitor to assess levels of irritability instead of the NBAS, they found that in a sample of 70 normal Anglo mother–infant pairs, spontaneous neonatal crying during the first 3 days of life was positively related to normal variation in maternal blood pressure during the third trimester of pregnancy ($r = .36$, $p < .01$). Multiple regression analyses showed that third trimester maternal blood pressure still accounted for a significant amount of the variance in spontaneous neonatal crying even after controlling for the effects of second trimester blood pressure, sex and weight of infant, length of first and second stages of labor combined, analgesic medication during labor, parity, and maternal age.

Finally, studying newborn Aboriginal and white Australian infants, I was able to provide still another replication of the pregnancy blood pressure–newborn irritability correlation (Chisholm, 1981b). This was performed in the Northern Territory of Australia because Freedman (1974) had reported that Aboriginal Australian newborn infants differed from Caucasian newborns on the same dimension as did the Oriental infants; they were "less excitable, less irritable, less labile in mood, less quick to cry, more consolable, and more likely to quiet themselves when left alone" (1974b:171). Independent studies had also demonstrated that Aboriginal Australians tended to have lower blood pressure than white Australians. They also showed that Aboriginal Australian blood pressure tends to rise toward white Australian levels with the acculturation stresses and changes associated with increased contact with the white Australian culture (Abbie and Schroeder, 1960; Casley-Smith, 1959; Edwards et al., 1976). A total of 51 Aboriginal

Australian and 47 white Australian newborns were examined on days 1 and 5 with the NBAS. On both days the Aboriginal Australian infants were significantly quieter and less irritable than the white Australian infants, as Freedman had reported. His gene pool differences hypothesis, however, was not supported by the analyses of the determinants of this group difference. On day 1 the group difference in neonatal irritability was best explained by individual differences in maternal age, even after controlling for the effects of the other significant covariates, namely duration of the first stage of labor, length of gestation, birthweight, APGAR score at 1 minute, minor abnormalities of the placenta and/or cord, and group (Aboriginal or white Australian). On day 5, the group difference in neonatal irritability was best explained by normal individual differences in maternal blood pressure during the fifth month of pregnancy, even after controlling for the covariates of maternal age, sex of infant, birth weight, and group. The finding that maternal midpregnancy blood pressure was related to day 5 irritability but not to day 1 irritability (although $p = .066$) is difficult to interpret, but one possibility is that day 1 irritability in this sample was different from day 5 irritability. Irritability on day 1 might have been affected more by the infant's recovery from the birth process than day 5 irritability. Not only were the irritability scores on both days unrelated to each other, but several perinatal variables were significantly related to day 1 but not day 5 irritability.

At the moment it is impossible to do much more than speculate on the reasons why the Navajo women in my sample had lower blood pressure during pregnancy than the Anglo women. Dietary factors cannot be ruled out, but while the connection between "elevated" blood pressure and cholesterol, clinical hypertension, and coronary heart disease are not clear, Cohen (1953) reports that hypertension and coronary heart disease are "rare" among the Navajo, in spite of high cholesterol levels in the foods they eat. Although I have no data with which to test the proposition, it is possible that the Navajo women had more physical exercise than the Anglo women during their pregnancies and that this contributed to their lower blood pressure. Another possibility, although the data to show it are lacking, is that the Navajo women were subject to less psychosocial stress than the Anglo women, and/or that they enjoyed more extensive coping mechanisms through the social support networks of their extended family and clan. A sizable number of studies have specifically implicated psychosocial stress in both within- and between-group differences in blood pressure. As mentioned, Abbie and Schroeder (1960), Casley-Smith (1950), and Edwards et al. (1976) have all accounted for Aboriginal–white Australian within- and between-group differences in blood pressure in terms of acculturation stress. Kaminor and Lutz (1960) have similarly implicated such stress in accounting for within- and between-group differences in Kalahari Desert San blood pressure, and Scotch (1960, 1963) has done the same for various Zulu populations. Alfred (1970) has even specifically shown that there was a significant increase in the blood pressures of recent male Navajo migrants from the reservation to Denver (females were not studied). To guard against the possibility of self-selection, Alfred cleverly measured the blood pressure of Navajo men on the reservation who *planned* to move off the reservation; he showed that higher blood pressure did not somehow "cause" Navajo men to migrate more often. Focusing equally on psychosocial stressors and coping mechanisms, Dressler (1980) has recently demonstrated a very direct association between psychosocial stress, the relative absence of coping mechansims, and elevated blood pressure in a large sample of blacks in St. Lucia. Finally, with special reference to Freedman's arguments about Oriental-Caucasian gene pool differences in neonatal irritability, it is interesting to note that Tung (1930) has reported that "the blood pressure of the Chinese, as well as that of the other Orientals, is distinctly lower than that of the western people of similar stature" (1930:126). Tung (1927) and Houston (1929) also note that the blood pressure of Caucasians residing in China usually tends to decrease toward Chinese levels.

However stress and/or coping mechanisms may affect blood pressure, there also exist a number of studies showing that maternal prenatal stress or anxiety affects a variety of behavior patterns in the infant. Sontag (1941), for example, found that maternal prenatal anxiety was associated with greatly increased fetal body movements during the stressful period itself. Ottinger and Simons (1964) found that prenatal stress on mothers produced more crying in their newborns, and Stott (1973), who implicated disharmonious marital relations especially, found that maternal prenatal stress was associated with fretful and hyperactive behavior in the children at a variety of ages. Barnes's work (1975) has already been mentioned; although not studying maternal prenatal stress or anxiety, she found that mothers of "poor birth status" infants were more likely to have had hypertension during pregnancy. Three years later these "poor birth status" children were more accident prone, had more trouble sleeping, showed more fear of strangers, and were more likely to be left handed or ambidextrous than were normal children. Jones and Dlugokinski (1978) report that mothers who scored higher on a test of anxiety or stress during pregnancy had newborn infants who received significantly lower APGAR scores. In a retrospective epidemiological study of psychiatric disorders in Finland, Huttunen and Niskanen (1978) compared 167 Finnish adults who had lost their fathers while their mothers were pregnant to 168 who had lost their fathers after they had been born, during their first year of life. Finding a significantly greater incidence of psychiatric disorders in the group which had lost their fathers prenatally, they suggest that maternal psychosocial stress during pregnancy increases the risk for the later development of psychiatric disorders. In another study, Turner (1956) reports that restlessness, irritability, vomiting and diarrhea, hypertonicity, and sleep problems are more commonly observed in children whose mothers were especially anxious during pregnancy. Finally, in a review of prenatal effects on neonatal behavior, Ferreira (1965) notes that several researchers have reported a link between prenatal maternal anxiety and complications of labor and delivery.

The epigenesis of neonatal behaviors of all sorts begins not at birth, but at conception, and there is no good reason why anthropologists, developmental pschologists, and evolutionary biologists must let the process of delivery stand as a conceptual and disciplinary barrier to a better understanding of human epigenetics. The sensitivity of the fetus to maternal blood pressure, circulating catecholamines, and other factors could constitute an important set of mechanisms in this epigenetic process. If the fetus is sensitive to its uterine environment then it is also at least partially sensitive to the effects of the mother's larger social-physical environment on her physiology. The sensitivity of the fetus to maternal stress or anxiety could be, for example, one of the mechanisms whereby the sex ratio at birth is determined. More males than females are conceived, more males are conceived than are born, and males are known to be more susceptible to gestational insult than females; under some circumstance the maternal physiological response to stress could constitute a gestational insult that selected against males *in utero* (Stott, 1973). An investigation of the relationships between particular environmental factors, maternal prenatal stress, the sex ratio at birth, and the reproductive success of male and female offspring could have immense implications for sociobiological theory. Conceivably, kin selection and parent–offspring conflict could even be operating *in utero*; Blurton Jones (1978) suggests for example, the parent–offspring conflict may account for the fact that mean birth weight in humans is slightly less than optimum birth weight. The higher incidence of aborted male fetuses might sometimes reflect the unborn male child's "attempt" to increase its inclusive fitness by virtue of the fact that a sister might have a greater reproductive potential than he. Although completely speculative, something like this is an intriguing possibility, especially since the womb serves as a unique indicator of kinship: whether simultaneously or sequentially, inhabitants of the womb are *guaranteed* to be at least half-siblings. A slightly less speculative possibility is that of "preadaptation" taking place *in utero*. It seems at least possible that natural selection would favor those fetuses who were sensitive to their mother's physiology such that they could respond to their mother's physiology and thus, at the same time, to the larger environment into which they were *going* to be born. An irritable infant, for example, might under certain circumstances be more successful in eliciting parental investment from parents under stress than a nonirritable infant.

In conclusion and without speculation, the hypothesis that Navajo—Anglo differences in neonatal irritability are due to Navajo—Anglo gene pool differences is not supported. In conjunction with the other studies which have reported strong effects of normal maternal blood pressure during pregnancy on normal neonatal irritability, the similar findings reported here for the Navajo indicate that this prenatal environmental effect on neonatal behavior may be especially robust. I make no claim that prenatal environmental factors cause all individual and group differences in neonatal behavior while genetic factors have no role. Blood pressure, environmentally labile as it is, does have a genetic component (Kass et al., 1977). My argument is simply that there is presently no unmambiguous evidence for the role of genetic factors by themselves in ethnic and racial group differences in neonatal irritability. Such a genetic explanation is too simple and tends to preclude the search for the epigenetic pathways whereby genotype and environment can be shown to interact to produce both individual and group differences. The nature-nurture dispute will be resolved only when it is shown how their components interact.

6

Navajo and Anglo Children's Fear of Strangers

MY reasons for administering the fear of strangers (FOS) test to Navajo and Anglo children were three. First, I hoped to obtain more objective, quantitative data with which to judge the validity of the common stereotype of Navajo children as more shy, fearful, or withdrawn than Anglo children. Second, I hoped to determine whether individual differences in fear of strangers were related to individual differences in cradleboard use, as might be expected if the cradleboard contributed to "anxious" attachment. Finally, I wanted to see if individual differences in fear of strangers might be related to individual differences in each child's larger social environment, and to determine whether cradleboard use or these larger social environmental differences was a better predictor of fear of strangers.

In general, my data support the common view that Navajo children are likely to be more fretful and less overtly friendly than Anglo children when meeting strangers. I must, however, immediately qualify this generalization with two observations. First, after my first FOS test on each child I was no longer a stranger to that child; thus, strictly speaking, I did not measure the development of fear of strangers, but the development of familiarity behavior. I do not, however, believe that this is an entirely valid objection to my generalizations because (1) there was a minimum of 2 months between the FOS tests I administered to each child, (2) I interacted with each child as little as possible throughout the 20 months of research, and (3) there was no relationship between a child's FOS score and either the time since the last FOS test or even the number of times that I happened to see the child since the last FOS test (calculated from the number of spot observations on each child since the last FOS test). The second, more valid objection, is that because I am an Anglo I was simply more of a stranger to the Navajo children than to the Anglo children. I attempted to at least partially circumvent this problem by speaking as much Navajo as I could to the Navajo children during their FOS tests, but I was still almost definitely more strange

141

to the Navajo children than the Anglo children. For this reason I will not stress the Navajo–Anglo differences in fear of strangers as much as others have, but will concentrate more on individual differences in fear of strangers within the Navajo sample.

SIMILARITIES AND DIFFERENCES IN NAVAJO AND ANGLO FEAR OF STRANGERS

Figure 6.1 is a schematic representation of the relative degree of fearful and friendly behavior shown by Navajo and Anglo children. As in the case of most of my analyses, Fig. 6.1 represents mixed cross-sectional and longitudinal data, and the FOS scores of any one child may appear in as many as eight or nine of the mean FOS scores for either group.

Two things of interest are immediately apparent in Fig. 6.1. First, there is virtually no difference in the age at which Navajo and Anglo children first begin to show a preponderance of fearful over friendly behaviors. Both groups show a clear preponderance of fear at about 8 to 9 months. This

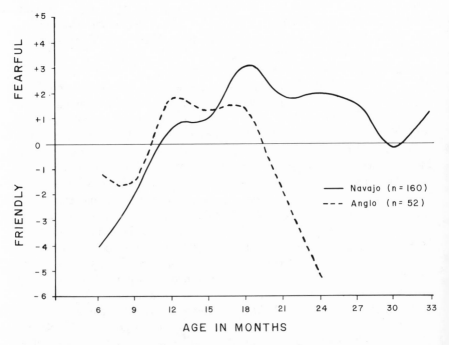

Fig. 6.1. Navajo and Anglo children's fear of strangers.

could be taken as evidence for the existence of a phylogenetically determined developmental course for fear of strangers that operates in very similar ways in children whose developmental environments are quite different. This point will be discussed later.

The second item of interest in Fig. 6.1 is the group differences in fear of strangers. These differences are significant ($p < .05$; one-tailed Mann-Whitney U test) at 6, 21, and 24 months. The significantly greater fear of Navajo children after 18 months of age was predicted, but as mentioned, these differences must not be overemphasized because of the fact that I was probably not equally strange to Navajo and Anglo children. The greater friendliness of the 3 to 6-month-old Navajo children, however, was not predicted, and I can think of no obvious explanation.

The picture of greater fear of strangers among Navajo children that emerges from a simple comparison of algebraically summed mean FOS scores emerges also from an analysis of group differences in the frequency with which individual behaviors were shown. Using a two-tailed chi-square test[3] of the significance of the group differences during the first and second years separately, it became apparent that there were no significant group differences in fear of strangers during the first year, but several in the second year, as Table 6.1 shows.

All of the second year differences reflect greater friendliness on the part of the Anglo children and greater fear, wariness, or ambivalence on the part of the Navajo children. One of the more intriguing group differences was in the behavior item *shake hands. Shake hands* never occurred in the Anglo sample but Navajo children as young as only 15 months initiated handshakes with me, either on their own or at their mother's instruction. In the third year of life nearly 25% of all Navajo children initiated handshakes with me. Among the Navajo, handshaking is ubiquitous and considered polite behavior at almost all encounters with non-coresidents of all ages; adult men and women will go quite out of their way to shake hands with everyone present, including small infants. Handshaking by infants is clearly a culture-specific behavior, and was seen to be specifically taught, but because of the similarities between *touch stranger* and *shake hands* I assigned a friendly numerical score to this behavior. It was not until I had completed all analyses making use of summed numerical FOS scores that I found I had wrongly interpreted *shake hands*.

In fact, shake hands seems to be neither friendly nor fearful. The great majority of *shake hands* that I received were initiated by the Navajo child as I made my approach. The child would typically take a step or two toward

---

[3] In spite of the fact that more fearful behavior had been predicted for the Navajo, two-tailed χ^2 tests were used because no predictions had been made as to which behavior items would necessarily constitute evidence of this fear.

Table 6.1. Behavior Items in Navajo and Anglo Children's Fear of Strangers

| Behavior item | First year | | Second year | | |
	Navajo ($n=50$)	Anglo ($n=19$)	Navajo ($n=63$)	Anglo ($n=33$)	$p<$
Laugh	8.0	.0	.0	3.0	
Touch stranger	30.0	21.1	7.9	12.1	
Smile	50.0	47.4	9.5	42.4	.001
Nonfret vocalization	30.0	13.2	5.6	55.3	.001
Shake hands	.0	.0	11.1	.0	.001
Arms up to stranger	6.0	5.2	4.8	3.0	
Approach stranger	.0	.0	11.1	6.1	
Stare at stranger	32.0	15.8	20.6	3.0	.05
Resist contact or restrain stranger	8.0	21.1	20.6	36.4	
Proffer or show to stranger	.0	.0	3.9	.0	
Hand at mouth	6.0	.0	.0	6.1	
Gaze avert < 2 seconds	14.0	26.0	19.0	27.3	
Coy[a]	.0	.0	.0	15.2	.001
Look at mother	40.0	52.6	52.4	24.2	.01
Withdraw from stranger	8.0	21.1	22.2	21.2	
Pucker face	14.0	.0	15.8	12.1	
Hide eyes	.0	.0	4.8	.0	
Approach mother	12.0	31.6	26.9	18.2	
Touch mother	2.0	.0	11.1	9.1	
Fret	14.0	21.1	46.0	6.1	.001
Cling to mother	.0	5.3	4.8	.0	
Cry	8.0	10.5	6.3	.0	

[a] Coy was defined as *smile* and *gaze avert* in rapid succession, and almost always also included *sideways glance* and/or *head on side* (see Marvin and Mossler, 1976).

me, holding out his or her hand, and usually looking at me. After I had shaken the child's hand, he or she would then almost invariably *resist contact*. After withdrawing, the child would then often *look at mother*, but was unlikely to *approach mother* or to *fret* or *cry*.

In many respects this pattern is similar to the pattern of adult Navajo handshaking: quick and gentle. The adult handshake, however, is further characterized by gaze aversion during the actual handshake; the Navajo children did not usually *gaze avert*. These infantile handshakes may have had some of the components of *coy* behavior, but true *coy* behavior involves *look*, *smile*, and *gaze avert* in rapid succession, often with some characteristic body posturing. Children who initiated handshakes had impassive faces, did not *gaze avert*, and tended to hold themselves straight and immobile before and after their quick approach and withdrawal. What may be similar to *coy* behavior is the ambivalence that seems to be a defining characteristic of this infantile handshaking. In classic *coy* behavior the apparent motivations to approach and to withdraw seem to be simultaneous (cf. Marvin and Mossler, 1976), whereas in this infantile handshaking, the culturally stereo-typed behavior pattern seems to offer a solution for the resolution of the presumed ambivalence by ritualizing the pattern itself and perhaps espe-cially its temporal sequence of quick approach, quick and light handshake, and quick withdrawal. Once having performed this little greeting ritual, the child may then "feel justified" in avoiding or resisting any further contact with stranger. The whole flavor of these handshakes was a preemptory move by the child to "get it all over with" as soon as possible and thereby perhaps to forestall my approach and/or to give full expression to his motivation to resist *contact.*

This pattern of handshaking by Navajo infants less than 2 years old is strongly reminiscent of the "cutoff" act or posture that Chance (1962) has described and analyzed in a variety of species. Infantile Navajo *shake hands* differs from classic cutoff behaviors, however, in that it seems to function through the cultural patterning of the quick sequential expression of op-posing motivations. It would be interesting to gather more longitudinal data to determine when and under what circumstances the adult pattern of gaze aversion during hand shaking appears. The epigenesis of fear of strangers behavior in Navajo children might be an especially interesting place to examine the processes whereby children learn to use culturally stereotyped behavior patterns to modulate conflicting motivations.

My mistaken scoring of shake hands as a friendly behavior is unlikely to affect the mean FOS scores of Navajo children substantially because only 11% of the children showed this behavior in the second year. Further, because it was accompanied by relatively more fearful behaviors, its some-what inflated friendly rating would tend to be canceled out. In any case, the bias would be toward making the Navajo children appear to be more friendly, thus tending to counteract their already greater scores on fearful-ness.

Just as there were no significant differences in the fear of strangers be-havior frequencies between Navajo and Anglo children in the first year, a varimax rotated factor analysis showed that the behaviors clustered together in similar ways in both samples. Factor analysis was carried out to explore the possibility that even if mean FOS test scores did not differ, Navajo and Anglo children might nonetheless organize their fear of strangers behavior in different ways. Because of the relatively small number of tests on Anglo children in the first year ($n = 19$), the number of behaviors entered as variables was reduced to the nine most common, and *resist contact* and

Table 6.2. Factor Analysis of Navajo and Anglo First Year FOS Test Behaviors

	Navajo (n = 50)		
Behavior item	Factor 1 (64.9%)	Factor 2 (23.7%)	Factor 3 (11.4%)
Touch stranger	−.25	.28	−.52
Smile at stranger	−.29	.72	−.29
Talk/vocalize to stranger	−.19	.61	−.20
Stare at stranger	.08	−.24	.26
Resist contact/leave stranger	.67	−.02	.13
Gaze avert < 2 seconds	.10	.11	.22
Look at mother	−.18	−.30	.24
Approach mother	.47	−.26	.13
Fret/cry	.74	−.12	.13

	Anglo (n = 19)			
Behavior item	Factor 1 (50.8%)	Factor 2 (20.5%)	Factor 3 (16.5%)	Factor 4 (12.2%)
Touch stranger	.81	−.27	−.62	−.12
Smile at stranger	.73	−.14	−.17	−.16
Talk/vocalize to stranger	.15	−.18	−.67	−.31
Stare at stranger	−.20	−.41	.22	−.29
Resist contact/leave stranger	−.24	.88	.19	−.15
Gaze avert < 2 seconds	−.20	.04	.18	.88
Look at mother	−.48	.36	.14	.07
Approach mother	.05	.11	.61	.22
Fret/cry	−.17	.64	.42	.16

leave stranger were grouped together. Table 6.2 presents the results of this factor analysis of the first year FOS test data.

The Navajo solution has a first, unambiguous fearful factor followed by two friendly factors. The Anglo solution has a first, unambiguous friendly factor followed by two fearful factors. A fourth factor emerged for the Anglo sample that is difficult to interpret. However, because its defining loading *gaze avert < 2 seconds* did not load on any of the Navajo factors and only on the least powerful Anglo factor, it may be an anomalous finding, perhaps a function of the relatively small sample.

Because the development of fear of strangers is by no means static during the first year of life, there is a danger in attempting to interpret too much from these factor analyses, which grouped children of all ages under 1 year together. However, while the child's age was not related, surprisingly, to any of the behavior items listed, there is nonetheless considerable variation in each sample in the precise age at which the children first begin to show a preponderance of fearful behaviors. Because fearful and friendly behaviors do not load together in the same direction on any factor in either sample, I think it is reasonable to make the common heuristic dichotomy of fearful and friendly behavioral subsystems for this age group. Beyond this it is probably not safe to infer much more, except that within these broad conceptually opposite categories the context of the FOS test itself (probably including the maturational context of age) may be of deciding importance. I feel, for example, that the difference between the two friendly Navajo factors and the two fearful Anglo factors may be explained in part by subtle differences in the way that I administered the test as I reacted to subtle differences in the larger social environment of the test which I failed to perceive and record.

Factor analyses of the second year FOS test behavioral data reveal a more complex picture of behavioral organization, and more inference is justified because of the larger sample sizes and because by the second year all children in both samples had begun to show a preponderance of fearful behaviors. The first four Navajo and Anglo varimax rotated factors are presented in Table 6.3.

In the factor analyses of the first year FOS test data, fearful and friendly behaviors were clearly seen to be the major dimensions of differences characterizing both samples. In factor analyses of the second year FOS test data, however, this simple dichotomy seems to be a less useful distinction. The major dimension on which Navajo children differed in the second year was the degree to which they avoided interaction with me by approaching their mothers. This is certainly suggestive of fearfulness, but *fret/cry*, for example, loads only minimally on this first factor while it was the factor-defining variable on the first factor for Navajo children in the first year. The second Navajo factor is an unambiguous friendly constellation of behaviors, including *approach stranger, proffer/show to stranger*, and *arms up to stranger*. The third Navajo factor is the *shake hands* factor discussed earlier, and the fourth Navajo factor seems to reflect a relatively passive dimension with weakly friendly and weakly fearful behaviors loading together, but in opposite directions. For heuristic purposes of quick conceptualization only, these four factors might be labeled "locomotory fear," "locomotory friendly," "culturally modified ambivalence" (the *shake hands* factor), and "passive facial-visual," respectively.

The first Anglo factor for the second year FOS test behaviors is also a generally fearful one, but whereas the first Navajo factor reflects the combination of locomotion (*approach mother* and *leave stranger*) and fear, the Anglo factor seems to reflect a simple refusal to interact without locomotion and without any other obvious indicators of fear. After the Navajo children

Table 6.3. Factor Analysis of Navajo and Anglo Second Year FOS Test Behaviors

Behavior item	Navajo (n = 63)			
	Factor 1 (23.9%)	Factor 2 (11.7%)	Factor 3 (11.3%)	Factor 4 (10.3%)
Touch stranger	−.19	.19	.05	−.05
Smile at stranger	−.24	.24	.08	−.46
Talk/vocalize to stranger	−.09	.12	.12	−.09
Stare at stranger	−.15	−.00	.19	.71
Gaze avert < 2 seconds	−.18	−.18	.07	−.15
Look at mother	.23	.00	−.21	.48
Leave stranger	.74	.03	−.01	.06
Resist contact/restrain stranger	−.04	.08	−.59	.03
Pucker face	−.01	−.02	−.16	−.00
Fret/cry	.33	−.37	.32	−.22
Approach mother	.63	−.20	.38	−.13
Touch mother	.00	−.04	.04	.07
Approach stranger	−.15	.77	.07	.02
Shake hands	.04	−.07	−.71	.03
Proffer/show to stranger	.09	.52	.04	−.09
Arms up to stranger	−.14	.15	−.09	−.02
Refuse pick up by stranger	.53	−.08	−.09	.14

Behavior item	Anglo (n = 33)			
	Factor 1 (27.6%)	Factor 2 (23.1%)	Factor 3 (16.1%)	Factor 4 (11.9%)
Touch stranger	−.26	−.12	.70	−.08
Smile at stranger	−.12	.53	−.09	−.38
Talk/vocalize to stranger	−.49	.15	.53	−.38
Stare at stranger	.17	.08	−.20	.17
Gaze avert < 2 seconds	−.07	.22	−.15	−.07
Look at mother	−.07	−.24	−.27	.56
Leave stranger	.10	−.13	−.10	−.09
Resist contact/restrain stranger	.59	−.24	−.05	−.22
Pucker face	.09	−.16	−.19	.12
Fret/cry	−.00	−.10	−.33	−.02
Approach mother	−.06	−.14	−.28	.51
Touch mother	−.00	−.01	.03	.85
Approach stranger	.20	−.18	.49	−.43
Arms up to stranger	.10	.34	.22	−.39
Refuse pick up by stranger	.86	.29	.12	−.04
Coy	.28	.79	.03	−.13

refused pick up by stanger they tended to move away from me and/or approach mother, but after the Anglo children *refused pick up by stranger* they tended to remain stationary. I suspect that the reason *resist contact/ restrain stranger* loaded positively with *refuse pick up by stranger* for the Anglo children (whereas it loaded with *shake hands* for the Navajo) was because they tended to remain stationary after refusing to be picked up but did not show other signs of fear, I often reached out to them, preparing to attempt another pickup, and thereby elicited more *resist contact/restrain stranger* behavior. My impressions are that the first Navajo factor and first Anglo factor are similar, but I think that simple "refusal" is a better heuristic label for the first Anglo factor than the alternative "nonlocomotory fear."

The second Anglo factor seems in many ways similar to the Navajo *shake hands* factor, for *coy* and *smile at stranger* load together on this factor, suggesting that it reflects a degree of ambivalence. *Smile* was recorded separately from those smiles that occurred together with gaze aversion to make *coy*. Whether *smile* or *coy* came first in the FOS test (which my event-sampling recording technique cannot show) may not matter, for *smile* and smiles in the context of *coy* behavior do not co-occur with the same behaviors and thus probably represent different motivations. The fact that they nonetheless load positively on the same factor here suggests either more ambivalence than simple *coy* behavior or another manifestation of the same underlying conflict in *coy* behavior. My impressions are that *smiles* occurred as I started the FOS test and that *coy* occurred moments later as I approached the child and/or attempted to interact with the child, a progression from "weak friendly" to "classic ambivalence." Thus, even though this factor probably reflects less ambivalence than the Navajo *shake hands* factor "ambivalent" is still a useful label for this factor.

The third Anglo factor reflects differences between children in the extent to which they *approach stranger, talk/vocalize to stranger,* and especially, *touch stranger.* This is an unambiguously friendly and active social interaction factor, similar to the Navajo "locomotory friendly" factor except that instead of *touch stranger,* the Navajo children show more *arms up to stranger* and less *talk/vocalize to stranger.* An heuristic label for this factor that reflects this slight difference might be "locomotory and vocal friendly."

The fourth Anglo factor is defined by high loadings by *look at mother, approach mother,* and especially, *touch mother.* That *leave stranger* does not load on this factor suggests that these children moved toward their mothers at the start of the FOS test before I could even begin to move toward them and thus record that they had moved away from me specifically. To the extent that this Anglo factor reflects individual differences in both locomotion and fear it is like the first Navajo factor ("locomotory fear"). The Navajo "locomotory fear" factor, however, does not include *touch mother* while this behavior is the one that best defines the factor for the Anglo children. Thus, this fourth Anglo factor might best be distinguished as a "physical contact with mother" factor.

In the first year FOS test behaviors there were no significant Navajo–Anglo group differences. Factor analyses of the FOS test behaviors in the first year revealed similar factors for both groups in which fearful and friendly behaviors were quite clearly separated on orthogonal factors and in which the most consistent indicators of fear were *fret/cry* and *resist contact*. In the second year FOS test behaviors, however, several significant Navajo–Anglo group differences appeared, all of which were indicative of more fearful behavior in the Navajo children. In the second year factor analyses fearful and friendly became less distinct categories of behavior and the major dimension of differences in both samples was in the extent to which children *leave stranger* and/or *approach mother*. One of the most striking differences between Navajo and Anglo children in second year fear of strangers behavior is that when Anglo children *approach stranger* they are likely to *touch stranger*, and when they *approach mother* they also *touch mother*, but Navajo children do not. When Anglo children *approach stranger* they are also likely to show *arms up to stranger*, which in some ways may be equivalent to *touch stranger*. But when Navajo children *approach mother* they are as likely to touch her as not. When Anglo children *approach stranger* they are likely to also *talk/vocalize to stranger* whereas the Navajo children tend to remain silent. Further, *smile at stranger* for the Navajo (which was seen in only 5.6% of all FOS tests) tends to go with immobility, and while *smile at stranger* loads on the Anglo "ambivalent" factor it also loads on the "physical contact with mother" factor, but opposite *approach mother* and *touch mother*, and in the same direction as *approach stranger*.

These factor analyses supported some of the impressions that I had formed during administration of the FOS tests: for the Navajo, movement toward the mother especially was a means toward the end of simple proximity. For the Anglo children, on the other hand, movement toward the mother or toward the stranger was a means toward the end of more active interaction through touching, talking, and smiling. Proximity to mother usually seemed to be sufficient for the Navajo children but not for the Anglo children. When the Navajo children showed *approach stranger* they were not so content to be merely close to me, but they tended nonetheless to be silent and interacted with me through an object *(proffer/show to stranger)* or via *arms up to stranger*.

Both groups showed a major "ambivalence" dimension of differences; the *shake hands* factor for the Navajo and the *coy* factor for the Anglo. I have labeled the Anglo *coy* factor "ambivalence" only to distinguish it from the "culturally modified ambivalence" Navajo factor, but it would be a mistake to assume that there is no cultural or social learning involved in the *coy* behavior of Anglo children. More cross-cultural developmental data are needed to establish better the range and variation in culturally modified manifestations of conflicting motivations to approach and avoid.

As an item of interest for other cross-cultural researchers in child behavior, in my samples it was the Navajo children who interacted with the stranger through *proffer/show to stranger* and not the Anglo children. Blurton Jones (1967) and Connolly and Smith (1972) have reported this to be quite common behavior in English children, and I have certainly seen it in Anglo-American children as well, but, for unexplained reasons, none of the Flagstaff Anglo children showed this behavior.

Finally, the first Anglo factor, "refusal," while clearly not friendly, should not be forced onto the fearful side of the usual fearful–friendly dichotomy which was so apparent in the analyses of the first year FOS test behaviors. By the time a child is a year old, he or she has many new behavioral capacities and assumed motivations (cf. Bretherton and Ainsworth, 1974) and this refusal to interact should be accepted as simply that, with perhaps even a hint of "aggression."

In sum, over 50% of the variance in the second year FOS test behavior of the Navajo children is accounted for by two fear factors (a weak one and a strong one), a friendly factor, and an ambivalent factor. Likewise, over 50% of the variance in the second year Anglo FOS test behavior is accounted for by a refusal factor, an ambivalent factor, a friendly factor, and a fearful factor. The mean differences in numerical FOS test scores indicate more fear among the Navajo children in the second year of life and the fear dimensions seem to account for more variance in the Navajo sample than they do in the Anglo sample. Given the problems in eliciting fear cross-culturally, however, I think the safest point to make about these group differences is not the differences in mean FOS test scores, not the factor labels, and not the amount of variance explained by each factor; instead, I think the safest point to make about these data is that the Navajo children are less "intrusive" than the Anglo children. The Navajo children are more content with simple proximity to mother and stranger than are the Anglo children, and the Navajo children are less likely to touch, smile, or talk/vocalize after approaching mother or stranger. There was indeed more *fret/cry* in the Navajo sample than in the Anglo sample, but *fret/cry* did not load highest on any of the first four Navajo factors (but by itself, on the sixth factor to emerge, accounting for only 8.0% of the total variance). If *fret/cry* is the best indicator of fear, and if one accepts that my methods were entirely appropriate in each culture, then Navajo children clearly showed more fear than Anglo children. But even if this is so, "pure fear," as measured by *fret/cry,* is not a major dimension of differences within the Navajo sample.

ENVIRONMENTAL CORRELATES OF NAVAJO FEAR OF STRANGERS

Having described patterns of Navajo and Anglo children's fear of strangers that are broadly consistent with the common reports of greater fear in Navajo children, the next step in data analysis was to investigate some of the determinants of within- and between-sample differences in fear of strangers. Because I am an Anglo I was most probably more fear-provoking for the Navajo children than for the Anglo children. For this reason, and because of the relatively small sample of Anglo children, I can discuss determinants of Navajo–Anglo differences in fear of strangers only with great caution, and will concentrate instead on the effects of the cradleboard and various aspects of each child's larger social environment on the expression of fear of strangers within the Navajo sample.

The Cradleboard and Fear of Strangers

Relating measures of Navajo fear of strangers to cradleboard use was straightforward but the results should be considered tentative because mothers' reports of how many months their children used the cradleboard is only a minimally acceptable measure for rank-order correlations with the numerical FOS test scores. The really fine-grain analyses relating cradleboard use to particular patterns of fear of strangers must wait until the independent variable—hours per *day* on the cradleboard—can be better quantified. Even so, from the analyses reported here I doubt that any very simple relationship will be found; all indications are that the cradleboard has little or no effect on fear of strangers.

First, there was no difference between the behavior frequencies or mean numerical FOS test scores of those children who were on the cradleboard and those who were not during the FOS test. However, inasmuch as all children given the FOS test while on the cradleboard were under 9 months old, this is not conclusive evidence because they would be expected to show little fear anyway. Second, there was no difference between the behavior item frequencies or mean FOS test scores of those children, Navajo or Anglo, who used the cradleboard and those who did not.

Reasoning next that the cradleboard might not begin to exert its hypothesized effects on fear of strangers until after this fear had developed at about 8 months, I searched for delayed or cumulative cradleboard effects on fear of strangers by relating total cradleboard use to the amount of fear of strangers shown by older children ($>$ 40 weeks) in the 4 months after they ended their cradleboard careers. None of the Anglo children used the cradleboard after about 9 months, and none had used it very extensively anyway, so I could not analyze the Anglo data in this way. Ten Navajo children, however, on whom I had sufficient FOS test data, had continued to use the cradleboard for varying lengths of time after the appearance of the classic "8 month's anxiety." The analysis then consisted of simply regressing total weeks of cradleboard use against each child's numerical FOS test score for each FOS test within the 4 months after cessation of cradleboard use.

The mean "fear" scores entered into the regression equation were simply the total of positively weighted behaviors that were judged to be indicative of fear, divided by the number of such behaviors. When averaging fearful and friendly behaviors together, some children's FOS test scores were zero because the fearful and friendly behaviors canceled each other out. For these more detailed analyses of the numerical FOS test scores I felt it would be important to distinguish between children who had actually scored zero (i.e., completely neutral) from those whose scores only averaged zero. In any event, fearful and friendly behaviors were highly correlated ($r = -.68$; $p < .001$), as were the total numerical FOS test score and fearful behaviors ($r = .90$; $p < .001$) and friendly behaviors ($r = -.92$; $p < .001$).

As Fig. 6.2 shows, there was a strong and significant relationship between total cradleboard career and the amount of fear shown in the 4 months after ceasing to use the cradleboard. However, this correlation turned out to be more apparent than real: when I identified the four children who scored the most on fearful behavior and total months of cradleboard career, it turned out that these four (represented by open circles in Fig. 6.2) were from a significantly different subpopulation than the other six. All of these four children lived more than 20 miles away from the trading post while the other six averaged only about 6 miles away. Three of these four children lived in isolated nuclear family camps and the other one lived in a very isolated three-hogan camp with his mother where the other camp residents were often absent. In contrast, the six children who showed relatively less fear and who used the cradleboard for fewer weeks in total all lived in larger extended family camps. The covariation of distance from the trading post and population of the camps with the children's fear scores and cradleboard use effectively destroys the apparent correlation between cradleboard use and fear of strangers.

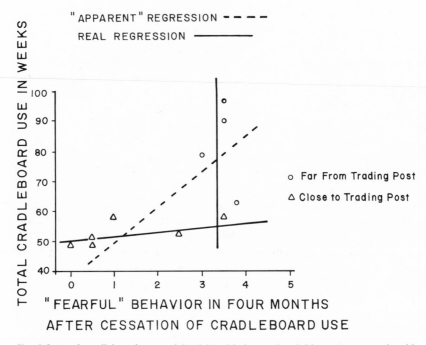

Fig. 6.2. Total cradleboard use and fearful and behavior for children over 40 weeks old.

Residence Patterns and Fear of Strangers

Having found no indication of any direct relationship between cradleboard use and fear of strangers, I turned to a deeper exploration of the relationship between Navajo children's fear of strangers and various measures relating to individual differences in residence patterns. It immediately became apparent that the number of FOS tests and spot observations on each child were not related to his or her FOS tests scores, or to the child's birth order, sex, or family size. However, two variables that turned out to be the best predictors of each child's fear of strangers were the population of the child's camp ($r = -.32$; $p < .001$) and the distance of the camp from the trading post ($r = -.28$; $p < .001$). The graphic regressions of both fearful and friendly FOS test scores against distance from the trading post (Figure 6.3) show that the r value of the distance from the trading post–FOS test scores correlation would be even higher were it not for a threshold effect in which children living more than 10 miles from the trading post show dramatically more fearful and less friendly behavior than children living less than 10 miles from the trading post.

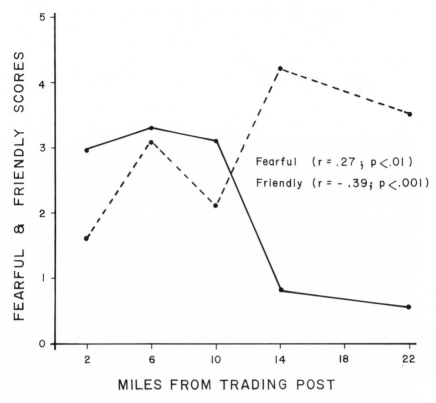

Fig. 6.3. Fear of strangers by distance from the trading post.

The reason I believe camp population and distance from trading post correlate with fear of strangers is that both are indirect measures of each child's opportunity for interaction with others, perhaps especially with strangers. Camp population and distance from the trading post are correlated with each other ($r = -.48$; $p < .001$), but my measure of camp population here does not exactly correspond to the definition of "camp" that I presented in Chapter 2. Here, instead of counting only those individuals who were coresident in the same nuclear or extended family camp, I also included an estimate of the number of immediate neighbors and probable passersby that children living in the trading post complex might encounter virtually any time they went outside. Thus, the correlation between camp population and distance from the trading post is strengthened by the three or four camps nearest the trading post where the children not only simply saw more strangers but where, because of their family's central location, they were also more likely to be visited by more family friends and relatives as they went to the trading post. At the opposite end of the scale, the most distant camps were widely separated, relatively small, and more difficult to get to and from. In some of the more distant camps, as mentioned, a child might conceivably never meet a stranger from the time it developed the classic "8 months anxiety" until it went away to school.

If the opportunity for interaction with others does have an effect on fear of strangers, there was another set of measures in my data that I felt might provide additional means for testing these effects. Given the significant differences in the number of coresidents between nuclear and extended family camps, I predicted that since nuclear family camp children are surrounded by fewer people and see fewer strangers, they might also be expected to show greater fear of strangers. Using the Mann-Whitney U Test (one-tailed) to test nuclear-extended family camp children's fear of strangers by 3-month age cohorts, it turned out that nuclear family camp children did not show more fear of strangers, but that they showed a preponderance of fearful behaviors on the FOS test about 2 months earlier than the extended family camp children. The nuclear family camp children showed significantly *less* ($p < .05$) fear of strangers during months 9–12 and 12–15 than the extended family camp children, significantly *more* fear ($p < .025$) during months 18–21 and 24–27, and then again significantly less fear ($< .025$) during months 30–33. Figure 6.4 is a graphic representation of these nuclear-extended family camp differences in FOS test scores.

Because so many factors may influence fear of strangers and because I feel that my FOS test provided only a gross measure of fear, Fig. 6.4 should not be overinterpreted. While significant nuclear-extended family camp differences in fear of strangers are apparent from 9 to 15 months, 18 to 24 months, 24 to 27 months, and 30 to 33 months, I feel that the most interesting points that can be reasonably inferred from Fig. 6.4 are that any differences exist at all and that nuclear family camp children seem to show unequivocal signs of fear of strangers about 2 months before the extended family camp children. Comparing Fig. 6.4 with Fig. 6.1, it also appears that there is as much variation within the Navajo sample as between the Navajo and Anglo samples, especially in the ages at which fear of strangers first becomes apparent.

DISCUSSION AND CONCLUSION

The comparison of Navajo and Anglo mean numerical FOS test scores and individual behavior item frequency counts both showed that the Navajo children were more fearful than the Anglo children—in the second year, but

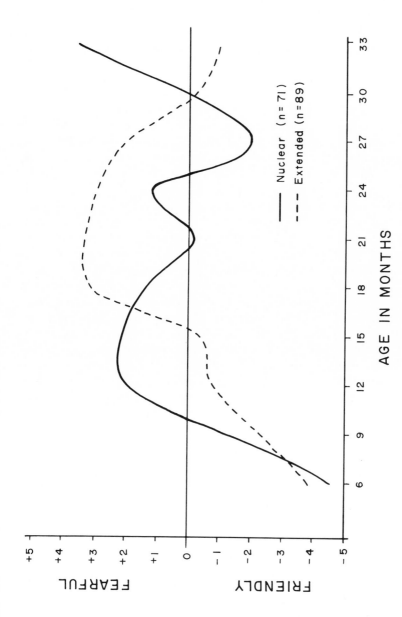

Fig. 6.4. Nuclear and extended family camp differences in fear of strangers.

not the first. Indeed, at 3 to 6 months Navajo children were more friendly than the Anglo children, although this numerical FOS test score was not mirrored in the analyses of any individual behavior item frequency counts. Factor analyses of the first year behaviors show markedly similar dimensions of individual differences in both samples. Factor analyses of the second year data suggested, however, that fear dimensions continued to best characterize dimensions of difference within the Navajo sample but that differences within the Anglo sample could not be so neatly conceptualized. Both groups showed a major ambivalence dimension as well, with the Navajo *shake hands* reaction to strangers representing the clear early influence of cultural patterns on the expression of fear of strangers. The most simple and conservative measures of fear of strangers showed no relationship to cradleboard use.

These same simple measures of fear of strangers did, however, show a strong relationship with the distance that children lived from the trading post and the population of children's camps. These variables are indirect measures, I suggest, of each child's opportunity for interaction and experience with others, perhaps especially with strangers. These variables also have an independent validity in the sense that they are more than purely social structural variables, but are material, environmental correlates of local kinship and residence patterns in the context of social adaptations to larger economic and ecological factors. In nuclear family camps the child is surrounded by fewer people than in the significantly larger extended family camps. In the nuclear family camps, where there is also a significantly shorter birth interval, not only will the child necessarily interact with fewer people of a smaller age range, chances are that he or she will also experience fewer interactions with strangers (non-coresidents) because there will likely be fewer visitors to smaller nuclear family camps than to larger extended family camps. I have no data to prove this point, but I believe it is a fair assumption: if non-coresidents visit a camp they probably do so most often to visit the adults in camp. If there are fewer adults in nuclear family camps there will probably be fewer visitors. Moreover, because extended family camps, by definition, include a core "head-of-camp" household, the couple in this household will serve as a social focus for a wider range of non-coresident kinsmen than is likely to be the case for a nuclear family camp couple.

That distance from the trading post correlates with camp population is, I think, partially an artifact of the way that I measured camp population for this set of analyses: the population density is simply higher near the trading post than far away. However, distance from the trading post clearly reflects the child's opportunity for meeting and interacting with strangers; the farther away he lives, the harder and more expensive it is for non-coresidents to visit a child.

The development of fear of strangers depends on maturational and experiential factors, and interaction and experience with strange and familiar persons is thought to be a major set of important experiential variables. The cognitive capacity to recognize an individual as strange is thought to involve the infant's perceptual capacities, his capacity to form an internally coded image or schema of what constitutes familiarity, and his capacity to compare perceptual input to this model of familiarity. When these capacities have sufficiently matured, a mismatch between stimulus input and the schema of familiarity produces an incongruence, a cognitive dissonance that is thought to be the basis for fear of strangers (Bronson, 1972; Kagan, 1974).

The development of this novelty-induced fear cannot proceed normally, however, until the child has had enough experience with what is familiar to formulate a sufficiently precise schema against which the stimulus qualities of the stranger can be compared (Hoffman, 1974). Bronson (1972) for example, showed that even as early as 4 months whether or not an infant smiled or cried at the approach of a stranger depended in part on the number of people who routinely cared for the infant. Those children in his sample who had been exposed to a greater variety of caretakers showed a later and sharper increase in fear of strangers than those who had daily experience with only one or two caretakers. Similarly, Rheingold (1961) found that institution-reared infants who had been exposed to a wide range of nursing staff showed less fear of strangers than a group of identically aged infants who had experience with only one or two caretakers at home. The general conclusion is that everyday exposure to a large number of other people may make it more difficult for the child to establish a schema of familiarity sufficiently detailed to exclude all strangers. This could account for the fact that at 3 to 6 months the Navajo children showed significantly more friendly behavior toward my approach than did the Anglo children. There was not a significant difference between Navajo and Anglo household size, but the Navajo camps were very much larger than the Anglo households ($p < .001$), and the camp is definitely a better measure of day-to-day interactive potential for Navajo children than the household.

The vitually identical ages at which Navajo and Anglo children began to show a preponderance of fearful over friendly behaviors (i.e., the "8 month's anxiety") is more apparent than real. The mean age for both groups was about 8.5 months, but this apparent similarity is the sort of finding that too often tends to be used in support of simple "ontogenetic-unfolding-of-phylogenetically-determined-propensities-to-behave" arguments that mask the crucial interplay of ontogeny, phylogeny, and environment. When the Navajo sample was divided into nuclear and extended family camps it appeared that there was at least as much variation in fear of strangers within the Navajo sample as between the Navajo and Anglo samples. The later emergence of fear of strangers in those children who lived in extended family camps (which were significantly larger than the nuclear family camps) tends to support the notion that the amount of contact and experience with familiar caretakers is inversely related to the child's capacity to recognize individuals as unfamiliar.

That the Anglo children showed less fear of strangers than the Navajo children in the second year of life, after both groups had presumably developed more-or-less adequate schemas of familiarity, is probably due to the fact that my appearance and behavior as a stranger could be more readily assimilated into the Anglo child's schema of familiarity than into the Navajo child's. The differences between novelty-induced fear and novelty-induced approach, exploration, and interaction is complex and subtle, but it is commonly accepted that too much novelty tends to elicit fear and withdrawal. I think there can be no question that I was more novel to the Navajo children than to the Anglo children. In addition to differences in skin and hair color, for example, I also had a moustache, an item of apparent interest or concern for many Navajo children, but not at all for the children of the usually hirsute Anglo fathers in Flagstaff. In addition to differences in language and accent, the very concept of a "fear of strangers test" is derived from common Anglo behavior patterns that are often unfamiliar to Navajo people: *complete* strangers rarely approach children and interact with them in such a familiar way. Finally, of course, regardless of differences in the behavior and appearance of strangers, Anglo children simply have a much wider variety of experiences with several classes of strangers than do Navajo children. Navajo children rarely see passersby in the street, usually have no immediate next-door neighbors, seldom see deliverymen, postmen, and repairmen, and rarely meet perfect strangers at the local trading post who fuss over how cute they are. Thus, as Konner says of the !Kung San, for most Navajo children, "the class of strangers, as well as the individual stranger, is strange" (1972:298).

Although my major points in this chapter are about the nuclear-extended family camp differences in fear of strangers among the Navajo, it is worth making another point about the Navajo–Anglo differences. In his study of the development of fear of strangers, Bronson (1972) refers to a number of clinical studies which give the impression that "extremely shy" children often seem to have been "hyperactive to stimulation" as children. In part because of Freedman's (Freedman and Freedman, 1969) earliest work on population differences in neonatal behavior, Bronson included Chinese, Japanese, Filipino, and Hawaiian infants in his study along with Caucasion infants in Honolulu. On a variety of measures at 3 months, these "Oriental" infants were significantly less reactive and irritable than the Caucasian infants. Bronson then found that a high degree of reactivity at 3 months predicted a high degree of fear of strangers at 4 months ($p < .02$). Further, although the strength of the correlation declined, the infants who were most reactive at 3 months continued to show more fear at 6.5 and 9 months. Bronson does not discuss, and does not appear to have found, any Oriental–Caucasian group differences in fear of strangers, but to the extent that my Brazelton scale data showed that Anglo newborns were significantly more irritable than the Navajo newborns, one might have predicted that the Anglo children would show more fear of strangers than the Navajo children. This was most certainly not the case, but it is interesting to note that the only age at which the Navajo children showed more "friendly" behavior than the Anglo children was 3 to 6 months—about the age when Bronson found the best positive relationship between earlier "reactivity" and fear of strangers. Within my Navajo sample there was a suggestive, but inconclusive association between average irritability on the Brazelton scale and fear of strangers at 3 to 6 months. The least irritable of the Navajo infants did tend to show the most friendly behavior ($r = .49$), but, perhaps because there were only six children on whom I had obtained both NBAS and early FOS test data, this correlation was not significant ($p = .14$).

In any case, whether or not neonatal irritability affects fear of strangers at 3 to 6 months, a great many factors besides the genetic and congenital have begun to operate by this age, and by the time that unequivocal fear of strangers appears toward the end of the first year, the amount of variance explained by these neonatal factors must be small. As Bronson concluded, I also feel that my data show that by the end of the first year the infant's response to strangers is best explained in terms of his or her previous experiences with familiar and strange persons and that specific environmental features such as cradleboard use have little or no impact on fear of strangers. Among the Navajo at Cottonwood Springs anyway, the major determinants of a child's opportunity for meeting strangers are the factors that determine residence patterns.

7

Mother–Infant Interaction
and the Cradleboard

THIS chapter specifically examines the immediate and longer-term effects of the cradleboard on mother–infant interaction. The previous chapter showed that there were significant differences between Navajo and Anglo children in their manifestations of fear of strangers in the second year of life, but that there was as much variation within the Navajo sample as between the Navajo and Anglo samples and that the factors that best accounted for the individual differences within the Navajo sample also seemed to best account for the differences between the samples. There was no indication that cradleboard use was related to fear of strangers. Chapter 5 showed that there were significant group differences in the behavior of Navajo and Anglo newborn infants, but also that whatever contributions gene pool differences may make to the explanation of these group differences, they cannot be the only explanation, for prenatal environmental factors (i.e., maternal blood pressure and uterine depletion) covaried with group differences in behavior and also with presumed gene pool differences. It now remains to be seen whether the cradleboard affects mother–infant interaction in a way that could independently affect fear of strangers and if newborn behavioral differences could affect either patterns of cradleboard use or patterns of mother–infant interaction. Finally, it also remains to be seen how aspects of the immediate environment of mother–infant interaction affect patterns of cradleboard use and patterns of mother–infant interaction and how larger, more pervasive or extensive social environmental factors may affect the immediate environment of mother–infant interaction. Many of the answers to these questions will be tentative, but the primary goal of this chapter is to provide a detailed description of Navajo mother–infant interaction as it is affected by the simple variable of cradleboard use.

THE IMMEDIATE EFFECTS OF THE CRADLEBOARD

Infant State

It was estimated in Chapter 3 that as much as 85% of the time that a child was on the cradleboard would be spent in sleep. It is true that Navajo mothers will place their infants on the cradleboard when they are sleepy, but mothers' reports and observations both clearly indicated that the cradleboard itself tends to help induce sleep in Navajo infants[4] as did swaddling in the experimental subjects of Lipton, Steinschneider, and Richmond (1965). First, mothers reported that their children slept longer on the cradleboard than when off, and that they slept better. When asked why she used the cradleboard one mother gave an answer that summarizes the answers of many: she used the cradleboard so that her 2-month-old daughter wouldn't "jerk and wake herself up." Second, over 400 spot observations on infants up to 15 months (the oldest that any were actually observed to still be using the cradleboard) showed a very strong correlation between cradleboard use and lower states. These spot observations were made between 7:00 AM and 9:00 PM and do not include more than a handful of children on the cradleboard for their regular night's sleep. Figure 7.1 shows the association between cradleboard use and lower states.

The state and/or activity-reducing effect of the cradleboard can be more immediately and graphically seen in the behavior of the child before and after he or she goes on and comes off the cradleboard ("cradleboard transition"). In 75.5 hours of direct observation and continuous recording of 23 children who were still using the cradleboard (all under 44 weeks old), there were 10 cases of a child being placed on the cradleboard and 22 of a child being taken off the cradleboard. There was an equal sex ratio in both cradleboard transition directions, but the sample sizes at 5 and 4 minutes before transition and 5 minutes after transition are only 8 and 20, respectively, because it was necessary to control for distance from mother. The zero point in each figure below marks the moment when the cradleboard was completely laced up or unlaced, depending on the direction of the transition. Figures 7.2 through 7.6 show the effects of the transition on a number of different infant behaviors. All tests of significance are two-tailed t-tests, except where noted.

Figure 7.2 is perhaps the clearest indication of the state-reducing effect of the cradleboard, in spite of the fact that, averaged over the full 5 min-

[4] There were too few observations of Anglo children on the cradleboard for most analyses, so unless otherwise noted, all discussion here refers to only Navajo children.

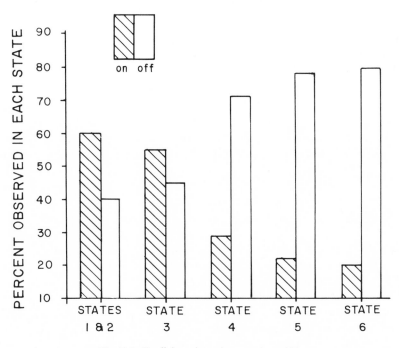

Fig. 7.1. Cradleboard use by state (n = 439).

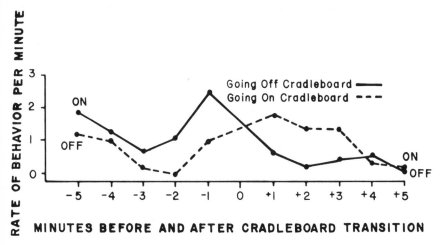

Fig. 7.2. Fret, cry, and pucker face before and after cradleboard transition.

utes, there is more *fret, cry,* and *pucker face* after going on the cradleboard than before. This increase in "upset" is not significant, however, and lasts for only 3 minutes, after which there is a sharp decline that probably reflects the fact that infants in general seem to protest swaddling, as Lipton, Steinschneider, and Richmond (1965) showed. This initial period of protest does not last, as is indicated both by the overall association between cradleboard use and lower states (Fig. 7.1) and by mothers' reports. Part of the Navajo tradition of cradleboard use is the accepted wisdom that babies often cry when first placed on the cradleboard and that one just does not worry about this—just as most Anglo mothers are not concerned when their babies cry for a few minutes after being put to bed alone in their rooms.

The decrease in fretting and crying from minutes 5 to 2 before going on the cradleboard represent the mother's approach to the child and picking up the child and preparing the cradleboard; at least a portion of the increase in crying and fretting after the cradleboard has been laced may be due to the fact that the mother is no longer so actively engaged with the child. Figure 7.2 also indicates very clearly that Navajo infants cry "in order" to be removed from the cradleboard.

Figure 7.3 shows that not only do infants tend to reach lower states after being placed on the cradleboard but that these states are associated with lower activity levels. Extension-flexion movements are simple movements of the limbs and/or head in an apparently nondirected and somewhat erratic way, although there may be shorter periods of rhythmic movements.

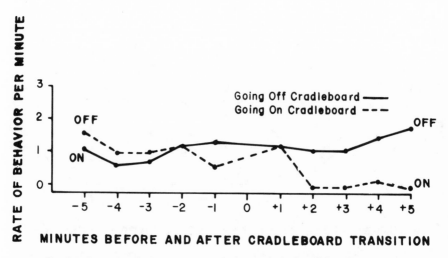

Fig. 7.3. Extension-flexion movements before and after cradleboard transition.

As Fig. 7.3 indicates, the cradleboard does not completely prevent the child from making these sorts of movements, for there is a high rate of such movements in the 5 minutes preceding removal from the cradleboard. These movements are circumscribed when the child is on the cradleboard, but it is easy to observe small body movements under the swaddling material of the cradleboard. Following the pattern of crying and fretting, there is a peak in extension-flexion movements in the first minutes after being placed on the cradleboard and then a sharp drop as they virtually cease altogether.

The increase in extension-flexion movements after removal from the cradleboard, although not significant, may nonetheless reflect the infant's "pleasure" at his removal. A clearer sign of this "pleasure" is more directly seen in Fig. 7.4 which shows a significant increase in the number of smiles after removal from the cradleboard. This does not necessarily mean, however, that the infant is happy specifically because he is off the cradleboard. As I will discuss below, coming off the cradleboard is a time of intense social interaction with mother, and most of these smiles after removal were in the context of social interaction with mother. The absence of smiles after going on the cradleboard seems to be due first to the fact that the child protests at being placed on the cradleboard for the first minute or so, and thus would not be expected to smile, and second, after the protest phase has passed, to the lower levels of arousal and activity that ordinarily go with a quiet, alert state.

Another indicator of reduced activity levels after being placed on the

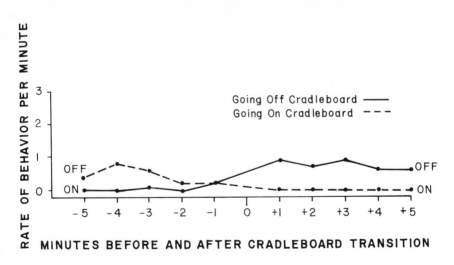

Fig. 7.4. Smiles before and after cradleboard transition.

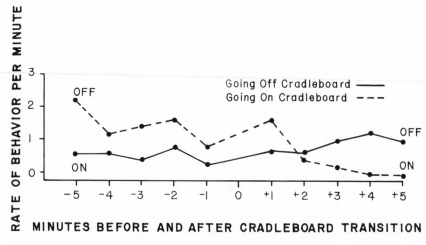

Fig. 7.5. Nonfret vocalizations before and after cradleboard transition.

cradleboard is the decrease in non-fret vocalization, as shown in Fig. 7.5. The same pattern holds true here as held true with fretting, crying, and extension-flexion movements: a drop from an initially high level 5 minutes prior to going on the cradleboard, with a sharp increase 1 minute after going on and then an equally sharp drop to very low levels, and finally zero, within 5 minutes. Figure 7.6 shows that in fact social interaction with mother in minutes 3 to 5 after going on the cradleboard is quite intense, and

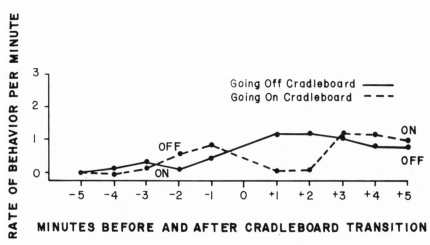

Fig. 7.6. Mutual gazing before and after cradleboard transition.

suggests that one might thus have expected smiling and nonfret vocalizing to also be high. Figure 7.6 shows that mutual gazing between mother and infant reaches a peak just when smiling and vocalizing are lowest—again suggesting that the infant has gotten over his period of protest and is not so much "unhappy" as in a quiet and alert state.

In the cradleboard transitions discussed above, most children on the cradleboard were either supine or being handled on their mothers' laps, so it was not possible to test for the last way in which the cradleboard might directly affect state—through the variable of posture. However, as mentioned in Chapter 3, in the 167 spot observations of children on the cradleboard, it was found that if the cradleboard was upright the child was much more likely to be in states 4 to 6 than if the cradleboard was laid flat ($p < .001$).

Mother–Infant Mutual Responsiveness

As we have seen in the previous section, there is good evidence that the cradleboard has at least short-term effects on infant state. Given this, it is not surprising that the cradleboard would also affect the infant's social interactions with others. Among the Navajo the cradleboard seems to exert its effects on mother-infant interaction in two ways: first, by directly affecting the behavior of the infant and mother, and second, indirectly by affecting the very opportunity for interaction. The direct effects will be discussed in this section and the indirect effects in the following section.

Returning to the same cradleboard transition periods discussed in the preceding section, it can be seen that a number of cradleboard effects on the infant's behavior are very closely paralleled by changes in the mothers' behavior. These transition periods are especially good places to see effects on interaction because not only are all infants on their mothers' laps or within arm's reach, but the very act of placing the child on the cradleboard or removing him from it forces a standardization of context that is often difficult to achieve in naturalistic observations. First, mother–infant interaction in these transition periods seems to be affected most directly through the effect of the cradleboard on the infant. For example, as the child's rate of smiling decreases as he goes on the cradleboard, so too does the mother's rate of smiling ($r = .84$; $p < .006$). As the child's rate of smiling increases as he is removed from the cradleboard, so too does the mother's rate increase ($r = .84$; $p < .006$). As the child's rate of nonfret vocalization decreases as he is put on the cradleboard, so too does the mother's rate of verbalization and vocalization decrease ($r = .72$; $p < .02$). As the child's rate of extension–flexion movements increases as he comes off the cradleboard, the mother's rate of vestibular stimulation of the child (rocking, bouncing, adjusting position) shows a markedly similar increase ($r = .62$; $p < .03$). Finally, as the extension–flexion rate of the child decreases as he goes on the cradleboard, the mother's rate of noninstrumental touching (simple *hand on*, stroking, patting, etc.) shows a similar decline ($r = .78$; $p < .009$).

These clear directional effects of the cradleboard on both mother and infant cannot be explained by the fact that nursing and other caretaking tend to preclude the more purely social behaviors listed above. This is the case because bouts of breast-feeding and bottle feeding and/or other forms of caretaking (cleaning, dressing, etc.) occur almost invariably both after removal from the cradleboard ($p < .05$) and after being placed on the cradleboard ($p < .02$). From the simple correlation between the behavior rates of mother and infant it is not possible to be certain whether the infant's behavior directly influences that of the mother or whether there is something a bit more subtle about the combination of the infant and the cradleboard that may, for example, have helped to establish patterns of interaction in the past which alter the mother's expectations and thus her behavior, which in turn affects that of her child.

The one clear effect that the cradleboard itself seems to have directly on the mother in these transition periods is the way that it apparently inhibits noninstrumental touching. Not only are mothers' rates of touching highly correlated with infants' rates of extension–flexion movements as they go on the cradleboard, mothers are also much less likely ($p < .001$) to touch their infants whenever they are on the cradleboard, regardless of whether it is before removal or after they go on, and in spite of the fact that the children were always in their mothers' laps or within arm's reach.

The cradleboard, however, does more than affect the rates at which mother and infant behave; it also influences the mutual responsiveness of mother and infant in interaction. In the case of maternal noninstrumental touching mentioned above, for example, the infant is not an object to be touched or not according to the mother's whim, but he or she is party to an exchange in which the behavior of mother and infant are more or less reciprocally contingent on each other. In this light, it is interesting to note that the infant on the cradleboard is significantly ($p < .05$) less likely to respond to the mother's touch within 15 seconds than an infant who is not on the cradleboard. ("Response" was defined as any behavior directed toward mother: any vocalization, any movement, any fret or cry, or any facial expression.) On the other hand, when her infant was on the cradle-board (as compared to off) mothers were significantly more likely ($p < .05$) to make a noninstrumental touch when her child had shown *no behavior at all* in the preceding 15 seconds. In other words, the cradle-board seems to have had the indirect effect of reducing the mothers' noninstrumental touching through its direct effect on the infant's responsiveness, which, in turn, would seem to be one aspect of the effect of motor restraint on the infant's level of arousal or reactivity.

The fact that mothers touched the children on the cradleboard most often when the child had shown no behavior at all suggests that the mothers may have been responding to the child's inactivity, and were perhaps trying to elicit a response in order to gauge their child's level of arousal. In any case, they usually did not elicit a response and non-instrumental touching was less common when the child was on the cradleboard. Another, perhaps clearer, example of the decrease in mothers' responsiveness is the fact that when the infant was on the cradleboard the mothers were much less likely ($p < .001$) to respond to the infant's frets and cries with any behavior at all within 15 seconds.

Although infants might cry less on the cradleboard in part because they learned that when they cried on the cradleboard mother did not respond, the work of Bell and Ainsworth (1972) suggests the contrary. Bell and Ainsworth found strong and consistent correlations between mothers' responsiveness to cries and *decreased* rates and durations of infant crying. The decreased frequency of crying on the cradleboard would seem to be due to the physiological effects of the cradleboard on infant state and the mothers' decreased responsiveness would seem to be due to the possibility that they expect the cradleboard to quiet the crying infant for them. Indeed, mothers quite often do place children on the cradleboard when they start crying for the specific purpose of quieting them.

On the other hand, it might also be possible that the cradleboard infant learns something from the temporal juxtaposition of being in an aroused, upset state with the soothing and quieting effects of the cradleboard bindings. The cradleboard infant might come to see the cradleboard itself as a "response" to his own crying, that is, crying when on the cradleboard (or at any time) might not be so specifically directed at the mother or any caretaker as we usually assume. If the child is upset and the cradleboard constitutes a relief from that upset, the cradleboard might be seen as both a very responsive "caretaker" and, moreover, a constantly responsive one. Sander and his colleagues (1970) have shown that the *length* of a response to crying (assuming that it is a positive response) can, under certain circumstances, be more effective in reducing crying than a speedy response. There is more to maternal sensitivity and responsiveness than mere speed of response, and as Bernal (1974) suggests, sensitivity may be no more than learning the characteristic response needs or expectancies of the individual infant in a particular situation, for instance, on the cradleboard. Something like this might underlie the not uncommon reports of Navajo mothers that older children, who have ceased using the cradleboard, will, when tired and irritable, sometimes ask to be placed on the cradleboard again.

In sum, the cradleboard does have the effects on mother–infant interaction that were predicted in Chapter 3. As Lipton, Steinschneider, and Richmond (1965) showed in their experimental work with swaddling effects, the cradleboard lowers the infant's activity or arousal levels, even for Navajo children whose levels of "irritability" at least, are lower to begin with. I believe that because of this lowered arousal level the infant is less reactive to his environment, including his mother, and that because of his higher response threshold and decreased activity level, his mother's responsiveness is reduced as well. Thus, because of their decreased mutual responsiveness, the Navajo cradleboard infant and his mother would seem to fulfill attachment theory's initial conditions for being at risk for "anxious attachment," with all the sequelae that may entail.

SOME SITUATIONAL DETERMINANTS OF CRADLEBOARD USE

This "microscopic" analysis of mother–infant interaction as it is affected by the cradleboard is, however, just that, and in addition to questions about the nature and developmental significance of "sensitivity" and "responsiveness," the fact remains that in order for these effects to influence mother–infant interaction, the child must be on the cradleboard. Even if the cradleboard does reduce mutual responsiveness, it also has an influence on the child's very *opportunity* for interaction that might prove to be as significant as the nature of the interactions themselves; certainly there must be an interaction before there can be any effects.

At the most proximal level of causation, probably the major determinant of cradleboard use is the infant. It must be stressed that when infants want to be removed from the cradleboard, they are, even if mothers sometimes seem to use the removal as a last resort. Not only were Navajo infants seen to fret and cry with great regularity a minute or so before they were removed from the cradleboard, mothers reported that this was the typical reason for removal from the cradleboard and moreover that the end of a child's cradleboard career was "up to him."

Further, as Kluckhohn (1947) observed, the cradleboard may inhibit or prevent some mother–infant interaction, but some of the interactions that will be prevented are those where the infant might "bother" his or her mother or distract her or raise her level of exasperation. This is especially true when their children are on the cradleboard, because Navajo mothers are then likely to be engaged in household tasks that are less easily inter-rupted than when the child is not on the cradleboard (see below).

On the other hand, the cradleboard clearly does not completely inhibit the close and warmly social sorts of interaction that ordinarily occur when the child is being held. In spite of the fact that mutual responsiveness is decreased when the child is on the cradleboard, and touching and close body contact are at a minimum, in 439 spot observations of cradleboard-aged children, those children who were on their mothers' laps were no more likely to be off the cradleboard than on it ($p < .20$).

Indeed, in the ordinary patterns of use at Cottonwood Springs, the cradleboard seems to have actually maintained or even increased mother–infant proximity even if it also reduced mutual responsiveness: while there was no difference between the number of children observed on their mothers' laps when on the cradleboard and when off, those who were within arm's reach of their mother were more likely to be on the cradle-board than those farther away ($p < .01$). Because of its rigid back and because it prevents locomotion and reduces state and activity levels, the cradleboard makes it easy to transport infants where they can be easily watched and cared for without any great demands on the caretaker's atten-tion. Cradleboard infants are easily and often carried short distances and "cached" almost anywhere while the mother works inside or outside, gathering piñon nuts, chopping wood, weaving, or simply doing the house-work. The infant is quiet, nearby, easily reached, looked at, and talked to—and the infant can easily watch his or her mother the whole time. If the parents must leave home for a few hours and cannot or do not wish to leave the infant behind, the cradleboard provides not only a good measure of safety for travel in the pickup, but the motor restraint and state- and activity-reducing functions of the cradleboard make the infant an easier and more pleasant traveling companion—and thus less of a burden on caretakers and less likely to be left at home. With the distances to be traveled, the frequent trips to the trading post, the visiting back and forth, and the weekend trips to and from the boarding schools, many Navajo children spend a great deal of time in the pickup and away from home, and in the 439 spot observations of cradleboard-aged children, those who were observed away from home were much more likely to be on the cradleboard than those observed within the boundaries of the camp ($p < .001$). Similarly, those that were within the camp boundaries, but out-of-doors, were more likely to be on the cradleboard than those that were inside a house or hogan ($p < .05$).

Thus, even thought the cradleboard has been shown to be capable of "disrupting" mother–infant interaction, infants have at least some control over how long they are on the cradleboard and the cradleboard itself is seen to have the effect of maintaining or even increasing mother–infant proximity. Moreover, as mentioned in Chapter 3 and above, of all the time that the child is on the cradleboard, as much as 85% may be spent in sleep. Even when the child is both awake and on the cradleboard—for probably no more than a couple of hours each day—the cradleboard tends to lower levels of arousal and activity, tends to promote mother–infant proximity, and tends to be used when the mother is engaged in activities than might make her less inclined to interact with her child anyway. Further, the cradleboard also seems to promote particularly intense bouts of caretaking and face-to-face social interaction with mother whenever the child is taken off the cradleboard. It follows then that before any statements about the effects of "disrupted" mother–infant interaction can be made, it will be necessary to examine some of the social and physical environmental correlates of the different patterns of mother–infant interaction that vary with cradleboard use. Not only is interaction off the cradleboard more common, the environment of mother–infant interaction may differ in more ways than the simple presence or absence of the cradleboard. The similarities or differences in the environment of interaction could tend to elicit behavior patterns that reinforced or acted synergistically with the cradleboard effects, or they could tend to counteract or negate them.

THE LONGER-TERM EFFECTS
OF THE CRADLEBOARD

In the "microscopic" analysis of mother–infant interaction during the cradleboard transition periods described above, the only variables controlled for were the cradleboard itself and distance from mother. Clearly, these are only two of a multitude of variables in the environment of mother–infant interaction. In my recording of each observation session a great many more environmental variables were noted, and some were reconstructed from the observational data after the fact. In order to see how the cradleboard variable affected grosser qualities of mother–infant interaction and how it covaried with other environmental variables, it was necessary to first separate out of my continuous observational data the periods of time when an interaction between mother and infant was actually occurring. Because mother and infant were not always interacting throughout an observation, and especially because the lengths of each chain of interactive behaviors varied so much, simple frequency counts of behaviors prorated for the length of the observation would not reveal very much. Thus, I felt that for describing patterns of interaction and for relating interactive behavior patterns to environmental variables, both within the Navajo sample and between the Navajo and Anglo samples, I first had to explicitly define an interaction in order to then give it a meaningful quantitative description.

Analysis of the Behavior Interaction Data

The computer programming language SNOBOL 4 (Griswold et al., 1971; Griswold and Griswold, 1973) is especially appropriate for the analysis of continuously recorded ethological data for it was designed for string manipulation, that is, the examination of a string of characters for predefined structural patterns. I designed two SNOBOL programs to search my data for particular patterns of interaction. The first program accepted as input raw observation data written in PRIMATE (Humpheries, 1974) grammar and subsequently verified by PRIMATE. This first SNOBOL program, which I called the data structures program (DSP), cycled through each observation and arranged the raw data into fixed-field format by each sentence. A sentence consisted of at least a subject and a verb (behavior), but could also include plural subjects, plural verbs, and single or plural objects (recipients of behavior). In addition, each sentence included three fixed fields for the various environmental conditions. If no behaviors at all occurred in a time block (a 15-second segment of observation) this too was counted as a sentence, but an empty or null sentence with only the environmental conditions entered. Each sentence was numbered consecutively within each time block, and each time block was numbered consecutively from the start of the observation to the finish. The purpose of this data structures program was to simplify the input for the second program, described below, which did all the actual counting of behaviors. With fixed-field format, processing time was greatly decreased.

Accepting as input the raw data in fixed-field format from the data structures program, my second program, behavior count program (BCP), functioned in the following manner. BCP searched each numbered time block, sentence by sentence, for either a mother-to-infant behavior or an infant-to-mother behavior. No restraints were placed on which behaviors were included in the search, only that something occurred that was the potential start of a chain of mother–infant interaction. Having found the potential start of an interaction, BCP would note the number of the time block in which it had occurred and whether it was the mother or the infant who performed the behavior. BCP then also began to count a number of variables in the DSP input and would continue through the observation, sentence by sentence, until it came to two consecutive time blocks in which there were no mother-to-infant behaviors and no infant-to-mother behaviors. This terminated the interaction, and the length of the inter-action was measured by subtracting the starting time block number from the ending time block number. This was an ad hoc, working definition of interaction, and the purpose of BCP was to simply standardize as much as possible the conditions under which it counted behaviors for each mother-child pair. This is not an empirically derived definition of interaction, but only a template placed over the raw data allowing only the most compar-able bits of data to appear for comparisons within and between groups. No mother-to-infant or infant-to-mother behaviors were lost because an inter-action (as defined above) did not occur. Even if there was no response to an isolated behavior by mother or infant another kind of interaction was scored as having taken place. In this event, of course, the behavior count record would show no behaviors for the one not responding and the inter-action would be minimally short.

All data reported here include the two time blocks at the end of the interaction, although, strictly speaking, the interactions themselves were in fact 30 seconds shorter. This 30-second period (actually, > 1 time block but < 2 time blocks $= 16$ to 29 seconds) of lag is, again, ad hoc, but necessary to allow for both slight variations in data recording and for possible variations in response time. Future analyses will systematically vary this criterion for the end of an interaction in an effort to more empirically determine the length of a "natural" interaction. Analyses of selected interactions by hand, however, showed that this ad hoc definition was valid in that it marked the end of interactions at the same place that my hand analyses did.

Having identified the start of an interaction, BCP was capable of count-ing any behavior that any subject showed, no matter how rare or common. BCP only counted each environmental condition once for each sentence. No restraints were placed on the degree of reciprocity involved in an interaction either. An interaction could consist of nothing but mother-to-infant behaviors with no response whatever from the child. In this event the interaction would continue until the mother ceased behaving toward the child for a full 30 seconds (two 15-second time blocks).

In addition to counting behaviors and environmental conditions, BCP attributed behaviors by subjects to objects while an interaction was taking place and while no interaction (between mother and child) was occurring. The following subject-to-object behavior counts were listed separately:

1. Mother-to-infant   (in interaction)
2. Infant-to-mother   (in interaction)
3. Infant-to-nobody   (in and out of interaction with mother)
4. Infant-to-other   (in and out of interaction with mother)
5. Other-to-infant   (in and out of interaction with mother)

Only the first three subject-to-object behavior counts in interaction are reported here, except where noted, and all subjects besides mother and child were grouped for these analyses.

I had no observations of children over 44 weeks old on the cradleboard, so for the analyses reported here only the first 48 weeks of life are considered. The Navajo and Anglo children were grouped into age cohorts of 13 weeks each, except for the final "quarter" of 9 weeks only. In order to keep the possible relationship between age and cradleboard effects roughly constant, the final "quarter" includes children no more than 4 weeks older than the 44-week-old child observed on the cradleboard. Table 7.1 shows the age by culture comparison cells used in data analysis.

Taken together, there were 151 separate observations (totaling 75.5 hours) on 21 different Navajo children (9 boys and 12 girls) of cradleboard age, and all 11 Anglo children (6 boys, 5 girls). None of the analyses reported here will focus on sex differences or culture × sex interactions, given the small number of Anglo girls observed in the first two quarters. Too few Anglo children were observed using the cradleboard to report many culture × cradleboard analyses, but the within-group Navajo analyses will, of course, focus explicitly on the social and physical environment correlates of cradleboard use. As will be discussed in detail later on, I was also fortunate that within each Navajo age cohort very nearly half of the total number of observations were on children living in traditional extended family camps and half were on children living in neolocal, nuclear family camps.

The output from BCP was analyzed using the packaged statistical program SPSS (Nie et al., 1975). A total of 686 variables were coded, including

Table 7.1. Navajo-Anglo Comparison Cells

Subject	First quarter (1-13 weeks)	Second quarter (14-26 weeks)	Third quarter (27-39 weeks)	Fourth quarter (40-48 weeks)
Navajo				
Subjects	12 (6B; 6G)[a]	11 (6B; 5G)	14 (7B; 7G)	6 (2B; 4G)
Observations	29	26	38	12
$\bar{X}$ age (weeks)	5.73	20.62	33.94	44.00
SD	3.24	3.40	4.04	2.63
Anglo				
Subjects	4 (3B; 1G)	5 (4B; 1G)	7 (3B; 4G)	6 (2B; 4G)
Observations	10	10	14	12
$\bar{X}$ age (weeks)	7.00	21.80	33.29	43.33
SD	2.92	3.19	3.15	1.21

[a] B, boys; G, girls.

raw behavior counts expressed as the rate of occurrence per 15 second
time block spent in interaction and environmental conditions expressed as
percentage of time in interaction during which each obtained.

Navajo–Anglo Similarities and Differences in Mother–Infant Interaction

Having shown that the cradleboard influences mother–infant interaction, as predicted, in the 5 minutes before and after the cradleboard
transitions was not enough. The next question was to determine whether
these immediate and "microscopic" effects last long enough to influence
measures that describe mother-infant interaction on a larger scale, and to
see if the cradleboard might be related in any way to similarities and
differences in patterns of Navajo and Anglo mother-infant interaction.

Preliminary analyses showed that a number of environmental conditions
and other more global characteristics of the interactions were common to
both Navajo and Anglo mother–infant interaction and reflected potentially
important dimensions of similarities and differences. Preliminary analyses
also showed that of the 62 mother behaviors and 71 child behaviors that
had been recorded, only a total of 51 appeared with enough frequency in
the first year of life to be useful in data analysis. Tables 7.2 and 7.3 give the
Navajo and Anglo means for the global characteristics of mother–infant interactions, the environmental conditions most frequently encountered,
and each of the 51 mother and infant behaviors expressed as their rate of
occurrence per 15 seconds of interaction. Some of these behaviors are
groupings of separately recorded behaviors that are conceptually very
similar and which individually occurred rarely, but in combination occurred frequently enough to be potentially important variables (e.g., *show*
and *demonstrate* were lumped, as were *crawl* and *walk*; *walk* occurred only
rarely toward the end of the first year).

The Interactive Behavioral Correlates of Cradleboard Use

Simple correlations of the amount of time during interaction spent on the
cradleboard with other overall characteristics of the interactions showed
that none of these global measures were related to cradleboard use in the
first quarter. In the second, third, and fourth quarters, however, there was
a small but significant negative association between cradleboard use and
the rate at which the infant behaved per 15 seconds of interaction
($r = -.20$, $p < .04$). This is in keeping with previously discussed findings
indicating that the cradleboard reduced arousal/activity levels. The

amount of time spent on the cradleboard during interaction was also negatively related to the rate at which the mother directed behaviors toward the child in all four quarters, but these correlations never reached significance. This finding is also in keeping with the cradleboard transition data which suggested that the mothers' behavior was keyed in some

Table 7.2. Characteristics of Navajo and Anglo Mother–Infant Interaction

	First Quarter			Second Quarter		
	Navajo	Anglo	$p <$[a]	Navajo	Anglo	$p <$
$\bar{X}$ interaction length	9.58	41.80	.06	11.74	17.65	
Interactions initiated by M per 100 time blocks	7.10	3.69	.01	6.49	5.02	
Interactions initiated by B per 100 time blocks	1.13	.89		2.66	3.63	
Interactions initiated by M (%)	77.06	76.52		71.87	62.94	
M rate of behavior	1.67	2.48	.03	1.66	1.96	
B rate of behavior	.18	.55	.03	.38	.65	.001
Interaction on cradleboard (%)	16.64	-0-		26.24	.83	.005
Interaction B fret/cry[b] (%)	9.89	8.51		9.91	8.52	
Interaction on lap M (%)	41.74	76.53	.005	44.82	40.74	
Interaction 3 feet M (%)	31.92	19.59		34.97	38.88	
Interaction 3–12 feet M (%)	21.02	2.90	.006	11.44	18.58	
Interaction nursing/feeding (%)	18.31	35.15		15.85	18.89	
Interaction other caretaking (%)	5.84	2.02		12.14	21.68	
All others rate of behavior to B	.56	.08	.008	.31	.14	
	Third Quarter			Fourth Quarter		
$\bar{X}$ interaction length	4.86	8.80	.001	8.41	5.72	
Interactions initiated by M per 100 time blocks	5.92	5.48		5.57	5.65	
Interactions initiated by B per 100 time blocks	5.81	5.24		5.48	7.24	.05
Interactions initiated by M (%)	50.93	49.27		54.52	45.87	
M rate of behavior	1.12	1.68	.02	1.32	1.26	
B rate of behavior	.55	.86	.001	.82	.88	
Interaction on cradleboard (%)	14.76	-0-		6.04	8.33	
Interaction B fret/cry[b] (%)	7.44	9.48		8.75	8.81	
Interaction on lap M (%)	10.68	24.29	.05	15.93	10.62	
Interaction 3 feet M (%)	33.42	30.23		39.56	45.45	
Interaction 3–12 feet M (%)	41.18	34.38		40.39	31.51	
Interaction nursing/feeding (%)	4.69	11.56		3.12	4.21	
Interaction other caretaking (%)	14.97	10.42		23.03	13.13	
All others rate of behavior to B	.46	.14	.001	.23	.19	

[a] All differences by two-tailed t-test.
[b] Summation of periods of fretting or crying that lasted continuously for more than 1 minute.

Table 7.3. Navajo and Anglo Rates of Behavior during Mother–Infant Interaction

Behavior item	First quarter			Second quarter		
	Navajo	Anglo	$p <^a$	Navajo	Anglo	$p <$
Mutual gaze	.1370	.2783	.02	.1039	.1630	
Mutual smile	.0006	.0037		.0107	.0384	
M show/demonstrate	.0009	.0600		.0327	.0405	
M feed B	.0047	.0042		.0127	.0237	
M place object for B	.0011	—		.0059	.0074	
M take/try take from B	.0002	—		.0028	.0046	
M reach to B	.0015	—		.0033	.0062	
M pat/rub B	.1206	.2402	.02	.1199	.1013	
M vocalize B	.0534	.1005		.0641	.0811	
M talk B	.1079	.3302	.04	.1640	.3228	.02
M hand on B	.0209	.0156		.0173	.0334	
M proffer B	—	.0018		.0212	.0113	
M bounce/toss B	.0518	.0051	.013	.0103	.0037	
M adjust position B	.1498	.1781		.1524	.1041	
M kiss B	.0159	.0672		.0282	.0519	
M look at B	.4258	.5898		.4261	.4882	
M watch B	.0893	.0185	.01	.0981	.0423	
M smile B	.1152	.1618		.1063	.1305	
M rock B	.1143	.2868	.034	.1064	.0173	.018
M approach B	.0410	.0224		.0316	.0504	
M leave B	.0347	.0191		.0271	.0478	
M lift on B	.0144	.0120		.0119	.0212	
M lift off B	.0127	.0103		.0122	.0224	
M clean/wipe/adjust B	.1177	.1247		.0791	.1587	
M call name B	.0083	.0013		.0053	.0111	
M laugh B	.0184	.0189		.0200	.0213	

	Third quarter			Fourth quarter		
Behavior item	Navajo	Anglo	p <	Navajo	Anglo	p <
Mutual gaze	.0938	.1328		.1407	.1267	
Mutual smile	.0121	.0175		.0122	.0132	
M show/demonstrate	.0175	.0232		.0193	.0196	
M feed B	.0199	.0268		.0141	.0625	
M place object for B	.0056	.0092		.0106	.0075	
M take/try take from B	.0074	.0037		.0069	.0059	
M reach to B	.0106	.0111		.0108	.0093	
M pat/rub B	.0259	.0430		.0303	.0400	
M vocalize B	.0381	.0449		.0359	.0330	
M talk B	.1273	.2628	.002	.1410	.1727	
M hand on B	.0269	.0172		.0207	.0043	
M proffer B	.0148	.0380	.002	.0414	.0149	
M bounce/toss B	.0078	.0034		.0042	.0018	
M adjust position B	.0475	.0779		.0760	.0282	.029
M kiss B	.0051	.0230		.0130	.0172	
M look at B	.2447	.4159	.01	.2558	.2850	
M watch B	.1244	.1135		.1563	.1055	
M smile B	.0876	.0983		.0924	.0967	
M rock B	.0221	.0308		.0187	.0059	
M approach B	.0408	.0958	.003	.0479	.0674	
M leave B	.0462	.1124	.001	.0552	.0928	
M lift on B	.0099	.0204	.031	.0122	.0164	
M lift off B	.0078	.0189	.006	.0145	.0129	
M clean/wipe/adjust B	.0540	.0363		.0917	.0244	
M call name B	.0196	.0083		.0154	.0113	
M laugh B	.0250	.0241		.0231	.0125	

Table 7.3. Continued

Behavior item	First quarter			Second quarter		
	Navajo	Anglo	$p <$	Navajo	Anglo	$p <$
B take/try take from M	—	—		.0053	.0070	
B vocalize M	.0086	.0523		.0126	.0163	
B touch M	.0220	.0869		.0448	.1744	
B refuse feed from M	.0088	.0542	.047	.0313	.0266	
B receive M	—	—		.0134	.0050	
B look at M	.0660	.0924		.0952	.0857	
B watch M	.0173	.0972		.0841	.1809	
B smile M	.0072	.0533		.0122	.0174	
B laugh M	—	.0007		.0007	.0056	
B approach M	—	—		—	.0033	
B leave M	—	—		.0005	—	
B crawl/walk	—	—		—	.0181	.007
B self touch	.1066	.0188	.011	.0619	.0337	
B vocalize nobody	.1185	.1725		.1728	.1885	
B extension-flexion	.4463	.3650		.3047	.2832	
B bang/flap	.0007	.0007		.0119	.0450	
B suck finger/object	.0045	.0135		.1127	.1674	
B smile at nobody	.0119	.0142		.0287	.0205	
B laugh nobody	—	.0007		.0109	.0054	
B pucker face	.0606	.0114	.013	.0247	.0161	
B rock self	—	—		—	.0178	.025
B adjust position	.0041	.0051		.0238	.0338	
B feed self	—	—		.0122	.0123	
B manipulate object	.0057	.0017		.1291	.1957	
B fret/cry	.0912	.0488		.0960	.0555	

	Third quarter			Fourth quarter		
Behavior item	Navajo	Anglo	$p <$	Navajo	Anglo	$p <$
B take/try take from M	.0035	.0010		.0069	.0059	
B vocalize M	.0363	.0552		.0654	.0813	
B touch M	.0155	.1120		.1008	.0606	
B refuse feed from M	.0080	.0204		.0078	.0168	
B receive M	.0098	.0218	.028	.0292	.0069	.022
B look at M	.1592	.1468		.1703	.1737	
B watch M	.1508	.2347		.2067	.2241	
B smile M	.0222	.0340		.0119	.0276	
B laugh M	.0026	.0056		.0041	.0022	
B approach M	.0285	.0699	.030	.0304	.1008	.001
B leave M	.0157	.0342		.0201	.0368	
B crawl/walk	.0562	.1474	.026	.0668	.2072	.003
B self touch	.0646	.0289	.055	.0397	.0212	
B vocalize nobody	.1606	.2663	.009	.1888	.2847	
B extension-flexion	.1940	.0909		.0779	.0789	
B bang/flap	.1172	.1038		.1287	.0634	.039
B suck finger/object	.0860	.1098		.1119	.0744	
B smile at nobody	.0305	.0370		.0117	.0192	
B laugh nobody	.0038	.0126		.0028	.0026	
B pucker face	.0153	.0030	.012	.0146	.0077	
B rock self	.0075	.0236		.0543	.0117	
B adjust position	.0644	.0387		.0831	.0619	
B feed self	.0399	.0307		.0600	.0267	
B manipulate object	.3551	.3397		.4933	.3656	
B fret/cry	.0392	.0661	.051	.0671	.0761	

[a] All differences by two-tailed t-test.

respects to that of the infant on the cradleboard. Finally, in the third quarter alone, cradleboard use was positively associated with the amount of time during interactions that the child was fretting and/or crying ($r = .37$; $p < .01$). At first glance this is contrary to other data which showed that the cradleboard reduced state and the frequency of crying/fretting. In all of the observations discussed here, however, the child was awake and there was thus a greater opportunity for the child to be seen crying. Further, the cradleboard transition data showed that children cried to be taken off the cradleboard as much as they showed that the cradleboard reduced crying when going on it. In the third quarter a number of children were in the process of being "weaned" (or weaning themselves) from the cradleboard, and it is during this time that they might be expected to "just not like it" the most. In the first quarter, on the other hand, cradleboard use was negatively associated with continuous periods of fretting/crying, as expected, but not quite significantly ($p < .12$).

From the fact that the cradleboard tends to "disrupt" mother-infant interaction by reducing mutual responsiveness and by tending to reduce the rate at which mothers and infants behave toward each other, it might also be expected that it would reduce the mean length of interactions, but this was not the case. There was essentially no relationship between amount of cradleboard use during interaction and the length of those interactions. To test the remaining possibility that there was an interactive effect between cradleboard use and other variables that might still affect mean interaction length, I carried out a series of multiple regression analyses to determine whether or not cradleboard use could explain any variation after the effects of these other variables were taken into account. In this set of analyses the third and fourth quarters were treated as one age group because of the relatively small number of subjects in the fourth quarter and their low rates of cradleboard use.

In a word, I could find no evidence of any direct or interactive effects of cradleboard use on mean mother–infant interactive chain length. The following variables were entered into the regression equations at each of the three age groups (first quarter, second quarter, and third and fourth quarters combined) with mean interactive chain length as the dependent variable.

Percentage of interactions initiated by M	(PCMIN)
Mother's rate of behavior to B	(MRATE)
Child's rate of behavior to M	(BRATE)
All others' rate of behavior to B	(ORATE)
Percentage of interaction on cradleboard	(PCBIN)
Percentage of interaction on mother's lap	(INLAP)
Percentage of interaction 3–12 feet from M	(INTWL)
Residence (nuclear or extended family)	(RES)

Table 7.4. Predictors of Navajo Interactive Chain Length

Variable	Individual variance	Simple r	Total variance	p <
First Quarter				
Percentage of interaction on mother's lap	.34	.58	.34	.001
Child's rate of behavior to M	.15	.50	.49	.001
Second quarter				.005
Percentage of interaction on mother's lap	.29	.54	.29	.005
Mother's rate of behavior to B	.05	.51	.35	.009
Third and fourth quarter				
Mother's rate of behavior to B	.49	.70	.49	.001
Child's rate of behavior to M	.11	.55	.60	.001

Other variables were not used because they were different ways of measuring almost the same thing (e.g., "percentage of interaction nursing/ feeding" was almost perfectly correlated with "percentage of interaction on mother's lap"). The global variable "percentage of interaction B fret/ cry" was not entered because it was low and showed such constancy across the four quarters. In stepwise multiple regression analyses for each of the three age groups the amount of interaction time spent on the cradleboard never accounted for more than 3.6% of the variance in mean interactive chain length and this small proportion of variance "explained" was never significant. The variables listed in Table 7.4 above were the ones that accounted for most of the variance in interactive chain length in each age group in the order in which they entered the equations.

Testing next the hypothesis that there were interactive effects between cradleboard use and the amount of time on the mother's lap during inter- action and the rates of behavior by mother and child to each other, I forced "percentage of interaction on cradleboard" into the equations before these items in each age-group analysis. In all cases these other variables con- tinued to show a strong effect and each improved the total variance explained and its significance. The conclusion remained that the cradle- board had no effect of any magnitude on the global characteristics of Navajo mother–infant interaction, nor did it interact in any way with the other environmental condition variables to exert an indirect effect on mean interactive chain length.

Reasoning then that because mean interactive chain length and these other global characteristics were *derived* from the actual behaviors of mothers and infants in interaction, I tested for direct correlations between cradleboard use and the specific behavior items seen in the interactions.

Table 7.5. Navajo Interactive Behavior Correlates of Cradleboard Use

First quarter			Second quarter			Third and fourth quarters		
Behavior item	r	p <[a]	Behavior item	r	p <	Behavior item	r	p <
M talk B	-.26	.086	M talk B	-.32	.058	M vocalize B	.28	.046
M watch B	.39	.017				M watch B	-.31	.027
			M touch B	-.026	.089	M touch B	.53	.001
			M rock B	.33	.049	M rock B	.35	.015
			M lift on B	-.35	.042	M lift off B	-.29	.036
			M pat/rub B	-.34	.087			
			M adjust position B	-.30	.069	M clean/wipe/adjust B	.40	.006
B fret/cry[b]	.44	.008				M laugh B	-.28	.066
			B vocalize nobody	-.31	.064	B vocalize nobody	-.25	.013
			B bang/flap	-.31	.062	B bang/flap	-.36	.013
			B adjust position	-.33	.053	B adjust position	-.27	.048
			B manipulate object	.34	.049	B manipulate object	-.46	.002
			B pucker face	-.33	.044			
						B crawl/walk	-.24	.077
						B suck finger/object	-.26	.055

[a]Pearsons r, two-tailed.
[b]Short, isolated frets or cries that were not continuous.

186

Table 7.5 shows which specific behavior items correlated significantly, or nearly so, with the amount of cradleboard use during interaction in each of the three age groups.

The majority of these correlations can be easily accounted for by the effects of simple physical restraint on the infant and how these effects change as the infant matures over the first year and develops new capacities for interaction. First, because of the simple motor restraint on cradleboard infants, mothers are less likely to adjust their childrens' position because, in a manner of speaking, it has already been adjusted for them by the cradleboard. Further, not only does the cradleboard tend to inhibit the child from adjusting his or her own position anyway, it also lowers the child's activity/arousal level, making him less reactive to proprioceptive stimuli that might otherwise result in such adjusting movements. Second, because the cradleboard is used for caching more than for carrying, mothers are also less likely to lift children on the cradleboard on or off their laps. When on the cradleboard, of course, the child cannot approach the mother or reach to her to be picked up. Because of the restraint of the cradleboard's swaddling material a child on the cradleboard cannot *bang/ flap*, *crawl/walk*, or *suck finger/object* as much as when he is off the cradleboard. Finally, because of the state and activity reducing effect of the cradleboard, the child is probably also less likely to *vocalize to nobody* during an interaction with mother (i.e., vocalizing, but not looking at anyone). Vocalizing to mother (i.e., vocalizing and looking at mother) is negatively correlated with cradleboard use throughout the first year, but these correlations never reached the level of significance.

Another class of the correlations between cradleboard use and specific interactive behavior items can be accounted for by the way that the effects of the cradleboard are altered during the first year as the child matures, begins to resist the cradleboard more vigorously, and as he becomes more capable of varied social interaction and object manipulation. In the first quarter, as mentioned, the cradleboard is negatively (if not quite significantly) related to the total amount of time that the infant frets and cries. Table 7.5, however, shows that the cradleboard does not also decrease the frequency with which the child makes short and isolated frets and cries, but in fact increases them. This phenomenon is probably due to the fact that the cradleboard soothes and quiets the infant and prevents these brief and intermittent periods of fretting from developing into full-fledged periods of continuous crying; at the same time, the cradleboard may *promote* these short periods of upset in that they almost invariably occur whenever a child is placed on the cradleboard. In addition, in the first few months of life, children are more likely to be placed on the cradleboard at the first sign of upset than they are later in the year, and any interaction involving a fret or cry during this period is thus more likely to also involve the cradleboard.

Toward the end of the first year, however, as the child has grown and is "weaning" himself from the cradleboard, it loses some of its effectiveness in reducing arousal level, and infants seem to protest longer and more vigorously when being placed on it and in order to be released from its increasingly greater confinement. Thus, in the first quarter, while cradleboard use is correlated with more short and intermittent frets and cries, it still lowers arousal level overall and tends to soothe and quiet infants, and mothers of quiet cradleboard babies tend to be silent and simply watch their infants more. In the second quarter the infants are still made quiet by the cradleboard and mothers are still silent and tend to not touch them or *pat/rub* them, although they now seem to be more likely to rock their children when they are on the cradleboard, possibly because they find that rocking an infant who has just gone on the cradleboard helps him to get over the initial period of protest that almost always follows going on the cradleboard—and which seems to last longer as the child gets older. In the second half of the year, however, things begin to change. Because being on the cradleboard now affects the infant in a slightly different way—by tending to prolong the initial period of upset—mothers appear to respond to cradleboard infants in a new way. For example, there is now a positive association between cradleboard use and mother vocalizing, for mothers tend to vocalize (more than verbalize) to small children who are crying, and a negative association with watching, for watching is more commonly associated with quiet play or inactivity on the part of children and less so with active crying. By the same token, touching and instrumental *clean/wipe/adjust* are associated with mothers' attempts to quiet the child, just as *M laugh B* is negatively associated with fretting and crying. Mothers continue to rock their cradleboard children in the second half of the year, but it is more likely now that this rocking also is related to mothers' attempts to quiet the infants' increasingly longer initial protests or more frequent periods of protest at the confinement of the cradleboard. The association between cradleboard use and the frequency with which children manipulate objects reverses from positive to negative between the second quarter and the second half of the first year, probably because in the second quarter mothers begin to leave their children's arms free when they are on the cradleboard specifically to play with objects that have been tied to the cradleboard bindings, while in the second half of the first year the kind of simple object manipulation possible when thus confined probably becomes less satisfying; in addition, my impressions are that children closer to 1 year of age may be less likely to have objects tied to the cradleboard than younger children.

The overall picture that emerges from these simple correlational analyses is that indeed the cradleboard does affect mother and infant behaviors shown during their interaction. The number of such behaviors affected, however, is small compared to the full range of interactive behaviors recorded, the effects of the cradleboard seem to be heavily influenced by maturation, and it is difficult to discern any patterns suggesting that the cradleboard has clear and consistent effects on mother–infant interaction over the first year. Moreover, many of the relatively small number of cradleboard effects are quite unremarkable in that they are the straightforward result of simple motor restraint, that is, that infants on the cradleboard are less likely to *bang/flap, adjust position, suck finger/object,* or *crawl/walk* than infants not on the cradleboard are hardly surprising findings.

The Cradleboard and Individual Differences in Navajo Mother–Infant Interaction

The next step in data analysis was to determine whether or not these behaviors affected by the cradleboard were important to the major dimensions of individual differences in patterns of mother–infant interaction in the Navajo sample. To arrive at these dimensions of difference the correlation matrices of the interactive behaviors in each of the three age groups were subjected to a factor analysis using a varimax rotation procedure. The behaviors loading highest on the first four factors to emerge from these analyses (which taken together accounted for more than 50% of the total variance in each age group) are presented in Table 7.6, and the single highest loading, or factor-defining variable, is italicized in each factor.

From Table 7.6 it can be seen that a number of mother and infant behaviors which correlate with the amount of time that the child is on the cradleboard during an interaction also load highly on one of the first four factors in each age group. These behaviors, however, may as easily have been affected by any of the other environmental conditions besides cradleboard use, and it may be also that when these behaviors are considered as part of a dimension of individual differences rather than as isolated, individual items, the strength of their association with cradleboard use may be overridden. To determine the relative importance of the amount of cradleboard use on each of these factors at each age, stepwise multiple regression analyses were carried out with the factor-defining behavioral variable entered as the dependent variable and the following global variables or environmental conditions entered as independent or predictor variables.

Percentage of interaction on cradleboard	(PCBIN)
Percentage of interaction initiated by M	(PCMIN)
Mother's rate of behavior to B	(MRATE)[5]
Child's rate of behavior to M	(BRATE)[5]
All other's rate of behavior to B	(ORATE)
Percentage of interaction on mother's lap	(INLAP)
Residence	(RES)

The most striking result of these analyses was that at no time in the first year, for any of the factors represented by the defining variables, did the amount of time during interaction that the child was on the cradleboard account for more than about 6% of the total variance, and the amount of variance accounted for by the cradleboard never reached the level of significance. Table 7.7 shows the predictor variables that individually made significant contributions to the total regression equation for each factor-defining independent variable, along with the total variance they accounted for and their overall significance.

In the first year of life, individual differences in patterns of mother–infant interaction among the Navajo are best predicted by aspects of the mother's behavior (her overall rate of behavior to her child and the percentage of interaction she initiates), the amount of time during interaction that the child is held on his or her mother's lap, the rate at which other people present during mother–infant interaction behave toward the child, residence type, and the child's overall rate of behavior to his mother. I will return to these findings later; the conclusion of most interest here is the apparent irrelevance of the cradleboard throughout the first year to these major dimensions of individual differences in patterns of mother–infant interaction. The cradleboard entered the regression equation of only one factor-defining variable (M smile B in the second half of the year) and was then (by itself) not quite significant ($p = .071$) and only accounted for 5.5% of the total variance.

A further check of this conclusion was provided by two additional analyses. First, using the amount of time on the cradleboard as the dependent variable in a series of stepwise multiple regression analyses in each age group with the four factor-defining variables entered as predictor variables, in the first quarter the four variables accounted for only 6.4% of the variance in "percentage of interaction on cradleboard," and neither the final solution nor any of the individual regressions were significant. In the second quarter B manipulates object accounted for 11.6% of the variance

---

[5] Because frequently occurring mother behaviors were obviously correlated with the mother's rate of behavior to her child and frequently occurring child behaviors obviously correlated with the child's rate of behavior to his mother, MRATE was not used to predict mother behaviors and BRATE was not used to predict child behaviors. Both, however, were used to predict each other's behavior.

Table 7.6. Navajo Mother–Infant Interactive Behavior Factor Analysis[a]

First quarter (60.9%)			
Factor I 20.1%	Factor II 16.4%	Factor III 13.7%	Factor IV 10.8%
M pat/rub B	M show/demonstrate B	M place object for B	M lift on B
M vocalize B	Mutual gaze	M adjust position B	M lift off B
M talk B	M take/try take B	M kiss B	B touch M
M bounce/toss B	M rock B	B adjust position	
M look at B	B vocalize M		
M smile B	B look at M		
M call name B	B smile M		
M laugh B			

Second quarter (56.7%)			
Factor I 19.6%	Factor II 15.5%	Factor III 12.5%	Factor IV 9.2%
M reach to B	Mutual gaze	M show/demonstrate	M place object for B
M bounce/toss B	Mutual smile	M talk B	M watch B
M adjust position B	M vocalize B	M proffer B	M watch B
M lift on B	M call name B	M look at B	B vocalize M
M lift off B	B smile M	B receive M	B look at M
B adjust position	B extension-flexion movement	B take/try take M	B suck finger/object
B vocalize nobody	B smile nobody	B bang/flap	B feed self
	B pucker face		B manipulate object

Third and fourth quarters (52.0%)			
Factor I 21.8%	Factor II 13.7%	Factor III 9.0%	Factor IV 7.5%
Mutual gaze	M call name B	M proffer B	B self-touch
Mutual smile	B crawl/walk	B receive M	B watch M
M vocalize B	B approach M	B touch M	B pucker face
M talk B	B leave M	B take/try take M	
M look at B			
M smile B			
M laugh B			
B vocalize M			

[a]Varimax rotated; all variables listed here loaded positively, that is, they were all positively correlated in each factor.

Table 7.7. Stepwise Multiple Regression Analyses of Navajo Mother–Infant Interaction Factor Defining Variables

Factor-defining variable	Predictor variable	r^2	$p<$
First quarter			
M smile B	PCMIN	.11	.079
B smile M	MRATE	.10	.063
M kiss B	INLAP		
	PCMIN	.31	.012
M lift on B	PCMIN	.30	.002
Second quarter			
M lift off B	INLAP	.21	.018
B smile nobody	(n.s)		
B take/try take M	MRATE	.17	.035
B manipulate object	(n.s)		
Third and fourth quarters			
M smile B	PCMIN		
	PCBIN	.24	.002
B crawl/walk	ORATE		
	RES	.38	.025
M proffer B	BRATE	.20	.001
B pucker face	(n.s)		

by itself, but was not significant, and none of the other variables added anything to the total variance or significance of the overall solution. In the second half of the first year the four factor-defining variables together accounted for only 11.8% of the variance in "percentage of interaction on cradleboard," and again the individual and multiple regressions were not significant. Second, returning to the use of the factor-defining variables as independent variables, cradleboard use was forced into the regression equations on the first step. For all four factor-defining variables at all ages, even when entered first, cradleboard use was never significant, never accounted for more than 11.6% of the variance, and the total regression solution was always improved by adding the other variables.

The Cradleboard and Navajo–Anglo Group Differences in Mother–Infant Interaction

Thus, the conclusion stands: the amount of time during interaction with mother that the child is on the cradleboard has very little effect on the major dimensions of Navajo mother–infant interaction. Even if cradleboard use does not account for any significant variance within the Navajo sample, however, given that there were marked Navajo-Anglo differences in both amount of cradleboard use and in many aspects of mother–infant interaction, might the cradleboard still be able to account for some of these Navajo-Anglo differences in patterns of mother–infant interaction? The lack of cradleboard effects on individual differences in Navajo mother–infant interaction does not imply that it is also unrelated to group differences, and given the lingering attraction of the swaddling hypothesis for some, it is worthwhile here to investigate the possible role of the cradleboard in accounting for Navajo-Anglo group differences in mother–infant interaction.

My procedure for investigating the relationship between cradleboard use and Navajo-Anglo group differences in patterns of mother–infant interaction was to enter as dependent variables in multiple regression analyses those mother and infant interactive behavor items on which the Navajo and Anglo mother–infant pairs differed most significantly and/or consistently over the first year. The following overall measures of mother–infant interaction and measures of the environment of interaction were entered as independent, predictor variables:

Percentage of interaction on cradleboard	(PCBIN)
Mother's rate of behavior to B	(MRATE)[6]
Child's rate of behavior to M	(BRATE)[6]
All other's rate of behavior to B	(ORATE)
Percentage of interactions initiated by M	(PCMIN)
Percentage of interaction on mother's lap	(INLAP)
Group (Navajo or Anglo)	(GROUP)

Table 7.8 lists the behavior items on which the Navajo and Anglo samples differed most in each of the three age groups (the third and fourth quarters were again combined). For each behavior the Navajo (N) and Anglo (A) means are given, along with the level of significance of any differences. Following this, the predictor variables that individually made a significant contribution to the total regression equation are listed in the order they entered the equation, along with the total variance for which they accounted and the level of significance of their contribution.

Of all the group differences in mother–infant interaction behaviors listed in Table 7.8, "percentage of interaction on cradleboard" made significant contributions to the regression equations of only six and was the best predictor of only two: *M watch B* and *B fret/cry* in the first quarter only.

---

[6]MRATE and BRATE were again used only to predict child behaviors and mother behaviors, respectively.

Table 7.8. Stepwise Multiple Regression Analyses of Navajo–Anglo Differences in Interactive Behavior

Behavior item	Group	X̄	p<	Predictor	r²	p<	Behavior item	Group	X̄	p<	Predictor	r²	p<
First quarter													
Mutual gaze	N	.1370		BRATE		.02	M kiss B	N	.0159		GROUP	.17	.004
	A	.2783		MRATE	.43	.001		A	.0672				
M talk B	N	.1079		BRATE		.04	M lift on B	N	.0144		PCMIN	.28	.001
	A	.3302			.23	.002		A	.0120				
M pat/rub B	N	.1206		INLAP		.02	M lift off B	N	.0127		PCMIN	.13	.026
	A	.2402			.21	.004		A	.0103				
M hand on B	N	.0209					M approach B	N	.0410		PCMIN	.27	.003
	A	.0156						A	.0224				
M look at B	N	.4258		ORATE			M leave B	N	.0347		INLAP		
	A	.5898			.33	.001		A	.0191		PCMIN	.32	.001
M watch B	N	.0893		PCBIN		.01	B vocalize M	N	.0086		GROUP	.16	.012
	A	.0185			.19	.006		A	.0523				
M bounce/toss B	N	.0518		GROUP			B watch M	N	.0173		GROUP		
	A	.0051		INLAP	.20	.001		A	.0972		INLAP	.25	.006
M rock B	N	.1143		INLAP		.03	B refuse feed from M	N	.0088		GROUP	.26	.001
	A	.2868			.37	.001		A	.0542	.05			
B approach M	N	—					B rock self	N	—				
	A	—						A	—				
B leave M	N	—					B extension-flexion	N	.4463		PCMIN	.20	.018
	A	—						A	.3650		INLAP	.20	.018
B crawl/walk	N	—					B vocalize nobody	N	.1185		MRATE	.17	.008
	A	—						A	.1725				
B self-touch	N	.1066		ORATE		.01	B fret/cry	N	.0912		PCBIN	.20	.004
	A	.0188			.45	.001		A	.0488				
B pucker face	N	.0606											
	A	.0114				.01							

Second quarter

Behavior	N/A	Value	Variable	r	p
Mutual gaze	N	.1039	MRATE	.34	.001
	A	.1630	INLAP	.14	.025
M talk B	N	.1640	GROUP		.02
	A	.3228			
M pat/rub B	N	.1199	INLAP	.22	.004
	A	.1013			
M hand on B	N	.0173	INLAP	.18	.01
	A	.0334			
M look at B	N	.4261	PCMIN	-.33	.001
	A	.4882	ORATE		
M watch B	N	.0981	INLAP	.42	.001
	A	.0423	PCMIN		
M bounce/toss B	N	.0103			
	A	.0037			
M rock B	N	.1064	INLAP	.41	.001
	A	.0173	PCBIN		.02
			BRATE		
B approach M	N	—			
	A	.0033			
B leave M	N	.0005			
	A	—			
B crawl/walk	A	.0181	GROUP	.30	.003
			PCMIN		.007
B self-touch	N	.0619			
	A	.0357			
B pucker face	N	.0247			
	A	.0161			

Behavior	N/A	Value	Variable	r	p
M kiss B	N	.0282	INLAP	.31	.001
	A	.0519			
M lift on B	N	.0119			
	A	.0212			
M lift off B	A	.0122			
M approach B	N	.0224	ORATE	.40	.001
	A	.0316	GROUP		
			INLAP		
M leave B	N	.0504	ORATE		
	A	.0271	GROUP		
	A	.0478			
B vocalize M	N	.0126	PCMIN	.51	.001
	A	.0163	MRATE		
B watch M	N	.0841	INLAP	.18	.041
	A		INLAP		
B refuse feed from M	N	.1809	GROUP	.34	.001
	A	.0313	INLAP	.13	.029
	A	.0266			
B rock self	N	—	GROUP	.23	.014
	A	.0178	MRATE		
B extension-flexion	N	.3047			
	A	.2832			
B vocalize nobody	N	.1728	MRATE	.20	.007
	A	.1885			
B fret/cry	N	.0960			
	A	.0555			

(Continued)

Table 7.8. *Continued*

Third and fourth quarters

Behavior item	Group	$\bar{X}$	p<	Predictor	r^2	p<
Mutual gaze	N	.1051		MRATE		
	A	.1300		BRATE		
				INLAP	.47	.001
M talk B	N	.1306	.01	INLAP		
	A	.2212		BRATE		
				PCMIN	.37	.001
M pat/rub B	N	.0270		INLAP		
	A	.0416		BRATE		
				PCBIN	.34	.001
M hand on B	N	.0254		PCMIN		
	A	.0112		ORATE	.36	.001
M look at B	N	.2474	.03	INLAP		
	A	.3555		ORATE		
				PCMIN		
				BRATE	.48	.001

Behavior item	Group	$\bar{X}$	p<	Predictor	r^2	p<
M bounce/toss B	N	.0069		INLAP		
	A	.0027		PCMIN	.19	.001
M rock B	N	.0212		INLAP		
	A	.0193		PCBIN	.33	.001
M kiss B	N	.0070	.04	INLAP		
	A	.0203		GROUP	.30	.001
M lift on B	N	.0105		INLAP	.30	.001
	A	.0186				
M lift off B	N	.0094	.04	INLAP		
	A	.0161		PCBIN	.22	.001

Behavior				Predictor		
M watch B	N	.1321		PCMIN		
	A	.1099		PCBIN		
				ORATE		
				INLAP	.31	.001
M leave B	N	.0483		GROUP		
	A	.1033	.001	PCMIN		
				INLAP	.33	.001
B vocalize M	N	.0433		ORATE	.10	.004
	A	.0672	.04			
B watch M	N	.1642		GROUP	.05	.043
	A	.2298	.04			
B refuse feed from M	N	.0080		INLAP	.40	.001
	A	.0187	.03			
B approach M	N	.0290		GROUP	.19	.001
	A	.0842				
B leave M	N	.0168		ORATE		
	A	.0354	.023	INLAP		
				MRATE	.20	.001
B crawl/walk	N	.0588		GROUP		
	A	.1750	.001	INLAP		
				MRATE	.30	.001

Behavior				Predictor		
M approach B	N	.0425		GROUP		
	A	.0827		PCMIN	.24	.001
B self-touch	N	.0586				
	A	.0253	.02			
B pucker face	N	.0152				
	A	.0052	.02			
B rock self	N	.0187				
	A	.0181				
B extension-flexion	N	.1662		GROUP		
	A	.0853	.02	INLAP		
				MRATE	.17	.003
B vocalize nobody	N	.0433		GROUP	.14	.001
	A	.0672	.04			
B fret/cry	N	.0459		GROUP	.05	.039
	A	.0707	.04			

Even here, amount of time on the cradleboard only accounted for 19% of the variance in the first and 20% of the variance in the second. Therefore, not only does the cradleboard have essentially no effect on the major dimensions of individual differences in patterns of mother–infant interaction within the Navajo sample, neither does it account for more than a tiny fraction of the differences in patterns of mother–infant interaction that exist between the two samples.

DISCUSSION AND CONCLUSION

The implications of these results will be dealt with in more detail in the following two chapters; here I will simply stress that the apparent lack of cradleboard effects on either within- or between-sample differences in mother–infant interaction does not contradict the conclusions drawn from the analyses of the cradleboard transition data (see above), which showed that the cradleboard did have an impact on mother–infant interaction, and in the directions that had been predicted. First, in the cradleboard transition data only 5 minutes of interaction on the cradleboard were considered, whereas in these analyses the total time in all interactions on and off the cradleboard were considered. Regardless of the cradleboard effects in these 5 minutes before and after transition, the transition itself is a relatively infrequent event in the daily life of the child and the effects might thus be expected to be transitory, washed out by other more pervasive influences during the course of interaction which occur in the space of a full observation period. Second, the major findings of the cradleboard transition analyses were that the cradleboard tended to decrease the child's arousal/activity level and thus also that of the child's caretaker, and their mutual responsiveness. Detailed sequential analyses of all interactions on and off the cradleboard might well reveal that the cradleboard in fact continues to have these effects, but even if they did, the conclusion would still have to be that lower arousal/activity levels and decreased mutual responsiveness were not such major dimensions of mother–infant interactions as many have argued, at least not in the environment of Navajo infancy.

8

The Determinants of Mother–Infant Interaction

IF the cradleboard is an aspect of the immediate environment of Navajo mother–infant interaction that does not significantly affect the major dimensions of their interaction or account for more than a small percentage of the differences between Navajo and Anglo interactive behavior frequencies, are there other features of the environment of mother–infant interaction that might? In the previous chapter it was shown that the major influences on both Navajo and Anglo patterns of interaction were the rate at which mother behaved toward child, the rate at which child behaved toward mother, the percentage of interactions initiated by mother, the percentage of interaction during which the child was held in mother's lap, and the dummy variable GROUP (Navajo or Anglo). It is insufficient, however, to simply report regression coefficients. In order to approach an explanation of the observed within- and between-sample differences in interactive patterns it is necessary to move more toward the analysis of causal pathways in an attempt to show by what processes the factors that influence these variables might also be employed to generate their observed effects. Thus, the purpose of this chapter is to outline the major interrelations among these variables and to better establish their validity by suggesting some of the ways that these variables are the product of larger Navajo-Anglo cultural ecological differences.

DERIVING THE DETERMINANTS

To outline the ways in which these variables are interrelated, another series of multiple regression analyses were carried out in order to determine the direction of influences between and among them and thereby to focus more explicitly on pathways of causation instead of simple correlations. My first step in untangling these causal chains was to enter the mother's rate of behavior to child and the child's rate of behavior to mother as dependent variables, entering the other variables in various orders as independent variables. Because MRATE and BRATE were derived after the fact from the measurements of interaction that occurred under different conditions of INLAP, ORATE, GROUP (and BRATE and MRATE, respectively), they were considered to be results or effects of the other variables and not direct causes. While there are very strong correlations between GROUP and both MRATE and BRATE, for example, it is obvious that having a high rate of behavior does not cause a mother or child to be an Anglo.

In any event, viewing the mother's and the child's rates of behavior to each other as the most significant independent variables is only a starting point, justified initially on the grounds that they are the most direct global measures of mother–infant interaction and on the heuristic grounds that in attempting to sort out complex causal pathways it is usually necessary to enter the system at an arbitrary point. Table 8.1 shows those independent variables that were significant predictors of BRATE and MRATE in stepwise multiple regression analyses. The significance of the independent predictor variable, the direction of its correlation with BRATE and MRATE, and the total variance explained are also listed.

Regardless of how other independent variables were forced into the regression equation for BRATE, none of them ever achieved significance or detracted significantly from the power of GROUP or ORATE. In the first quarter for MRATE, however, when INLAP was forced into the regression equation ahead of ORATE, it was significant but still did not detract from the overall power of ORATE, meaning that even when the enhancing effect of INLAP on MRATE is taken into account first, ORATE still has a significant reducing effect on MRATE.

From these two multiple regression analyses a number of potential causal chains can be ruled out and some interesting general patterns begin to emerge. Of most interest is the fact that in spite of the significant differences in Navajo and Anglo BRATE and MRATE, the dummy variable GROUP is the best predicator of BRATE but never enters the equation for MRATE. Even in the second half of the first year, when ORATE becomes the best predictor of BRATE, GROUP continues to have a significant effect on BRATE after the effect of ORATE is removed. What this means is that if you know whether the child is Navajo or Anglo you can predict the child's rate of behavior to mother with a high degree of confidence, but knowing whether the mother is Navajo or Anglo will not allow you to predict her rate of behavior to her child. In other words, there is something about the differences between Navajos and Anglos that is more related to BRATE than to MRATE. Moreover, there appears to be no relationship between MRATE and BRATE, leading to the tentative conclusion that they are not directly causally related.

Another set of findings from these multiple regression analyses is that whereas INLAP is the most consistent predictor of MRATE throughout the year (with the partial exception of the first quarter when its effects are

Table 8.1. Stepwise Multiple Regression Analyses of BRATE and MRATE by Quarter

Dependent variable	First quarter			Second quarter			Third and fourth quarter		
	Predictor	$p <$	r^2	Predictor	$p <$	r^2	Predictor	$p <$	r^2
BRATE	−GROUP (A > N)	.001	.26	−GROUP (A > N)	.002	.26	−ORATE −GROUP (A < N)	.001 .010	.31
MRATE	−ORATE +INLAP	.001	.35	+INLAP	.002	.25	+INLAP (−ORATE)	.001 .002	.39

swamped by ORATE) it is never a significant predictor of BRATE. This suggests that the child has a greater impact on his mother's rate of behavior when she is holding him, but that her impact on the child's rate of behavior is not any greater when she is holding him than it is when she is not. This finding fits nicely with attachment theory's view of the functions of proximity to or contact with mother, but the real question here concerns the nature of the interaction itself and not simply the rate at which mother and infant direct behaviors toward each other (this is undoubtedly why the global measures MRATE and BRATE do not predict each other at any time during the first year). What this effect of INLAP on MRATE means, I think, is that when the child is on his mother's lap he is better able to elicit (and she to give) a number of behaviors that simply do not occur with any frequency when the child is not on her lap (e.g., rocking, cuddling, clinging, nursing, and the close facial–visual–vocal sorts of interaction that are so important for the establishment of patterns of mutual reciprocity). On the other hand, in these data at least, the only Navajo or Anglo child behavior that is clearly positively correlated with INLAP throughout the year is *B vocalize M*. This is an important interactive behavior without question, and doubly interesting because the Anglo mother–infant pairs, who have higher INLAP scores, also have higher rates of *B vocalize M*. But the increase in Navajo *B vocalize M* that is associated with an increase in INLAP is not enough to also raise the Navajo BRATE score.

   The only other independent variable that entered these multiple regression equations was ORATE, and it was the only one that entered the equations for both MRATE and BRATE. Like the other independent variables under consideration here, the rate at which other people present during mother–infant interaction directed behavior toward the child was very different for the Navajo and Anglo samples. Yet ORATE had an effect on BRATE only in the second half of the year (and even then GROUP continued to have a significant effect) while it was the best predictor of MRATE in the first quarter and of secondary importance in the second half of the year. The direction of its effects was always the same however; it always decreased both MRATE and BRATE. Now it might seem that in this case MRATE or BRATE could cause ORATE instead of the opposite, but for two reasons I do not think this is the case. First, BRATE and MRATE were derived only from periods of mother–infant interaction, and it is my impression that others (siblings especially) were more likely to interact with the child during his interaction with mother when these interactions were most intense, that is, when the interaction between mother and infant was most "interesting." Second, and more important, I think the biggest part of the Navajo-Anglo differences in ORATE is due to the simple fact that there were ordinarily many fewer other people present during my observations of Anglo mother–infant interaction. No matter how intensely he behaved, for example, an Anglo child could not cause more brothers or sisters or grandparents to be present, or could a Navajo child cause them to disappear.

On the other hand, I suspect that the reason ORATE becomes an important predictor of BRATE in the second half of the year is because after a child is roughly 6 months old he becomes a more interesting playmate than he was earlier. Prior to 6 months, and especially in the first 3 months of life, infants are, of course, very attractive to their siblings, but they are usually not especially responsive playmates by the standards of most children under five or six, who are often too vigorous in their attempts to show affection or elicit response. Thus, in the first part of the year, mothers' behavior toward their infants will tend to be disrupted as they ward off the overtures of older siblings toward the infant, and in the later part of their year their behavior will tend to be disrupted more to the extent that they allow other children more leeway in interacting with the bigger, stronger, and more competent infant, something that will obviously also affect the child's rate of behavior to his mother.

Summarizing briefly to this point, these regression analyses have helped to sort out some of the causal pathways among the variables considered and have thus suggested aspects of the environment of mother–infant interaction where it might be productive to look for the causes of Navajo-Anglo differences. All of the independent variables entered in these equations were measures on which Navajo and Anglo mothers and infants differed significantly, yet some were shown to affect mothers and others to affect infants. The task now is to relate these abstract causal pathways to concrete measures of mother–infant interaction and its environment. This will be attempted by moving from the general to the particular, illustrating the proposed causal pathways by suggesting how the significant predictors BRATE and MRATE are concrete manifestations of very real aspects of the Navajo and Anglo social-physical environments of interaction, and further, by suggesting how specific items of observed behavior that correlate with these predictors also relate to BRATE and MRATE.

NAVAJO NEONATAL BEHAVIOR AND MOTHER–INFANT INTERACTION IN THE FIRST QUARTER

One likely candidate for explaining at least part of the large effect of GROUP (Navajo or Anglo) on BRATE is the fact that Navajo and Anglo infants are different at birth. While we disagree on why Navajo and Anglo infants differ in behavior at birth, Freedman and I are agreed that Navajo newborns tend to be quieter and less irritable than Anglo newborns (see

Chapters 3 and 5). The definitive study of long-term sequelae of neonatal behavioral differences remains to be done, but longitudinal studies of at least a few months have shown continuities in neonatal behavior (for example, Bakow et al., 1973; Hall and Pawlby, 1981; Osofsky, 1974, 1976). Because of the small numbers involved, I could not relate Anglo Brazelton scale scores to measures of mother–infant interaction, but of the 12 Navajo infants observed in interaction with their mothers during the first quarter, 11 had also been examined with the Brazelton scale at birth. The simple correlations between Navajo newborn behavior and mother–infant interactive behavior frequencies during the first three months that I report here must be accepted as tentative and only generally illustrative of how GROUP effects on BRATE might reflect continuities in Navajo-Anglo neonatal behavioral differences, for I cannot say what the Anglo correlations are, or even if they are in the same direction. Table 8.2 shows the significant ($p < .05$) correlations between measures of Navajo neonatal behavior and mother–infant interaction during the first quarter.

The Brazelton scale items listed in Table 8.2 are those on which Navajo and Anglo infants differed most. The "+" or "−" after each correlation coefficient indicates whether a knowledge of the direction of Navajo-Anglo neonatal behavioral differences and a knowledge of the direction of the Navajo correlation would allow one to predict the direction of Navajo-Anglo differences in mother–infant interactive behavior frequencies in the first quarter. The Navajo newborns, for example, had significantly lower predominant states on the NBAS than the Anglo newborns, and there was a positive correlation between Navajo predominant state and M pat/rub B during the first quarter; all other things being equal, one might thus expect the Navajos to score lower on M pat/rub B just as they scored lower on predominant state—which is in fact the case.

There are 32 significant correlations between these Navajo NBAS scores and first quarter mother–infant interactive behavior items, and a knowledge of the direction of the correlation and of the original Navajo-Anglo differences would allow one to predict the direction of the later Navajo-Anglo differences in mother–infant interactive behaviors in 21 instances. To be sure, one also needs to know the direction of the correlation for the Anglo sample as well, and even then, of course, correlation is not causation. But the main point here stands: there is a relationship between the behavior of the newborn Navajo infant and aspects of his or her interaction with mother during the first three months of life. Moreover there is a specific relationship between BRATE and rapidity of buildup and irritability—two NBAS items on which the Navajo infants most consistently scored lower than the Anglo infants. The fact that it is a negative correlation is not any major stumbling block; the correlation might also be negative for the Anglo sample as well, which would suggest the kind of "inversion of intensity" noted by Bell et al. (1971) in other aspects of behavioral development. It is quite possible too

Table 8.2. Correlations between Navajo Brazelton Scale Scores and First Quarter Mother–Infant Interaction Behavior Frequencies

First quarter interactive behaviors[a]	Brazelton scale items						
	Predominant state (A)[a]	Consolability (N)	Peak of excitement (A)	Rapidity of buildup (A)	Irritability (A)	Activity (A)	Lability of states (A)
M *pat/rub* (A)	.60c (+)					.47b (+)	.65c (+)
M adjust position (A)	.60c (+)	−.54b (+)	.55b (+)		.52b (+)		.55c (+)
M smile B (A)						.80d (+)	
M *rock* B (A)	.60c (+)						
M clean/wipe/adjust (A)						−.64c (−)	
M laugh B (A)						.54b (+)	
M *talk* B (A)						.75c (+)	
M vocalize B (A)			.50b (+)	.63c (+)	.42b (+)		.45b (+)
B look at M (A)					−.42b (−)		−.55b (−)
B smile M (A)							−.48b (−)
B *self-touch* (N)	−.60c (−)						
B extension-flexion movements (N)	−.52b (+)		−.50b (=)				
B fret/cry (N)	.52b (−)	.49b (+)			.48b (−)		
Mutual gaze (A)						−.42b (−)	−.45b (−)
Length of interaction (A)	.57c (+)						
BRATE (A)				−.45b (−)			
Interaction fret/cry (N) (%)	.57c (−)				−.39b (−)		

[a] N or A = Navajo or Anglo *higher*; when italicized group difference is significant.
[b] = p < .05.
[c] = p < .01.
[d] = p < .001.

that the relationship between neonatal irritability and later BRATE is curvilinear: infants who are the least irritable and the most passive may have mothers (and others) who stimulate them more in attempts to elicit more satisfying interaction, whereas infants who are the most irritable and reactive may have mothers who try to maintain them in a quieter, more peaceful state.

But again, taking these simple correlations at face value suggests that the effects of GROUP, on Navajo children at least, may in large part be the sequelae of lower irritability and its correlates at birth. It is not known how long the effects of lower neonatal irritability may last, and I have no direct evidence that they continue even into the second quarter. Incomplete though my data are on this point, however, I strongly suspect that these effects do continue at least into the second quarter, even if the pathways through which they work are obscure. To take only one example, low irritability at birth predicts low *M vocalize B* for the Navajo in the first quarter, and in the first quarter *M vocalize B* is positively correlated with *B vocalize M* ($r = .39$; $p < .01$). Thus, the effects of lower irritability at birth need not be continuous in the child, but may feed back to the child through the child's effects on the mother and vice versa.

THE CHILD'S OPPORTUNITY FOR INTERACTION WITH OTHERS

Navajo–Anglo Between-Sample Differences

There is not such an obvious candidate for explaining how INLAP comes to exert such consistent effects on MRATE as there was for suggesting how GROUP comes to affect BRATE. This is because MRATE, ORATE, and INLAP are all highly intercorrelated. In an attempt to further sort out the relationship between INLAP and ORATE (which were consistently negatively correlated in both samples, although not so significantly in the second half of the first year), INLAP was used as the dependent variable in a series of multiple regression analyses. However, due to the known relationship between INLAP and MRATE, MRATE was forced into the regression equations on the final step. Table 8.3 shows those independent variables that were the best predictors of INLAP when the effects of MRATE were not allowed to exert their effects until after all the others.

In the first half of the year, when MRATE is forced into the regression equations on the last step, ORATE is the best predictor of INLAP, as it is also in the second half, but not significantly. In the first quarter, however, even after the effects of ORATE have been taken into account, GROUP still has a significant effect on INLAP. Thus, the general conclusion is that whatever determines ORATE also has a strong effect on INLAP, and that in the first

Table 8.3. Multiple Regression Analyses of INLAP[a]

Dependent variable	First quarter			Second quarter			Third and fourth quarter		
	Predictor	$p <$	r^2	Predictor	$p <$	r^2	Predictor	$p <$	r^2
INLAP	−ORATE	.001		−ORATE	.035		(−ORATE	.105	.04)
	GROUP			+BRATE	.043	.21			
	(A > N)	.025	.34						

[a]MRATE entered on last step.

quarter (when Navajo-Anglo INLAP differences are greatest) there is something about the differences between Navajos and Anglos that helps to explain INLAP differences.

The consistent negative effect of ORATE on INLAP is best explained, I feel,
by the fact that when the child is on the mother's lap, others that are present
are less likely to interact with the child for very long. In this way INLAP tends
to decrease ORATE. At another level of analysis, INLAP cannot cause more
or fewer people to be present. The fact that other people are present and
available for interaction means that they can care for or entertain the child
and hold the child themselves, thus reducing the amount of time that the
mother may have to hold her child.

But what determines ORATE? In a word, the factors that determine ORATE
(and thereby also influence INLAP, MRATE, and BRATE) are those factors
which conspire to present the Navajo child with a greater opportunity for
interaction with larger numbers of familiar people than the Anglo child. As
mentioned, while there may well be Navajo-Anglo differences in the way
that these people behave toward the child, the essence of Navajo-Anglo
differences in ORATE is the greater availability of familiar others for the
Navajo child. These differences exist in large part because of the larger
social-cultural, historical, economic, and demographic factors that make for
larger Navajo families, short birth intervals, and an ideal of extended family
camp residence that is supported (or has been) by the material realities of
sheepherding in poor and over grazed land. These factors tend to place the
Navajo child in a social environment that is dense with individuals of a wide
variety of ages who are closely related and/or familiar.

These residence and family demographic patterns mean that for most
Navajo infants there are a number of siblings/cousins nearby who are often
expected to care for the child or help his mother and who in any case often
come visiting simply to play. The security and familiarity of the Navajo
camp also means that these other children can visit by themselves, without
their own mothers. Given the Anglo residence and family demographic
patterns, siblings and cousins are rare to begin with and because of the
age-grading that is so pervasive in Anglo society (especially in early schooling), even neighboring children rarely come to play with an unrelated infant.
The major part of the Navajo-Anglo difference in ORATE was due to the
presence of boys and girls under 12 years of age and girls under 16 years
among the Navajo and their virtual absence among the Anglo. Anglo infants
find themselves in social environments where, except for mother, the opportunity for interaction with others is much more diffuse—limited almost entirely to people who are unrelated and/or familiar only to the extent that
neighbors and family friends are common visitors.

A final aspect of Navajo-Anglo differences in the social context of early
interactions is related as much to the physical qualities of the residence itself

as it is to the number and identity of its inhabitants. The Anglo homes in Flagstaff had more rooms than the Navajo homes ($p < .05$), more stairs, more doors, more furniture, and many more dishwashers, toasters, telephones, TV sets, and so on. These differences mean that there are more, and more varied, physical settings for Anglo mother–infant interaction and a greater likelihood that the Anglo mother and infant will be separated or out of sight altogether in separate rooms. The electrical appliances, TV sets, telephones, doorbells, and the like, also mean that the Anglo mother will be called away from interactions with her child more often to attend to the demands of burning toast, the telephone, or a record that will not eject properly. It is interesting to note in this cultural ecological context that in the second half of the year, when infants are crawling and beginning to walk, Anglo mothers and infants both approach and leave each other significantly more often than do Navajo mothers and infants.

Returning briefly to the family demographic causes of differences in ORATE, there is another aspect of the differences between Navajo and Anglo families in my sample that merits discussion. As numerous developmental psychologists have reported (e.g., Moss, 1967; Zajonc, 1976), many components of mother–infant interaction can be affected by parity, and certainly with higher parity there will be more siblings around to contribute to a higher ORATE. Thus, a portion of the Navajo-Anglo differences in ORATE, MRATE, INLAP, and even BRATE and some specific individual items of interactive behavior could be due to the fact that my Anglo sample consisted almost entirely of first-born children while all but three of the Navajo children considered here were later-born. Even though the small number of primiparous Navajo mothers makes it impossible to check statistically, I do not believe that these group differences in parity account for a very large portion of the differences in the other measures. My reasons for suspecting that parity differences have little overall influence is that with only two first-born nuclear family Navajo children and only one first-born extended family Navajo child, the nuclear-extended family differences in mother–infant interaction still almost exactly parallel the Navajo–Anglo differences, as I will describe in the following section. Thus, the fortuitous way that my Navajo sample divided itself into equal proportions of nuclear and extended family camp children provided a further check on my interpretations of how ORATE, MRATE, BRATE, and INLAP and a number of specific behavior items may be interrelated.

Navajo Within-Sample Differences

For the purposes of this discussion, the most significant dimension of differences between the Navajo nuclear and extended family camps is the extended famly camp child's greater potential for interaction with more people of both sexes and a wider age range who are also related and/or very familiar. By the same token, the extended family camp child may have a greater potential for interaction with his or her mother because there are more people to help with her children and her other duties about the camp. As I mentioned in the description of the Navajo sample, the extended family camp child lives not only with his siblings, but also with another 1.6 peers (ages 0 to 3 years), another 2.9 potential child caretakers/playmates (aged 3 to 12 years), and another 3.6 teenaged or adult caretakers. The extended family camp mother, on the other hand, has an additional 6.5 people over the age of three who may not only help her with her own children, but who may relieve her from some of her regular camp duties for more exclusive time with her children. As I also mentioned in the discussion of Navajo and Anglo children's fear of strangers, except for the few nuclear families who live near their jobs in the trading post area, most nuclear family camp children will also have less experience with strangers than most extended family camp children. This is because there is a greater potential for movement and travel in the larger extended family camps where there are more pickup trucks and more potential drivers. In the nuclear family camps there are not only fewer trucks and drivers but fewer potential babysitters to mind the other children if the parents wish to make a trip to the trading post.

All of these points were corroborated by data from the 1100 spot observations. Comparing nuclear and extended family camp children, the nuclear family camp children were observed at home more often than the extended family camp children ($p < .001$); they were observed actually inside their house or hogan more than the extended family camp children ($p < .001$); their mothers were observed to be with them more often ($p < .01$); but they were less likely to be held or carried by mother throughout the first 3 years of life ($p < .001$). As expected, the nuclear family camp children were observed in the presence of fewer other people than the extended family camp children ($p < .001$). Each of these observations is consistent with the interpretation that the extended family camp mother has more help both with her own children and with her domestic duties around camp.

In order to examine the effects of these larger social-contextual differences on within- and between-culture differences in patterns of mother-infant interaction, multiple regression techniques were again employed. The dependent variables were those mother and infant behaviors during interaction, and global measurements of these interactions as a whole, which showed the most significant and/or consistent nuclear-extended family differences averaged over the children's first year of life. These are listed in Table 8.4, along with the Anglo scores on each variable for comparison.

Not all of these within- and between-group differences are significant, but most were significant for at least two of the four quarters of the first year.

Table 8.4. Within- and Between-Culture Comparisons of Aspects of Mother–Infant Interaction[a]

Aspect	Navajo nuclear family	Navajo extended family	Anglo
Mutual gaze	.12	.13	.18
Mother talk to child	.10	.17	.33
Mother touch, pat child	.07	.11	.12
Mother approach, leave child	.07	.09	.12
Child vocalize	.13	.19	.23
Child vocalize and look at mother	.03	.04	.05
Child approach, leave mother	.01	.04	.06
Mean interaction length (minutes)	1.68	2.60	4.63

[a] Expressed as the rate of occurrence per 15 seconds of interaction, averaged across all interactions observed.

The most striking aspect of these differences, however, is not so much in their degree, but in the fact that they were so consistent throughout the year, that is, the rank-ordering of the three groups was the same on each variable at each quarter. In every instance Navajo nuclear family patterns of interaction were less like Anglo nuclear family patterns than those of the Navajo extended families. The three groups did not differ significantly on all of the nearly 80 behavior items that occurred with enough frequency to be analyzed, nor was the pattern of differences identical for some of the more rare behaviors, but the behaviors listed here represent fundamental and theoretically highly significant dimensions of mother–infant interaction.

The independent variables entered into the regression equations as predictors of the mother and infant interactive behaviors listed in Table 8.4 were those which were expected to influence the behavior of mother, infant, or both. They were: the mother's rate of behavior to her child, the child's rate of behavior to mother, the rate at which all other people present during interaction directed behavior toward the infant (ORATE), the percentage of the interaction during which the child was held on the mother's lap, the percentage of the interaction devoted to caretaking (e.g., nursing, dressing, cleaning), and whether the mother or the infant initiated the interaction. In the end, four of these independent variables proved to be significantly related to the mother and infant behaviors on which the three groups differed most. These variables, averaged over the first year, are listed in Table 8.5.

Table 8.5 shows that the distinctive pattern of within- and between-culture differences so evident in the dependent variables is just as evident in

Table 8.5 Within- and between-culture comparisons of aspects of the social environment of mother–infant interaction[a]

Aspect	Navajo nuclear family	Navajo extended family	Anglo
Mother rate of behavior	1.28	1.61	1.80
Child rate of behavior	.46	.50	.74
All others rate of behavior	.43	.32	.15
Interaction on lap (%)	23.32	33.52	38.05

[a] Except for "percentage interaction in lap," expressed as rate of occurrence per 15 seconds of interaction, averaged across all interactions observed.

these independent variables. Again, the Navajo extended family pattern is more like the Anglo nuclear family pattern than is the Navajo nuclear family pattern.

Together these four variables accounted for far more of the variance in the mother and infant interactive behavior variables than any combination of all the other independent variables. For example, they accounted for as much as 47% of the variance in *mutual gaze,* 40% of the variance in *mother approach, leave child,* and 37% of *mother talk to child.* In the first quarter they accounted for 49% of the variance in mean interactive bout length, 35% in the second quarter, and fully 60% in the second half of the first year.

Furthermore, another series of multiple regression analyses showed that of these four variables, the single most powerful was ORATE, the rate at which all others present during mother–infant interaction directed behavior toward the infant. Averaged over the entire first year, this variable accounted for 39% of the variance in MRATE and nearly 30% of the variance in BRATE. During the first quarter of the year ORATE also accounted for 34% of the variance in INLAP (but this figure dropped to 21% in the second quarter and was negligible in the second half of the first year).

DISCUSSION AND CONCLUSIONS

The analyses reported in this chapter warrant two overall conclusions. The first conclusion is the tentative one that Navajo-Anglo neonatal behavioral differences probably contribute to Navajo-Anglo differences in patterns of mother–infant interaction. Navajo infants, who were significantly less irritable and reactive than Anglo infants at birth, also scored lower on BRATE throughout the first year, and a major determinant of BRATE scores within the Navajo sample was shown to be levels of neonatal irritability. BRATE, in turn, as shown in the previous chapter, had a significant influence on Navajo-Anglo differences in patterns of mother–infant interaction. This conclusion about the contribution of neonatal differences to later group differences in mother–infant interaction is tentative, however, because it was not possible to relate measures of Anglo neonatal behavior to measures of mother–infant interaction any time during the first year and because it was possible to do so for the Navajo sample only in the first quarter of the year. In any case, whatever the contribution of the neonate to later patterns of mother–infant interaction, at least 30% of the variance in BRATE was accounted for by ORATE, the rate at which other people present during mother–infant interaction directed behavior toward the infant.

The second conclusion to be drawn from these analyses concerns the singular role of ORATE in influencing patterns of mother–infant interaction. Specifically, the nature of mother–infant interactions was shown to differ both within and between the two cultural groups according to residence patterns, and the analyses reported above showed that these differences were most directly accounted for in terms of the impact of the behavior of other people present in these residential groupings on the behavior of mother and infant. The fact that ORATE differentiated nuclear and extended family patterns of interaction within the Navajo sample as well as it differentiated between the Navajo and Anglo samples suggests that ORATE may operate largely independently of other Navajo-Anglo social-cultural differences. In sum, Navajo nuclear family mother–infant interaction was characterized by the shortest interactive bouts, the children spent the least time on their mothers' laps, the mothers and infants alike both did the least *approach, leave* to each other, and both vocalized/verbalized to each other the least. They were also subject to the highest rate of behavior from others (the child's siblings) present during their interaction. At the opposite extreme were the Anglo nuclear families, with the longest interactive bouts, most time on mothers' laps, the highest rates of both *approach, leave* and vocalizations/verbalizations by both mother and child, and the lowest rate of behavior from other people present during their interaction (who were very few in number anyway). Intermediate on all these behaviors, and other important dimensions of mother–infant interaction, were the Navajo extended family mothers and infants, who were similar to the Navajo nuclear families in having many others around them during interaction but similar to the Anglo families in having more opportunity for exclusive attention to each other. The Anglo mothers not only had many fewer other children to make demands on their time, they also had more time for exclusive attention to their children because of their economic and technological advantages.

In the following, concluding chapter I will discuss further the significance and implications of these conclusions and will integrate them with the various conclusions from the preceding chapters according to the view of development that I advanced in Chapter 1.

9

Summary and Conclusions: Development as Adaptation

SUMMARY

Responses to the Cradleboard

ONE of the hypotheses that guided the research discussed in the preceding chapters was based on experimental data and theoretical considerations which suggested that the cradleboard might constitute a perturbation in the environment of Navajo mother–infant interaction. The experimental data came from studies which demonstrated that motor restraint tended to reduce infants' arousal and activity levels, and considerations of attachment theory suggested that these reduced arousal-activity levels might tend to disrupt mother–infant interaction and thus impair the attachment process by decreasing the mutual responsiveness of mother and infant.

This hypothesis received empirical support from analyses of the cradleboard transition data (Chapter 7). The cradleboard did in fact lower infants' levels of arousal and activity; these changes in infant state were closely paralleled by changes in a number of maternal behaviors. Moreover, sequential analyses of mother–infant interaction while the infant was on the cradleboard showed that mother and infant were both less responsive to each other when the infant was on the cradleboard.

But do these immediate cradleboard effects constitute a perturbation? Certainly not a lasting one, for further analyses showed that regardless of how much stress might be associated with these cradleboard effects, they were highly transient. These analyses were of three sorts. First, factor analyses of mother–infant interactive behaviors averaged over the total length of all interactions revealed a cradleboard factor, but this factor accounted for only a negligible portion of the overall variance. Second, a series of multiple regression analyses showed that use of the cradleboard during mother–infant interaction predicted only a tiny fraction of all mother and infant behaviors entered as dependent variables. In addition, many of the small number of interactive behaviors thus predicted were hardly surprising (e.g., high cradleboard use during interaction predicted low levels of infant *approach* and *leave* mother). Third, another series of multiple regression analyses were carried out in which the dependent variables were only those mother and infant interactive behaviors on which the Navajo and Anglo samples differed most. Again the cradleboard could account for virtually no cultural differences in patterns of mother–infant interaction. Taken together, these analyses suggest that the observed effects of the cradleboard on mother–infant interaction were transient, operating only while the infant was on the cradleboard and not generalizing in any obvious way to affect patterns of interaction between mother and infant when the child was not on the cradleboard.

In spite of the fact that there is no good evidence for long-term cradleboard effects on infant behavioral development the immediate effects of the cradleboard on infant behavior and mother–infant interaction are clear and a substantial corpus of theory suggests that these immediate effects should last. The question now becomes why don't these clear immediate effects of the cradleboard last?

The strategy that I used to approach this question was a logical extension of the view of development as adaptation discussed in Chapter 1. In that chapter it was argued that the process of adaptation is best seen in terms of hierarchically interconnected environmental tracking systems and that the process of adaptation is not limited to changes in the genotype over generations but that it includes, may depend upon, and begin with the most immediate behavioral responses of individuals to environmental perturbations. This concept of adaptation predicts an evolutionary trend toward increased behavioral plasticity, most evident in *H. sapiens,* and the process of *K*-selection, along with its concomitant, neoteny, is a likely evolutionary mechanism whereby this greater plasticity has been achieved in the human line. Viewing the process of development itself as one of adaptation makes it possible to study development as evolutionary biologists study adaptation. The strategy that many evolutionary biologists use to study adaptation is simply to determine what the environment will "do" to an organism if it does not perform the particular behavior in question. As mentioned in Chapter 1, the steps in this sort of research are (1) the identification of an environmental perturbation; (2) analysis of the relative success of responses to the perturbation in removing the stress associated with the perturbation; and (3) analysis of the mechanisms whereby the successful responses are preserved.

Applying this strategy to the question of why the theoretically perturbing effects of the cradleboard do not last, I looked for responses to the cradleboard that might constitute a corrective adaptation and prevent these effects from becoming a more stressful perturbation to which the infant could not successfully respond. In this context, a successful response is one in which the immediate effect of the early experience is a response which prevents that early experience from causing later or long-term effects that decrease the child's capacity to successfully respond to future environmental perturbations. Such an immediate successful response (immediate effect) might also be viewed as the child's first step on some hypothetical alternate development pathway.

I found three responses to the cradleboard that might qualify as corrective or successful responses. Although the first is obvious, its very obviousness might suggest that the concept of goal correction by the infant is not such a developmental *deus ex machina* as some seem to feel. My data showed unequivocally that while the cradleboard does lower infants' state, arousal level, and reactivity, infants nonetheless also cry in order to be released from the cradleboard. There was a significant ($p < .02$) increase in fretting and crying in the 2 minutes prior to removal from the cradleboard. Moreover, Navajo mothers were unanimous in reporting that except for special circumstances (e.g., traveling away from home) removal from the cradleboard was "up to" the child and that the child evidenced his decision most often by crying. In addition, in the second half of the first year, when the cradleboard seemed to account for more of the Navajo-Anglo behavioral differences, most of the behavior items correlated with cradleboard use reflected dimensions of the infants' protests and mothers' attempts to quiet the child. In other words, the effects of the cradleboard seemed to be most marked at the end of the child's cradleboard career as he or she demanded more clearly to be removed. The child may want to be removed from the cradleboard for more reasons than that the cradleboard binding becomes more stressful with simple age or size. As the child matures and develops more sophisticated schemata of social interaction and object manipulation, simply watching mother and other children may be more arousing later in the year than earlier, and when aroused thus by his perception of a social situation, the cradleboard binding may be perceived by the child as relatively more uncomfortable. In any case, the infant is a social person with an effect on the behavior of others, and crying or fretting to be removed from the cradleboard is probably sufficient for explaining why the cradleboard is not used enough (however much that may be) for it to have many lasting behavioral effects.

The second possibly adaptive response to the immediate effects of the cradleboard involved mother–infant interaction although it is difficult to establish the separate roles of each. Nonetheless, at the end of virtually every cradleboard session, after the infant cried to be set free, the mother and infant engaged in a particularly intense 2 or 3 minutes of affectionate face-to-face interaction and/or nursing. The regularity with which these bouts of intense sociability followed release from the cradleboard suggest that they could function as a sort of behavioral equivalent of the catching up in growth children seem to undergo after a period of growth retardation due to illness or malnutrition (see Prader, Tanner, and Von Harnack, 1963).

The third potentially adaptive response to the cradleboard cannot be credited only or directly to the infant's behavior either, but depends for its possible efficacy on those factors which conspire to bring the infant on the cradleboard into greater proximity to mother than those infants not on the cradleboard. The evidence for this greater mother–infant proximity for children on the cradleboard is especially strong. In the 439 spot observations of cradleboard-aged children, it will be recalled, infants who were observed away from home were much more likely ($p < .001$) to be on the cradleboard than those observed at home. To the extent that the activity and arousal reducing effect of the cradleboard make it easier to travel away from home with infants on the cradleboard, the cradleboard can also be said to increase mother–infant proximity. Likewise, infants who were observed within the camp boundaries but still out-of-doors, were more likely ($p < .05$) to be on the cradleboard than those observed inside the hogan or house. Finally, regardless of where they were observed, infants on the cradleboard were significantly more like ($p < .01$) to be within arm's reach of mother than infants not on the cradleboard. For Navajo mothers the cradleboard's primary function seems to be that of a baby-minding device. It makes travel with the infant easier and it makes it easier for the mother to watch her child—and have the child out from underfoot—while she carries out her various tasks in and around the home. A good example of how the cradleboard functions as a baby-minding device that increases mother–infant proximity comes from a family in which the only child, a 5-month-old boy, actually never used the cradleboard. One warm fall day after I had completed my observation inside, the boy's mother took him outside to a spot under a tree where for the past several days she had been shelling and sorting piñon nuts. She placed her son in a large cardboard box and sat down next to him and began her work. He was unable to crawl about and could not play with the piñon nuts, scattering them in the sand, yet he was nearby and could watch his mother and she could talk, look, and smile at him. In countless other situations of this sort the cradleboard fuctioned as the cardboard box did for this mother. By immobilizing the infant in these situations the cradleboard may also function to prevent the negative or unhappy sorts of interactions that might occur if the child were free and able to reach the mother's work, scattering the piñon nuts, pulling on strands of yarn, spilling the coffee, and the like.

The factors that conspire to bring the infant on the cradleboard into greater proximity to mother than those not on the cradleboard may be to some extent epiphenomenal, that is, an accidental but beneficial result of the human tendency to conserve energy and do things the easy way. Thus, after placing her child on the cradleboard, the mother then sets the cradle-board down—where else but within arm's reach?—and continues with the cooking, weaving, and shelling piñon nuts. In addition, however, it also seems likely that infants in close proximity to their mothers will tend to be happier and quieter than infants who do not enjoy such proximity; mothers may learn that if they want to immobilize their children so that they can get on with their work without interruption, an infant immobilized nearby may be quieter and more content than one immobilized farther away. In any case, regardless of how and why such proximity is achieved, the greater proximity to mother of the cradleboard child may itself tend to counteract the theoretically negative effects of the cradleboard. In other words, even if mother–infant interaction on the cradleboard is characterized as less mutually responsive, the increased proximity itself may offer an acceptable alternate pathway to the set-goal of secure attachment. This is an empirical question for attachment research, but it seems that under some conditions secure attachment might be achieved as well through proximity as through the mutual responsiveness that is presently stressed so much.

Thus, while data and theory both suggested that the cradleboard might constitute a perturbation for the Navajo child and while observation showed that the cradleboard did in fact have a theoretically negative effect on the behavior of both mother and infant, there was no evidence that these immediate effects lasted beyond the time the child was on the cradleboard. I cannot demonstrate that the three responses to the cradleboard I have dis-cussed above are the ones (or the only ones) that prevent the theoretically negative effects of the cradleboard from having any obvious impact after the child is removed from the cradleboard, but I believe that they are likely candidates for the adaptive (successful) responses we would predict from an evolutionary view of development as adaptation. Phrased in terms of a general hypothesis, I would predict that the observed and hypothetically negative effects of the cradleboard do not last because of the way that the Navajo child responds to them so quickly, either alone, through his effects on the behavior of others, and/or because of the way that the cradleboard is used in the larger context of Navajo daily activities.

Responses to the Social Context of Mother–Infant Interaction

Having established that the cradleboard has the effects that had been predicted but that these effects do not last and are essentially unrelated to either within- or between-culture variance in patterns of Navajo and Anglo mother-infant interaction, the next step in data analysis was to determine which variables best accounted for both the within- and the between-culture variance. A number of measures and analytic procedures showed that the best predictor of both kinds of variance was differences in each child's opportunity for interaction with others besides mother. At the most basic level of analysis, the frequencies of many items of mother and infant inter- active behavior were shown to systematically differ both within and between the two cultural groups according to residence patterns, and the operative within- and between-culture difference in residence patterns was shown to be differences in the number and age/sex/kinship identity of each infant's coresidents. Multiple regression analyses showed that the variable ORATE (the rate at which all others present during mother–infant interaction directed behavior toward the infant) was the best single predictor of the interactive behavior items on which the Navajo nuclear, Navajo extended, and Anglo nuclear families differed. As mentioned in Chapter 8, the fact that this variable differentiated between the Navajo nuclear and extended families just as well as it differentiated between the Navajo and Anglo families suggests that the impact of differences in each child's opportunity for interaction with others besides mother may not depend very much on other kinds of cultural differences that also differentiate between and among the three groups.

However, the fact that the Navajo nuclear families and the Anglo nuclear families were on opposite ends of the distribution of mother-infant inter- active behavior frequencies means that abstract social structural variables such as residence classifications might not always serve as adequate indirect measures of social opportunity, especially for cross-cultural comparisons. For example, spot observation data showed that Navajo nuclear family mothers held their infants less than did the Navajo extended family mothers. Precisely the same picture emerged from the continuous observation of mother–infant interaction: again the nuclear family mothers held their children less than did the extended family mothers. This nuclear-extended family differences is a good replication of the finding reported by Munroe and Munroe (1971) that in large Logoli households in Kenya, infants were held more often than in small households. In this study, however, the Anglo nuclear families were the smallest, yet the Anglo mothers held their infants the most. So it is not only the number and identity of others that affect holding and other aspects of mother–infant interaction, but the way that these factors may interact with others which also affects the opportunity for interaction (daily routines, work loads, etc.).

In addition to the systematic within- and between-culture differences revealed by continuous observation of mother–infant interaction, spot observations also revealed clear parallel differences in social opportunity for infants in the three groups. To summarize, the data from these spot observations indicate that the Navajo extended family infant has more opportunity for exclusive interaction with mother because she has more help both with her other children and with her various domestic duties about the camp. At the same time, the extended family camp infant also has more opportunity for interaction with more other people and people of a wider variety of age/sex/kinship identities simply because of the extended family camp structure. The Navajo nuclear family infant is at the opposite end of the scale on all these variables because of the structure of the Navajo nuclear family camp and the ways that this structure affects the mother's work loads and other daily activities which in turn affect the infant's opportunity for interaction with mother and others. The Anglo nuclear family infant, on the other hand, has the lowest opportunity for interaction with others besides mother because of the minimal size of the Anglo coresidential unit. He also has the greatest opportunity for exclusive and very long interactions with mother because of, for example, the Anglo mother's economic and technological advantage over most Navajo mothers.

Another aspect of the differences between the Navajo nuclear and extended families that may be at least partly related to the differences in infants' social opportunity in these families are the significant differences in birth interval and length of breast-feeding. It is impossible to know from my data whether the shorter period of breast-feeding in the nuclear families is causally related to their shorter birth interval, but the shorter birth interval in combination with the nuclear family mother's relative social isolation and dearth of mother's helpers might make it more difficult for her to maintain breast-feeding as long as the extended family camp mother. In any case, all of this reflects again the Navajo nuclear family infant's lesser opportunity for exclusive and/or very long interaction with his mother. The significantly longer period of breast-feeding in both the Navajo extended families and the Anglo nuclear families reflects the opposite condition in those families where the mother has more opportunity for such exclusive attention to each of her children.

Finally, the impact of differences in each child's opportunity for interaction with others besides mother is also seen in the Navajo nuclear-extended family differences in the development of fear of strangers. Here the "others" are strangers, and the nuclear family children, who had less opportunity for meeting and interacting with strangers than the extended family children, also manifested fear of strangers earlier than the extended family children.

These consistent effects of differences in infants' social opportunity on a variety of measures of infant behavior are ultimately best understood in terms of differences in the larger social contexts of the infants' residence groups. There is nothing very significant, of course, about any residence classification per se, but the Navajo nuclear and extended families and the Anglo nuclear families are specific adaptations to specific economic, ecological, social-cultural, and historical factors that result in significant within- and between-group differences in the number and age/sex/kinship identities of coresidents. The greater availability of the pickup truck, for example, means that more Cottonwood Springs families may now be residing neolocally in small, isolated nuclear families than was the case only 20 or so years ago. While the pickup truck could not figure in any definition of Navajo residence types, the many causes and correlates of the increase in the number of pickup trucks are at least tangentially related to differences in infants' social opportunity, and the effect of the pickup at Cottonwood Springs is "packaged" into the residence-type variables.

My overall conclusions about the impact of differences in infants' social opportunity on their interactions with mother and others constitute good support for the Whitings' argument that knowing the number and age/sex/kinship identities of potential interactors in the social settings which occupy most of the child's time will allow one to predict characteristic patterns of interpersonal behavior. My study focused on mother–infant interpersonal behavior and infant–stranger interpersonal behavior, and not only were these children younger than most studied by the Whitings and their colleagues, the interactions themselves were described in ethological terms quite different from those used in the Whiting studies. The fact that the same overall conclusion was reached in spite of these differences in focus and method suggests that the central finding of both approaches may be especially robust.

One of the more significant implications of this finding is the way that it stresses the necessity of "unpacking" culture as an independent variable. As Leiderman and Leiderman argue in their work on the differential developmental effects of mono- versus polymatric households among the Kikuyu, ". . . it is no longer possible to assume either a homogeneity of caretaking arrangements or a constancy of social forces within a relatively homogeneous society even over the short time span of the infant's first year" (1977:430). The material I have presented here on the impact of differences in infants' opportunities for interaction with others besides mother showed that in many respects there was as much variability within Navajo culture as between Navajo and Anglo culture. Thus, using "culture" as an explicit or implicit variable may obscure as much as it reveals.

By focusing on the social settings in which a child spends most of his or her time, and on the number and age/sex/kinship identities and specific roles and functions of the individuals in these settings, one is in a much better position to relate both within- and between-group similarities and differences in behavior not only to common patterns and styles of interaction learned in these settings, but also to the larger historical, economic, and ecological factors which so greatly determine the nature and composition of these social settings through their effect on subsistence activities, work loads, the sexual division of labor, daily routines, and so forth. With such an approach, one is then able to test hypotheses about specific developmental pathways whereby the infant responds to the larger social and physical environment he or she will face as an adult through the effects of this larger environment on the infant's early social environment.

Further, just as group differences in behavior which happen to parallel group differences in known genetic markers cannot themselves be logically attributed to the genetic differences, group differences in behavior which happen to parallel group differences in obvious cultural markers (language, religion, kinship, etc.) cannot themselves be attributed to the vague gestalt of cultural differences. Instead, one must approach the problem in such a way that one can test the hypothesis that these group differences in behavior exist because of simple group differences in the distribution of larger economic and ecological factors that cause individual differences. Explaining group differences in terms of "culture" is too simple and tends to preclude the search for the developmental/causal pathways whereby behavior may be generated from the interaction between the infant and his environment.

Navajo–Anglo Neonatal Behavioral Differences

My Brazelton scale data on Navajo and Anglo infants agrees in all important respects with Freedman's earlier findings: Navajo infants are quieter and less irritable at birth than Anglo infants. My data also suggest, however, that Freedman's genetic explanation of these Oriental-Caucasian neonatal behavioral differences is incomplete at best for he failed to adequately control for prenatal factors which in my analyses were shown to be correlated with individual differences in levels of newborn irritability. The most significant prenatal correlate of newborn irritability in my sample was mother's blood pressure during pregnancy. The Navajo women had lower pregnancy blood pressure than the Anglo women, in spite of their greater age and parity, and blood pressure is known to be affected by a variety of environmental factors, including stress, at least as much as by genetic factors. Furthermore, while the specific physiological mechanisms whereby maternal blood pressure affects the developing fetus are not clear, a number of recent studies have demonstrated this same effect in several different populations.

Any purely genetic explanation of neonatal behavior is too simple and effectively precludes the search for the epigenetic pathways whereby genotype and environment interact. The genotype is subject to environmental influences from the moment of fertilization and the science of human epigenetics begins then. Numerous studies have noted that not only do maternal nutrition and exposure to a wide variety of drugs and other chemical substances affect newborn physiology and behavior, so also may maternal psychosocial stress during pregnancy. There is no reason to believe that the fetus cannot or does not respond physiologically to changes in its uterine environment, just as newborns respond physiologically and behaviorally to changes in their external environment. The sensitivity of the fetus to its uterine environment thus admits the possibility that the fetus may respond to the effects of its mother's environment on *her* physiology, with the result that the science of human epigenetics would have to include analyses of the mother's environment during pregnancy, how she perceived this environment, and how it affected her physiology. In turn, this suggests that developmental pathways may begin *in utero* and that the fetus's response to changes in maternal physiology (the effects of these changes on the fetus) could represent the first step on an alternate developmental pathway that might be more adaptive in the environment into which the child was going to be born—the environment which triggered the changes in maternal physiology.

The point here is not whether the Navajo–Anglo differences in neonatal irritability have a genetic component (for there is a genetic component to all behavior); the point here is only that the degree of irritability shown by Navajo and Anglo newborn infants could be adaptive in their respective environments. Certainly the Anglo children, whose mothers were more isolated during pregnancy and who themselves were more irritable at birth and who right from the start had to rely almost exclusively on their mothers for any social interaction at all, also seemed to be better able to engage their mothers in longer and more intense interaction than the Navajo children. Adaptation does not occur only at the level of the genotype; it may occur there when perturbations eliciting the response are severe, widespread, and lasting enough. Adaptation may also occur during development, without alerting the gene pool, as the child responds to some perturbation in such a way that the next time he meets that perturbation his response is quicker, easier, or in any way "less costly." The possibility suggested by my data on newborn irritability is that this adaptation might occur *in utero* because the fetus responds to the mother's stress and because the manifestation of this response at birth might be adaptive in the larger social environment that contributed to the mother's stress in the first place.

Because the birth process still stands as a conceptual and disciplinary barrier to all but a few behaviorally oriented pediatricians and developmental psychologists, our knowledge of the cross-cultural range of variability in normal newborn is inadequate, and we have only general ideas of how best to quantify the crucial dependent variables of newborn behavior. Research with the Brazelton scale and other studies of neonatal behavior, however, all suggest that irritability is a major dimension of both individual and group differences. But even more than adequate measures of neonatal behavior we need collaborative research among the psychologists and anthropologists who could measure the pregnant woman's environment and her perceptions of it and the physiologists and endocrinologists who might specify the mechanisms whereby her physiology was affected by the environment and how it affected the fetus. The results of this sort of epigenetic research, should it come to pass, might be important not only for maternal and child health but also for such specific questions as those about individual and group differences in temperament, an area of study undergoing a recent renaissance in developmental psychology. I shall have more to say on the subject of temperament shortly.

SYNTHESIS AND IMPLICATIONS

What, then, is the significance of my major conclusions that the cradleboard has no obvious lasting effect on the behavior of Navajo children, that within- and between-culture differences in patterns of Navajo and Anglo mother–infant interaction are best explained in terms of differences in each child's opportunity for interaction with others besides mother, and that Navajo and Anglo infants differ in behavior at birth? How do these general conclusions relate both to Navajo society and culture, in which the research was carried out, and to the evolutionary and developmental theories outlined in Chapter 1, which guided the research? These are the broad topics to be covered in this section.

Cosocialization and Adaptation

Perhaps the easiest way to draw implications from the first two of my general conclusions and to establish their relationship to the larger theories which guided the research is simply to ask why they *should* be true. Asking why the cradleboard should have no lasting effects and why differences in early cosocialization (opportunities for interaction with others besides mother) should be the major determinant of individual and group differences in patterns of mother–infant interaction is another way to further outline the value of an epigenetic approach to questions about gene-environment interaction.

Children learn particular behavioral styles from habitual interaction with others of particular age/sex/kinship identities but there is no way that an infant can influence the actual number or particular age/sex/kinship identity of others with whom he may interact. The behavioral styles learned in the context of interactions with these others should thus have lasting effects, as the Whitings have argued and as my data also suggest. On the other hand, because the cradleboard tends to reduce mother–infant mutual responsiveness, which seems to be so crucial for the attachment process, and because the infant can respond to these short-term effects in an adaptive way, as my data indicate, we should not expect the cradleboard to have any long-term effects. In other words, the effects of the cradleboard constitute a short-term perturbation with a potentially maladaptive long-term developmental outcome to which the infant (and/or his caretakers) is simply *able* to respond adaptively by keeping its use within safe limits. The effects of early cosocialization patterns, however, represent simple alternate developmental pathways that are likely to be the most adaptive in the child's particular society, as is the child's general capacity to follow them.

The child's capacity to follow such alternate developmental pathways (i.e., to learn different styles of interaction as well as substantive cultural content) may be a long-term adaptive consequence of natural selection for retarded development because such a capacity would seem to be a prerequisite for culture. Thus, from an evolutionary perspective, the neurobiological mechanisms underlying developmental plasticity (the capacity to follow a variety of developmental pathways) became important biological bases for learning culture. With the evolution of these neurobiological mechanisms and their effects there would be a marked increase in nongenetic inheritance—the preservation of successful responses to environmental perturbations through increasingly complex social-cultural and linguistic means. In this view of behavioral evolution, the hominid infant might be thought of as increasingly "hard-wired" by natural selection (especially its K-selection mode) to be "sensitive," "responsive," or "affected by" enduring aspects of his early environment to which he cannot respond, that is, those aspects of his early environment which he cannot "affect" or "influence" by his own behavior (either directly or through others). The ultimate reason that differences in enduring patterns of early cosocialization have such apparent long-term developmental effects may thus be that there was natural selection for a sensitivity or responsiveness to different numbers and age/sex/kinship identities of others. This is because the child could not affect or influence these numbers or identities and because this sensitivity-responsiveness made it *possible* for children to be socialized to fit the enormous variety of adult behavior patterns which throughout hominid evolution have been established by the vagaries of human ecology, economy, history, and all the other determinants of cultural diversity. The *K*-selected and neotenous neurobiological mechanisms underlying the infant's capacity to be socialized in a variety of ways, to follow a variety of developmental pathways, would also have had unique adaptive consequences with the increasing speed of cultural evolution. The behavioral flexibility of adult humans has resulted, especially in the last 10,000 years, in a velocity of culture change that rapidly altered developmental environments and would have greatly increased the adaptive value of infants' capacities to follow any of a wide variety of developmental paths. The sensitivity of infants to different patterns of early cosocialization would mean that they could develop normally almost regardless of the development environment created by adult subsistence activities, work loads, patterns of the sexual division of labor, residence patterns, child-care practices, and so forth. Further, since these institutions actually are the more-or-less successful responses of the adults to their environment, these institutions also function to help preserve these responses in their developing children.

In the midst of all this diversity in developmental environments, however, all hominid infants have also always had certain biologically essential developmental tasks that could not be interfered with. Primary among these tasks has been the one of forming attachment bonds to mothers or their substitutes. The manifest capacity of human infants to be socialized in a variety of ways is not so great that normal development can be achieved without some minimum quantity and quality of "mothering" behavior. If the infant is not a passive *tabula rasa,* and if the infant has any influence on his social environment, then we might expect infants to maximize the quality of their interactions with others so as to better ensure the formation of these attachment bonds. Natural selection for behavioral-developmental plasticity might better enable the infant to form attachments under a wide variety of the many circumstances that affect the amount and quality of mother–infant interaction, including such things as use of the cradleboard.

What may be most important to the infant, as attachment theory suggests, is the general quality of mutual responsiveness in his interactions with others, but what may need more systematic attention is the possible relationship between the quality of the infant's interactions with others and the opportunity for any interaction at all with specific numbers and particular identities of others besides mother. By conducting most of their research on European and white American middle-class families, attachment theorists may have somewhat neglected an important source of variation in patterns of interaction, and more important, may therefore have missed the possibility that these variations are adaptive in the particular environments where they are found. Because isolated mother–infant pairs have likely been the exception rather than the rule throughout human evolution, definitions of "normal" attachment on the basis of their behaviors toward each other might be misleading, even more so if these researchers assume that the nuclear family child's previous experience with others is either constant or irrelevant. My data on Navajo and Anglo patterns of mother–infant interaction, for example, suggest a relationship between more intense interaction and fewer opportunities for interaction with others besides mother, both within the Navajo sample and between the two samples. The generally longer and more intense Anglo mother–infant interaction might be adaptive in the sense that because these mothers and infants have only each other as interactive partners for the most of the day, their interaction becomes the only means by which the infant may affect or influence his environment and the only means by which the mother may invest care and attention in her child. Among the Navajo, on the other hand, the slower and less intense nature of mother–infant interaction might be a function of the fact that greater proximity and access to others besides mother is adaptive because of the way that quiet and relaxed interactions with a number of others is a good strategy for eliciting (and bestowing) care and attention in a relatively dense and crowded environment where the state and behavior of one individual has an impact on several others at once.

By focusing so much attention on *how* mother and infant influence each other attachment theorists may have neglected the crucial question of *why* they influence each other so much. By focusing on mother–infant interaction as something of a closed system in which earlier mother or infant behaviors affect later patterns of interaction, attachment research may have been looking at the means of adaptation or the results of adaptation, but may have overlooked just what it was that the mother and/or infant were adapting to. Certainly they adapt to each other, and certainly early responses may directly cause later responses, but my data suggest generally that a major influence on how mother and infant behave toward each other may be the mother's and the infant's opportunity for interaction with others. Understanding the relationships between their patterns of interaction and the determinants of these opportunities may make it possible to specify patterns of interaction that are *adaptive* in particular social and physical environments rather than vaguely "normal," "abnormal," "secure," or "anxious." Understanding the broader social context in which particular patterns of mother–infant interaction occur might also begin to outline the developmental pathways whereby cultural differences arise from an original similarity in the capacities by which infants respond to particular perturbations and conditions in their developmental environments. If there is a systematic relationship between aspects of mother–infant interaction and the child's opportunity for interaction with different numbers and age/sex/

kinship identities of others, this might, for example, provide a framework for relating infants' strategies for eliciting parental investment from others (parents or not) to larger social-cultural factors like subsistence activities, work loads, patterns of the sexual division of labor, and residence patterns, which my data showed was a significant correlate of many differences in the environment of mother–infant interaction and their interactive patterns as well.

My data on the effects of differences in early cosocialization agree in general form with the conclusions of the Whitings and their colleagues about the effects of behavioral styles learned in the enduring social contexts encountered during development. There is, however, another body of data from a very different kind of research that also suggests long-term behavioral effects according to differences in patterns of early cosocialization, and these data may provide some additional insight into why infants should be sensitive or responsive to at least some aspects of differences in these early cosocialization patterns.

The data to which I refer are the accumulating reports and analyses of incest avoidance in humans as a direct result of the early cosocialization of boys and girls regardless of their genetic relatedness. Spiro (1954), Talmon (1964), and Shepher (1971), for example, working in Israeli kibbutzim where all children are reared together in communal nurseries and dormitories from birth on, and where there is actually an ideal of kibbutz endogamy, found in their combined samples of over 3000 marriages not one (and little or no evidence of mating) between adults who had been cosocialized from the newborn period to age six. Wolf (1966, 1968, 1970) has provided exactly parallel data from Taiwan, where there exist two forms of marriage. In the more prestigious major form, a woman joins her husband as an adult; in the minor form, she joins her future husband's family when both she and her future husband are small children, usually under 1 year old. Though jurally unrelated, the future couple are raised as brother and sister until they marry years later (often only after more than a little pressure from their parents). Wolf's ethnographic and census data clearly indicate that marriages between adults raised as brother and sister suffer from significantly more divorce, more adultery, fewer children, and a greater incidence of a variety of marital difficulties.

In addition to these studies of human incest avoidance, there are studies showing similar patterns of incest avoidance after early cosocialization in a number of nonhuman primate species (e.g., Demarest, 1977) and other mammalian species (e.g., Bischof, 1975a). The mechanisms underlying incest avoidance caused by cosocialization are not known, but Demarest (1977) has outlined a neurophysiological model for the socialization of incest avoidance that includes the developmental effects of differences in the intensity of early experience on brain centers known to be involved in the control of attention, fear-aggression, and sex. In this light, Fox's (1980) recent discussion of incest avoidance is especially intriguing. Analyzing several additional ethnographic reports relating to incest avoidance as a function of early cosocialization patterns, Fox suggests that cosocialization per se may be something of a "packaged" variable and that considerations of the *style* or quality of interaction during cosocialization may lead to more refined predictions about later incest avoidance behavior. He notes that intense physical interaction (e.g., rough and tumble play) between boys and girls being reared together may more often lead to their later positive aversion toward sex, but that simple physical proximity coupled with prohibitions on intense physical play may actually lead to a later desire for sex. He notes further that incest prohibitions should be lax in societies permitting intense physical interaction between cosocialized boys and girls but that these prohibitions should be stronger in societies that prevent such intense physical interaction. Thus, along with those factors that determine the composition of early cosocialization groups, cultural attitudes and beliefs about juvenile play and sexuality may also influence later incest-avoidance behavior.

The selective advantage of the infant's capacity to have his choice of adult sexual partner limited by his patterns of early cosocialization is that this form of learning would tend to prevent the genetic problems associated with close inbreeding (see Bischof, 1975a and Demarest, 1977 for discussions of these problems). Early cosocialization seems to serve as an idiom of genetic relatedness in a very wide range of species, including humans, because in the vast majority of cases individuals that are reared together from infancy will in fact be close genetic relatives. As Fox puts it, "nature assumes a certain learning environment in order that the avoidance can indeed be learned" (1980:19).

This material on incest avoidance as a function of early cosocialization has an important implication for sociobiological studies (or those by any other name) which seek to describe the phylogenetic and ontogenetic interaction of nature and culture. A major issue in the continuing debate over the usefulness with which sociobiological principles may be applied to analyses of human social behavior is just how kin selective and altruistic humans may be. One problem is that for every case in which close biological relatives behave altruistically to each other, there seems to be another case in which they do not and still another in which individuals behave altruistically to others with whom they share only that fraction of genes that all humans share. Another problem is that it seems very doubtful that natural selection could store enough high quality information in the genotype to enable individuals to reckon coefficients of relatedness with anywhere near the accuracy implied in many sociobiological models. The answer of most sociobiologists, of course, is that there is no need to postulate such a "kin-recognition gene," that kin recognition need only be probabilistic, and that cosocialization serves as a perfectly adequate kin-recognition mechanism. This being so, sociobiological studies of kin selection in humans might do well to relate the altruistic behaviors of adults not only to biological kinship and social kinship, but also to patterns of early cosocialization. To my knowledge, no such "developmental sociobiological" studies have been conducted, but if cosocialization is indeed one kin-recognition mechanism, as it appears to be for incest avoidance, the "felt kinship" arising from early cosocialization might be a better predictor of altruism than either biological or social kinship. On the other hand, it might not, or not always, and the behavioral and emotional plasticity of humans might render the application of sociobiological principles to human social behavior very complex indeed, for it seems possible that under certain circumstances the human capacity to become emotionally attached to cognitive categories might "fool" the cosocialization kin-recognition mechanism into believing that an individual was kin simply because he belonged to a kinship category that also included cosocialized real kin.

In sum, this material on incest avoidance after early cosocialization is exactly analogous to my own conclusions about the effects of differences in children's opportunities for interaction with others besides mother and the conclusions of the Whitings' and their colleagues about the effects of behavioral styles learned in the social settings that occupy most of a child's time during development. Despite very great differences in theoretical orientations, research problems, methods, and samples, all of these various studies indicate that infants and small children are sensitive or responsive to differences in the social context of early cosocialization groups and that the effects of these early differences are significant and long lasting. I argued above that the capacity of the infant to embark on different developmental paths according to these differences in early cosocialization would be adaptive because this capacity made it possible for hominid infants to be socialized to fit any of the highly variable and rapidly changing adult behavior patterns which are so largely determined by the large-scale ecological, economic, and historical factors that in turn so largely determine the patterns of early cosocialization. In the same vein, the capacity of the child to learn incest avoidance as a result of early cosocialization would be adaptive in the way it provides a workable mechanism for avoiding the genetic problems of close inbreeding. In other words, developmental plasticity is put to good evolutionary use through the epigenetic rule which specifies that the infant human should be capable of developing in a number of different ways depending on the nature of the social group in which he finds himself.

Similar kinds of arguments have recently been made by Draper and
Harpending (1982).

Temperament and Values

Despite wide differences in theoretical orientation and method, there exist
three bodies of research on aspects of Navajo culture or behavior that have
reached conclusions tantalizing in their otherwise unexpected similarity. In
pointing out these similarities and discussing them in terms of my arguments
about developmental plasticity I hope to accomplish three purposes. The
first is the simple one of tying together some loose threads of data and theory
left dangling until now. The second is to relate some of my conclusions
about Navajo child development more explicitly to Navajo culture, especially to a set of beliefs and values about behavior derived from emic
research with the Navajo. My most general purpose, however, is to outline
one way in which behavior and meaning might be related in an evolutionary
context, that is, how successful responses to environmental perturbations
may be preserved in culture and in the infant's capacity to readily learn
behavior patterns prescribed by certain cultural beliefs and values.

The first of these three bodies of research includes those highly objective
etic studies which have shown that Navajo infants (and Mongoloid or
Oriental gene pool infants in general) are quieter and less irritable than
Anglo (Caucasian) infants at birth and perhaps for some time during development. The second body of research, only hinted at thus far with
mention of the Navajo concept *nila,* includes those studies which emphasize Navajo cultural values about freedom of choice, the inviolability of the
individual, and prohibitions about imposing one's will on others. For simple
ease of expression I am going to speak of the common denominator of these
studies as consistent reports of Navajo "nonintrusiveness." The third body of
research includes those studies, also conducted from an etic, outside
observer's point of view, which emphasize anxiety, depression, withdrawal,
shyness, and reserve among Navajo adults. It is obviously difficult to make
comparisons among such radically different kinds of data, but with a
developmental perspective on the interaction of biology and culture I
believe that their interrelationships may be profitably explored.

While the concept of temperament, and especially its measurement, need
a great deal of refinement, a number of studies suggest that placidity, low
levels of irritabiliity, and nonintrusiveness may be especially characteristic
of Oriental peoples. Freedman's gene pool differences explanation of
Navajo–Anglo differences in neonatal irritability rests entirely on the fact
that Chinese, Japanese, and Navajo infants all showed more quietness and
less irritability at birth than Anglo infants. For Freedman this is a priori

evidence of genetic influences on neonatal behavioral differences, because Chinese, Japanese, and Navajo people are known to be genetically more closely related to each other than to any Caucasian group. While my data on Navajo–Anglo neonatal behavioral differences agree with those of Freedman in all important respects, of course, they do not support his specific gene pool differences explanation. It should be stressed here, however, that there is nothing in the concept of temperament that requires any simple genetic explanation of temperamental differences; temperament refers only to an individual's habitual way of responding to stimuli, and the nature-nurture issue is as complex in temperament research as it is anywhere else.

Besides Freedman's work, however, there is additional evidence for the existence of an "Oriental temperament." Wolff (1977) has documented group differences in autonomic nervous system responsivity between Oriental (Chinese, Taiwanese, Vietnamese, Japanese, Korean, and Native Americans) and Caucasoid subjects. Specifically, he reports that Oriental infants and adults both exhibit significantly greater and faster vasomotor responsivity (skin flushing) to small amounts of alcohol than do Caucasian infants and adults. (Wolff presents convincing arguments showing the "absurdity" of any claims that these genetic differences in autonomic responsivity are directly related to group differences in alcoholism rates.) While his data reveal clear Oriental-Caucasian group differences in one aspect of physiological functioning, he also notes that his observations of *greater* autonomic responsivity in Oriental infants and adults are not entirely consistent with Freedman's reports of greater quietness and lower levels of irritability in the neonatal behavior of Oriental infants. The problem, of course, is the biobehavioral one that plagues all temperament research: mechanisms. The relationship between autonomic function and behavior in the neonate is not well known.

Kagan and his colleagues (Kagan, Kearsley, and Zelazo, 1980), however, provide data that may be consistent with both Wolff's data on greater autonomic responsivity in Oriental peoples and Freedman's data on Oriental infants' lower levels of irritability or intrusiveness. In a longitudinal (3½ to 29 months of age) comparison of the effects of day care versus home care on child development, Kagan and his associates tested a sample of 53 Chinese and 63 Caucasian children in Boston. While they found essentially no effects of day care versus home care on behavior or development, they did find significant and consistent Chinese–Caucasian group differences. These differences are best summarized in the author's words:

> The Chinese children, both day care and home control, were less vocal, less active, less likely to smile to many, but not all, of the laboratory episodes, and were more apprehensive in the social and separation situations. The Chinese children were quieter, stayed closer to the mother, played less when they were with unfamiliar

children or adults, and cried more often following maternal departure. Finally, the
Chinese consistently showed more stable heart rates during the laboratory episodes.
This cluster of qualities implies a disposition toward inhibition among Chinese
children, a disposition that may have a partially biological basis (Kagan, Kearsley,
and Zelazo, 1980:268).

Kagan and his associates speculate that a likely explanation of this
"disposition toward inhibition" is that the autonomic arousal that accom-
panies apprehension and inhibition is not necessarily greater in Chinese
children, but that it persists longer. They suggest that behavioral inhibition is
mediated by physiological systems activated by perception of the unfamiliar, and argue that

> If it is true that this physiological feedback persists longer in the Chinese than the
> Caucasians, their behavioral inhibition should persist for a longer period of time. The
> more stable heart rates of the Chinese children could be regarded as supportive of
> this idea, for under conditions of continued vigilance adults tend to maintain a steady
> heart rate with low variability for a long period of time (Kagan, Kearsley, and Zelazo,
> 1980:271–272).

Some additional support for this hypothesis about the greater persistence of
autonomic arousal in Oriental peoples comes from research on Japanese-
white American differences in electrodermal activity. Both Lazarus et al.
(1966) and Crider et al. (1966) report that in their experimental situations
Japanese subjects maintained high levels of skin conductance longer than
white American subjects, and Lazarus et al. note that the "Japanese subjects,
both young and old, were much more apprehensive about the total experimental situation" (1966:631). Neither research team rules out genetic
causes of these differences, but both favor an explanation in terms of
Japanese culture and standards of behavior.

Kagan and his colleagues conclude that there is an "inborn disposition"
toward wariness and inhibition in Chinese children, at least toward the class
of stimuli presented in their laboratory. They do not conclude, however, that
experience cannot alter this disposition, ". . . only that the Chinese infant
initially displays a behavior profile to his caretakers and to other children
that is likely to elicit reactions that strengthen rather than transform the
original disposition" (Kagan, Kearsley, and Zelazo, 1980:272). The conclusions of Kagan and his colleagues are consistent with Wolff's conclusions
in that both studies indicate Oriental–Caucasian group differences in autonomic responsivity, which Kagan et al. relate, at least tentatively, to group
differences in behavior. And their conclusions are entirely consistent with
those of Freedman because both studies demonstrate greater inhibition,
greater placidity, and less intrusiveness in Oriental than Caucasian infants.

Another set of studies that are central to any discussion of Oriental–
Caucasian infant temperament differences are those carried out by Caudill

and his colleagues in Japan and the United States (Caudill, 1972; Caudill and Frost, 1973; Caudill and Schooler, 1973; Caudill and Weinstein, 1969). Comparing mother–infant interaction in the two countries, they report Japanese–Caucasian behavioral differences that precisely mirror the differences discussed above: Japanese infants cried and vocalized less than the Caucasian infants and the Caucasian infants were more motorically active than the Japanese infants. In addition they report that Caucasian mothers provided more stimulation to their infants, especially verbally, while the Japanese mothers spent more time in body contact with their infants and provided them with more soothing and quieting kinds of stimulation like lulling and rocking.

Throughout their work Caudill and his co-workers stress that conscious and unconscious socialization goals and values of caretakers will affect the behavior of even very young infants, and they state that by 3 or 4 months the infants in their samples had learned "to be Japanese and American babies in relation to the expectation of their mothers concerning their behavior" (Caudill and Weinstein, 1969:39). Admitting that they cannot rule out inborn temperamental differences as a cause of their observed group differences, they nonetheless report that mothers and infants of recent Japanese descent living in the United States showed interactive behavior patterns more similar to those of Anglo-American mothers and infants than to those of Japanese mothers and infants living in Japan. Specifically, the Japanese mothers living in the United States verbalized to their infants *more* than did Anglo-American mothers, and their infants engaged in more "happy vocalizing" in return (Caudill and Frost, 1973).

The overall conclusion reached by Caudill and his colleagues is that Japanese and American infants respond to their mothers' conscious and unconscious socialization goals and values and that Japanese and American mothers have different goals and values. As Super put it in a recent review:

> One of the Japanese mother's goals is to help her infant become integrated into the fabric of social life in the family and, by anticipation, in the larger society. She therefore encourages a close and solicitous relationship with the purpose of rearing a passive and contented baby. In contrast, the American mother bears in mind the need to assist her infant's emerging independence, to facilitate individual activity, assertiveness, and self-direction (Super, 1981:230).

The evidence for general Oriental–Caucasian differences in infant temperament is thus strikingly consistent. It is unacceptable to argue, however, that even these consistent Oriental–Caucasian differences constitute evidence for simple gene pool differences in temperament. As I stressed in Chapter V, group differences in behavior may be observed because of simple group differences in the distribution of nongenetic factors causing indivdual differences. Further, even when genetic factors are implicated in behavior, their effect may vary from group to group because such genetic influences are unlikely to be static but very likely to develop along complex epigenetic pathways which do not exclude significant environmental input—and not just from the moment of birth, but from the moment of conception.

Indeed, the long-term evolutionary significance of hominid developmental plasticity lies in the very capacity of the infant (and perhaps also the fetus) to embark on that developmental pathway which is most appropriate in his or her social-cultural environment. There *is* a genetic basis for temperament, just as there is a genetic basis for any and all aspects of the phenotype, but even if there is a very direct and significant genetic basis for population differences in infants' "inborn dispositions toward inhibition" this manifestly only provides the basis for differences in infants' readiness to learn, while the proximal cause of the developmental path they take will be the nature of their social-cultural environments. Caudill's sample of Japanese mothers and infants living in the United States behaved more like Anglo–American mothers and infants than they did like Japanese mothers and infants living in Japan. Even if we postulate that it is easier for Oriental infants to learn nonintrusive, placid, and quiet behavioral styles in Japan because of some "inborn disposition toward inhibition," and thus harder to learn the more intrusive and less placid Anglo–American style of behavioral interaction in this country, these infants nonetheless appear to have done so.

Clearly there are limits to develomental plasticity. The human infant cannot develop normally along just any pathway, and it is entirely probable that there are "inborn dispositions" in the infants of various populations that incline them to develop along a certain range of developmental pathways. Given the worldwide and historical variability in developmental environments however, even within large racial groups, it is difficult to imagine the selection pressures that could make these inborn dispositions either very specific or very determining of adult behavior styles. Racial differences in anatomy and physiology are well-documented, and there is no reason to believe that these differences in the infant could not affect newborn behavior and patterns of development. It is something entirely different to say that the neonatal behavioral-temperamental differences were *themselves* specifically selected for. In spite of all the evidence that the infant can and does affect the behavior of his caretakers, it is also difficult to imagine that the infants of any particular racial group, simply because of their inborn dispositions, could significantly affect interactive behavior styles or beliefs and values about what constitutes appropriate behavior. Infants do affect the behavior of adults, but the behavior of adults is more broadly affected by their particular ecology, economy, and history. The behavior of adults toward their children is also affected very immediately by their perceptions of the environment in which their children will be developing, as the behavior of the Japanese mothers in Caudill's American sample demonstrates. The *capacity* of their infants to embark on the new Anglo–American kind of developmental path is what would be adaptive in their new American environment, regardless of what their inborn dispositions might otherwise "prefer."

Thus, while the evidence for Oriental–Caucasian group differences in "inborn dispositions" is fairly good, the evidence for their developmental significance remains obscure. Not only does an evolutionary perspective on development lead us to expect developmental plasticity (the capacity to embark on a wide variety of developmental pathways), longitudinal studies of early temperamental differences have generally failed to reveal convincing continuities (Kagan, 1975; Rutter et al., 1964; Rutter, Korn, and Birch, 1963; Rutter, 1970; Sameroff, 1975; Sameroff and Chandler, 1975; Sameroff et al., 1982). In their study of the longitudinal effects of day care versus home care, Kagan and his colleagues conclude that "the available information indicates either that the obvious variation among infants during their first year is of no future consequence or that the threads of continuity are few in number and extremely subtle" (Kagan, Kearsley, and Zelazo, 1980:274). With reference to the specific Chinese–Caucasian differences in early "inborn disposition toward inhibition," they conclude that

> The Chinese children, as a group, remained more inhibited than the Caucasians, as a group, over the period from twelve to twenty months. This fact implies that conditions in the homes of both the Chinese and the Caucasian families were more stable than the qualities of individual children, for within each ethnic group there was considerable individual change over time. The conditions of rearing in both Chinese and Caucasian homes appeared to impose specific behavioral profiles on children although each child remained receptive to some change (Kagan, Kearsley, and Zelazo, 1980:278).

This brings us to the question of what "conditions of rearing" in Navajo homes might help to maintain the newborn Navajo infant's originally greater quietness and low levels of irritability. One such condition has already been mentioned: my data on Navajo and Anglo patterns of mother–infant interaction indicate a relationship between the intensity of interaction between mother and child and the child's opportunity for interaction with others besides mother, that is, the fewer the opportunities, the more intense the interaction, and the Navajo children had significantly more opportunities for interaction with others than the Anglo children.

There is, however, another most pervasive "condition of rearing" among the Navajo which may be even more powerful in the maintenance of non-intrusive behavior patterns in Navajo children. This condition is a fundamental dimension of Navajo beliefs and values about interpersonal behavior that is, in its own way, precisely analogous to the beliefs of Caudill's Japanese mothers (in Japan) that "interdependence and reliance on others" is a more appropriate behavioral style than the American goal of "independence and self-assertion," and that therefore the infant must early on "be drawn into increasingly interdependent relations with others" (Caudill and Weinstein, 1969:15). Or, as Super put it, the Japanese mothers encourage a "close and solicitous relationship" with their infants "with the purpose of rearing a passive and contented baby" (Super, 1981:230). The parallel Navajo belief about appropriate behavior is best approached through analyses of the Navajo concepts *nila* and *t'áá bee bóholníih*. *Nila* ("it's up to you") and *t'áá bee bóholníih* ("it's up to him to decide" or "it's his business) are Navajo phrases that one hears continuously in the context of decision making, especially group decision making about cooperative activities and especially when one person asks another about a particular course of action that should be taken. The essence of their meaning is that one should not impose one's will on others, that one cannot make unilateral decisions that are binding on others, that the individual is inviolable, and that "everyone is their own boss." As Lamphere puts it, "the phrase *t'áá bee bóholníih* combines Navajo emphasis on both autonomy and consensus, and it entails egalitarian rather than hierarchical authority relations" (Lamphere, 1977:41).

In her penetrating analysis of Navajo concepts of cooperation and autonomy, two aspects of human social behavior that to Anglos are in potential conflict, Lamphere (1977) begins by noting that cooperation (interdependence) is consistently revealed as one of the most explicit and powerful of Navajo values on behavior. She cites Ladd's (1957:253–255) enumeration of behavioral prescriptions in Navajo ethics:

1. Take care of your possessions.
2. You ought to take good care of your children.
3. Children should take care of their parents.
4. In general, people ought to help the aged.
5. One ought to help a person who is in dire need.
6. There are other people whom it is particularly important to help; one's wife and her family.
7. In general, you ought to help anybody who needs it or requests it.

Lamphere also cites the work of Keith (1964:32) who arrived at a similar listing of Navajo prescriptions for cooperative behavior:

1. Work hard.
2. Be generous.
3. Don't be mean.
4. Don't laugh too loud.

5. Be helpful.
6. Be happy and cheerful.
7. Be gentle with children.
8. Be dependable.
9. Be respectful.
10. Be kind.

From her own fieldwork, Lamphere (1977:37) lists Navajo behavioral proscriptions which describe their view of uncooperative behavior:

1. One is not stingy.
2. One is not mean.
3. One is not mad.
4. One is not envious or jealous of someone's possessions.
5. One is not sexually jealous.
6. One is not lazy.

Opposed (in the Anglo view) to these generalized obligations to be cooperative are equally strong values on individual autonomy. Lamphere argues that the Navajo concept *t'áá bee bóholnííh* actually "fuses" these values on cooperation and autonomy. First, the phrase describes the individual's exclusive rights over the use and disposal of property. If the owner of a piece of property is not available and the would-be borrower asks even a close relative of the owner, the relative will likely respond *t'áá bee bóholnííh,* ("it's up to him") which suffices as an answer because of the implication that the would-be borrower must ask the owner himself; no one has the right to dispose of another's property. Second, this phrase also describes the individual's exclusive rights over his own time, energy, and action. Lamphere notes that Navajo people rarely make direct requests for aid or generosity but prefer to wait for another person to notice their need and, following the generalized obligation to be cooperative and helpful, to make a spontaneous offer. This recognizes the inviolability of the other individual and preserves his decision rights over his own actions. She notes further that there are reflections of this value on autonomy and individual decision rights in the Navajo language itself:

> Sentences such as "I made the horse trot" or "I made my wife sing," can be rendered in Navajo only by "I made the horse trot, even though he did not want to do so," and "Even though she did not want to do so, she sang when I told her to do so." Where the subject is an agent causing an action to be performed by another agent, the latter's will or desire must be considered (Lamphere, 1977:39).

In the same vein, Lamphere also notes that most Navajo people are unwilling to violate another person's autonomy by presuming to speak for them, for instance by telling a third person what the other person thinks or feels about a particular topic.

The first two uses of t'áá bee bóholníih emphasize the individual's autonomy, and so does the third, but the third also shows how consensus and
cooperative group action can be achieved without violating the autonomy
of others. Lamphere cites a number of examples (of which two will suffice)
in which consensus and cooperation were reached through judicious use of
the phrase t'áá bee bóholníih:

> As one young Navajo woman said, in discussing the possibility of a second marriage,
> "If somebody wants to get married with me, I'd say shimá bóholníih or shizhé'é
> bóholníih (It's up to my mother or my father to decide). Making such a statement
> implies both the girl's own willingness and the necessity of asking her parents. If she
> had no interest in the marriage, she would discourage the suitor immediately
> (Lamphere, 1977:40).
>
> If someone comes to the chapter secretary asking to be placed on a list of workers for
> the next Tribal Works Project, the secretary may say, Ńleí bóholníih 'áájí bidiní (That
> one, he is the boss, ask him), referring to the chapter president. Upon asking the
> president, the individual will be given the same answer and sent back to the secretary
> or to the vice-president. This seems like the proverbial run-around, but if all three
> officers indicate agreement, the name will be added to the list. In other words, the
> individual will be sent back and forth until it is clear that none of the officers object
> and consensus is reached (Lamphere, 1977:40).

Thus there is no inherent or necessary conflict between a high valuation of
mutual cooperativeness or interdependence and an equally high valuation
of individual autonomy. Potential conflicts can be circumvented by striving
for consensus, for while it is always up to the individual, each individual's
autonomy is preserved through individual valuation of cooperation and
through consensus decision making.

Two others who have commented specifically on Navajo individualism or
autonomy and nonintrusiveness are McAllester (1954) and Witherspoon
(1975, 1977). McAllester notes that in Navajo group singing there is no
recognized leader and that it is considered appropriate for each singer to
sing in his own way. He also notes that among the Navajo there is a culturally stereotyped "silencing sound" that "in the case of children . . . was
usually timed so as to forestall any noise or exhibitionism . . ." (1954:78).
And in the conclusion to his description and analysis of Navajo epis-
temology, Witherspoon states:

> Navajos attempt to keep their emotions under control and seldom verbalize intense
> emotions of either love or hate, kindness or anger. Navajo emotional life proceeds in
> a low key and at a slow pace. Even the tremendous emphasis on humor leads only to
> restrained, never boisterous, laughter. This emphasis on moderation is also exhibited
> in Navajo speech patterns which are not characterized by the superlatives to which
> many Americans are accustomed (Witherspoon, 1977:186).

Witherspoon suggests that all of this seems "designed to maintain and
enhance social order" (1977:188), and that "this cultural belief in, or an

emphasis upon, individualism is uniquely complemented by a belief in, or emphasis upon, communalism" (1975:95).

In an entirely different kind of analysis, but one which was also carried out from an internal observer's point of view, Basso (1979) arrives at a similar picture of Southern Athabascan beliefs and values about appropriate behavior in general, and the inviolability of the individual in particular. Although he is writing about the Western Apache, in my own experience what Basso says about them also holds for the Navajo (another Southern Athabascan group); elsewhere, Basso himself has said that in these respects the Navajo and Western Apache are "strikingly similar" (Basso, 1970; see also Chapter 2). The unique beauty and special value of Basso's internal observer's model of appropriate Western Apache behavior is that it is derived from the cultural symbols appearing in Western Apache "portraits of the Whiteman," which amount to a series of ethnic jokes about Anglos told by Apaches. Thus, the contrast between Western Apache beliefs and values about appropriate behavior and the typical behavior patterns of Anglo–Americans in the Southwest makes these Western Apache beliefs and values especially clear. The most prominent Western Apache belief about appropriate behavior that emerges from Basso's analysis of these "Anglo jokes" told by the Apache themselves is that of "nonintrusiveness." For example (Basso, 1979:51–60):

> . . . they are forcefully struck by the speech of Anglo-Americans, which is regularly described as being too fast, too loud, and too "tense" (ndóó; a commonly drawn analogy is with a muscle stretched to the point of pain).
>
> [quoting an Apache] Whitemen make lots of noise. With some who talk like that —loud and tight— it sounds too much like they mad at you. With some, you just can't be sure about it, so you just got to be careful about it, so you just got to be careful with them all the time.
>
> [quoting another Apache] Even it's something little—like they want you to close the door—even for something like that, some Whiteman talk like they bossing you around. It's like shooting rabbits with a .30-.30.
>
> Apaches agree that Anglo-Americans are inclined to ask too many questions and to repeat the same question (or minor variants of it) too many times. This gives them the appearance of being in a state of extreme hurry and aggravated agitation, which, besides being distinctly unattractive, sometimes causes them to lose sight of what Apaches take to be an obvious and important truth: carefully considered replies to questions are invariably more reliable (because less likely to be retracted or modified) than replies that have been rushed.
>
> To insist that [a] visitor come inside, to command him, is to overrule his right to do as he chooses, thereby implying that he is a person of little account whose wishes can be safely ignored. "When you talk to people like this," one of my consultants said, "you run over them. You make them feel small." To avoid such displays of disrespect, Apaches either refrain from issuing directives or construct them in ways so circumlocutional and oblique that they typically carry the force of observations rather than [orders].

> Backslapping and vigorous handshaking are regarded as direct and unwarranted encroachments upon the private territory of the self. . . . Prolonged eye contact, especially at close quarters, is typically interpreted as an act of aggression, a display of challenge and defiance . . . By Apache standards, Whitemen are entirely too probing with their eyes and hands, a distasteful tendency that Apaches take to be indicative of a weakly developed capacity for self-restraint and an insolent disregard for the physical integrity of others. As one of my consultants put it: "Whitemen touch each other like they were dogs."

> Whitemen lack self-awareness, a form of ignorance that blinds them to the effects their actions may have on other people.

> Whitemen lack circumspection and restraint, a shortcoming that leads them to behave with a kind of reckless self-centeredness that implies a basic disregard for the worth of other people.

> Whitemen lack tolerance and equanimity, a deficiency that causes them to make harsh and precipitate judgments of other people.

> Whitemen lack modesty and humility, a characteristic that causes them to adopt an attitude of imperiousness and condescension when dealing with other people.

> Whitemen lack an understanding of inadequacies inherent in their own forms of reasoning, a failing that leads them to assume that they know what is best for other people. In acting upon this assumption, they insult the intelligence of those they presume to advise.

> Whitemen fail to appreciate the encompassing virtue of actions that affirm the dignity of other people . . .

The picture that emerges from these studies of Navajo (or Southern Athabascan and perhaps Native American) beliefs and values about appropriate behavior is that cooperation and interdependence are simply and fundamentally necessary and good, but that the individual has exclusive rights over the use and disposal of his property, time, and action. The road to cooperation and interdependence must therefore be through the individual's own positive valuation of cooperation ("behave as if everyone was your relative") and through recognition of the individual's rights ("it's up to you"). The inviolability and inherent dignity of the individual are recognized in part by not imposing on the individual through loud or fast speech, "tense" speech, too many questions, commands, or invasion of personal space. The necessary research has not yet been done, but it would be surprising indeed to learn that Navajo caretakers did not modulate their own behavior toward their children according to these beliefs about appropriate behavior, or to learn that they did not encourage these kinds of behavior in their children. It is also true that even during the first year of life Navajo infants vocalize less than Anglo infants, have shorter and less intense interactions with their mothers, engage in less mutual gazing with their mothers, and have mothers who talk to them less and touch them less. The only apparent effects of these early differences is that one set of infants becomes more recognizably Navajo while the other becomes more recognizably

Anglo. This seems to be the entire evolutionary point behind infants' sensitivity to their early environment and their capacity to develop in different ways according to the nature of this early environment.

There is presently no evidence that early Oriental-Caucasian temperamental differences are themselves the product of specific selection pressures and no evidence that infants of one temperament have a greater inclusive fitness than those of the other. It is entirely possible that these early temperamental differences are an epiphenomenonal correlate of other racial/ethnic group differences in anatomy or physiology, but even this very direct genetic basis would seem to indicate no more than an "inborn disposition" which does not imply any narrow developmental path. There is also no evidence that these early temperamental differences can in any way make more likely the particular beliefs and values about appropriate behavior that help to guide (consciously or unconsciously) caretakers' behavior toward their children.

I think, then, that we are left with only two possible conclusions about why Navajo infants are quiet and nonirritable at birth and why Navajo beliefs and values about appropriate behavior emphasize cooperation and reserve, quietness, and nonintrusiveness. The first conclusion is that this apparent similarity is simply coincidence, or even that this similarity is more apparent than real and that we see it at all only because the "apple" has an orange tinge and the "orange" a reddish tinge, and because of our apparent need to see continuity in development. The second conclusion is speculative, but I think it is less speculative than the notion that the great variation in adult beliefs and values about behavior can be significantly influenced by the single dimension of irritability in newborn infants. Although it has not been demonstrated, low levels of irritability may well make it easier for infants to learn nonintrusive adult behavioral styles, but I find it difficult to believe that nonintrusive adult behavioral styles are derived from them in any direct way. If this were the case, the independent variable (levels of neonatal irritability), which has essentially only two values (high or low irritability), would somehow have to determine the dependent variable (adult behavior styles), which has innumerable values. The second conclusion, or better, hypothesis, is that adult behavior styles and beliefs and values about cooperation and reserve, quietness, and nonintrusiveness may influence the level of irritability shown by the newborn. In this case the independent variable has innumerable values while the dependent variable can take only a very few values. There is no need for me to emphasize the speculative nature of this hypothesis, but in Chapter 5 I showed that levels of irritability in newborn Navajo infants were related to their mothers' blood pressure during pregnancy, and I reviewed other studies showing similar blood pressure effects on irritability. I have no special faith that future research will show that it is maternal blood pressure itself, or by itself, that affects neonatal irritability, but in Chapter 5 I also reviewed a number of studies indicating in a general way that diet and psychosocial stress during pregnancy can affect the behavior of the neonate. I also suggested that epigenesis begins before birth and that natural selection might even favor the capacity for facultative adaptation *in utero*. Caution demands that I add the remaining possibility: that adult beliefs and values about behavior begin to influence the infant at first breath, but before the neonatal behavioral examinations are administered. I admit this possibility, but find it doubtful because of the evidence for Oriental-Caucasian neonatal behavioral differences that exist in spite of the range of differences in adult behavior and beliefs and values about behavior, as Freedman has shown. But neither do I believe that these early Oriental-Caucasian differences in behavior can have significant developmental continuity unless they are maintained by the environment in which they develop. And I know of no reason why this environment could not include the prenatal environment.

Turning back now to my discussion of Navajo beliefs and values about cooperation and autonomy, I want to make some additional points about the adaptive value of developmental plasticity and about the "conditions of rearing" which help the Navajo child maintain his early quietness and low levels of irritability. It is difficult to conclusively establish causal connections between a people's past and details of their present-day behavior and values, but, as outlined in Chapter 2, the conditions of Navajo history have been such that it cannot be surprising that the Navajo today value cooperation and individual autonomy. For perhaps as much as 500 years the Navajo lived under constant and great ecological, economic, and military/political pressures. I think it must be nearly impossible for most middle-class people in the industrial nations to grasp the encompassing necessity of cooperation for a band level, hunting-gathering society living under these conditions. The word "cooperation" itself can hardly do justice to the social and economic security that could be achieved only through joint action. At the same time, however, balancing a mixed hunting-gathering-herding-farming-raiding economy under these constant pressures demanded that each person have the right to exploit whatever resources were available, whenever and wherever they appeared, and until their release from prison camp at Ft. Sumner, the Navajo had not even the beginnings of a tribal government to limit their movement. The right of the individual to freedom of action would have been one way of ensuring the most effective harvesting of widely scattered and only intermittently available resources that might support only a few families for a short time. The high valuation of individual autonomy and cooperation might thus have provided individual Navajos with an emotional and philosophical basis for the more or less frequent movement, dissolution, and alliance of social groups of a variety of types, and for the sharing and redistribution of goods and services in spite of fluid and shifting patterns of social organizations (cf. Aberle, 1963). Rushforth (1982) has recently arrived at the same conclusion about the role of autonomy and cooperation among a Northern Athabascan group, the Bear Lake Indians. It is also true that the great majority of band level, hunting-gathering societies in Native North America, as well as throughout the world, have egalitarian political philosophies that emphasize cooperation and the necessity of consensus decision making.

On top of four or five centuries of economic stress and uncertainty the Navajo have suffered an equally long history of dangerous or discouraging relations with their various neighbors. On entering the Southwest they also entered a long period of raiding, and being raided by, the Pueblo Indians, the Ute and Paiute, the Spanish, and the Mexicans. With the coming of American power in 1848 this raiding escalated to virtual war in which the Navajo suffered complete military defeat and after which they were forcefully removed from their land and held in prison camp for 4 years. Since 1868 relations with Anglos have improved, but the past century of Navajo–Anglo relations has also been characterized by insensitivity, suspicion, and more than a little racial prejudice. With this history it is all too easy to understand why Anglo ethnographers and others observe that the Navajo suffer from a "high degree of tension," "morbid melancholia," and "endemic uneasiness." What they have described, however, from their outside observer's point of view, may be only the outward manifestation of Navajo beliefs and values about appropriate behavior to strangers, to outsiders, and perhaps especially to Anglos, who have been the historical source of much Navajo tension, melancholy, and unease. From the Navajo point of view not only does the interpersonal behavior of Anglos often seem to reflect a lack of regard for the dignity and autonomy of the individual, so also does the history of Navajo–Anglo group relations. Thus, if Navajo people often seem silent and reserved, or even melancholy and uneasy, around Anglos, it may be that they feel there are good reasons for such behavior. A relaxed quietness is appropriate behavior among familiars, and so too may it be among strangers and outsiders, but for understandable reasons many Navajos may find it difficult to relax among Anglos. At least in a historical sense, maintaining a certain level of wariness around Anglos has probably been appropriate and adaptive behavior.

In summary, it is worth requoting (Chapter 2) LeVine on the theme of child rearing as cultural adaptation:

> ... cultural evolution within human populations also produces standarized strategies of survival for infants and children, strategies reflecting environmental pressures from a more recent past, encoded in customs rather than genes and transmitted socially rather than biologically (LeVine, 1977:16).

Navajo beliefs and values about cooperation and autonomy would seem to constitute "survival strategies" under the special "environmental pressures" facing the Navajo for the past several hundred years. Instead of saying these "survival strategies" were "transmitted socially rather than biologically," however, LeVine might better have said they were "transmitted socially rather than genetically." The apparent opposition of "social" to "biological" tends to perpetuate the nature-culture dichotomy, and it is also true that the social transmission of beliefs and values *does* involve biology. Not only must beliefs and values be represented in particular neural structures, the human infant also has the genetic capacity to have these neural structures organized by experience. This is the entire point of natural selection for developmental plasticity: the infant's sensitivity or responsiveness to his developmental environment and his capacity thus to follow any of a wide range of developmental pathways, is what makes culture both possible in the first place and "easy to learn" in the second. It is too much to suppose that natural selection could endow Navajo infants with a high valuation on cooperation and individual autonomy, but natural selection does seem to have endowed all infants with the genetic capacity to learn the behavioral styles that are the expression of these values by their caretakers. Developmental plasticity provides for the nongenetic transmission or preservation of the parental generation's successful responses to the environmental perturbations that they have encountered, and is also, of course, why the highly K-selected and neotenous hominid line has been so successful. It does not matter for the process of adaptation *how* a successful response is preserved, only that it *is* preserved. Because social organizations and cultures can store information necessary for the successful response of any individual to the environmental perturbations that members of that culture have encountered in its history, natural selection would largely be for the elaboration and sophistication of infants' genetic capacities to quickly and easily learn the culture of the group into which it was born. This genetic capacity for culture is ultimately adaptive because it provides *Homo sapiens* with a most sensitive and flexible environmental tracking mechanism.

Epigenetics and Culture

All of this by no means implies that the human infant is a *tabula rasa*. We already know, for example, that normal development requires some degree of "warmth" and responsiveness in early infant-caretaker interactions. My data on the lack of long-term cradleboard effects on behavioral development also imply significant infant behavioral effects on caretakers, and thus the possibility of epigenetic control mechanisms. More generally, Hamburg (1963) has suggested a natural selective basis for human emotions and emotionality in the way that these emotions have helped motivate humans to learn what they have had to learn in order to survive and reproduce. Hamburg's argument foreshadows a more recent one by Ruyle (1973, 1977) who has suggested a selective advantage for hominid neurophysiological structures which provided for the perception of "satisfaction" when acts were performed that promoted survival and reproduction. As Ruyle says, "Square wheels, crooked spears, and sickly children are unlikely to provide much satisfaction" (Ruyle, 1977:54). Many others have discussed the likelihood of, and natural selective basis for, various "predispositions to learn" and cases of "prepared learning" in humans (e.g., Lumsden and Wilson, 1981; Durham, 1979; Draper and Harpending, 1982).

On the contrary, far from implying that the human infant is a *tabula rasa*, natural selection for developmental plasticity necessarily entails epigenetic rules of development. Epigenetic rules are regularities in the developmental interaction of genes and environment which establish particular developmental pathways leading to the most adaptive phenotype in a particular environment. Developmental plasticity is simply the genetic capacity to develop in a variety of ways according to these regularities. Thus, the relationship of the genotype to the phenotype is a developmental one, and questions about the relationship of nature to culture become questions about developmental process and how genes and environment may influence development. Lumsden and Wilson have argued that "Epigenetic rules are ultimately genetic in basis, in the sense that their particular nature depends on the DNA developmental blueprint" (1981:370). They are in one sense completely right, but in another, more important sense, they are only half right. They are completely right in the sense that there is an ultimate genetic basis for everything we are and do, but this is a truism. More importantly, they are only half right in the sense that some regularities in the developmental interaction of genes and environment that channel development along certain pathways may arise from regularities in the developmental environment itself. While we remain woefully ignorant of the details, there is now little doubt that the human genotype more-or-less narrowly prescribes the development of anatomical, physiological, emotional, cognitive, and behavioral patterns and capacities so that the optimum phenotype in any given environment is more likely to be achieved. As a result, there are universals of human behavior, universals of culture, universal response to similar problems, and some things are easy to learn and some things are hard to learn. However, regularities in the developmental environment itself may also tend to ensure that children in particular cultures embark on the developmental pathways which have the greatest chance of leading to the optimum phenotype. Durham (1979), who has also stressed this point, puts it this way:

> . . . where the natural selection theories of sociobiology have been right in their
> prediction or explanation of human behavior, it has often been for the wrong rea-
> sons. The apparent consistency between biological theory and human behavior
> suggests *not* that there is necessarily an underlying biological basis that guides,
> steers, controls, programs, predisposes, or inclines every human activity, but rather
> that the traditions and customs produced by cultural processes are often adaptive in
> the "biological sense" (Durham, 1979:41; original emphasis).

For example, even though it cannot now be demonstrated, I believe there can be no real doubt that during the past 500 years Navajo beliefs and values about cooperation and individual autonomy would tend to have been adaptive—"in the biological sense." Such beliefs and values would tend to increase inclusive fitness by decreasing conflict, anxiety, and uncertainty and promoting resource exploitation and the exchange and redistribution of goods and services in a highly mobile society with a fluid pattern of social organization. While other beliefs and values might also work as well, once these were established variant "belief-value phenotypes" would have less success. The human capacity to create and hold models of the world is a genetic capacity, and given its universality its development is likely to be highly resistant to environmental influences. The human capacity to establish and follow rules for behavior that are consistent with these models is also a genetic capacity, equally likely to be resistant to environmental influences. It is, however, the *content* of these models and rules that make them adaptive in any particular environment. Since natural selection operates on phenotypes and not on genotypes, and since there is no known way that the content of models and rules can be represented genotypically, whenever the content of these models and rules led to behavior that promoted survival and reproduction natural selection could only work to improve the capacity to formulate such models and for a greater readiness to learn them. The DNA developmental blueprint may limit the neural structures whereby these models and rules can be represented cognitively, and it may also lead to a predictability about some general features of their content insofar as it influences the development of human perceptual and emotional patterns, but in the end there is an "essential indeterminacy" in the relationship of the genotype to the phenotypical content of these models and rules. This indeterminacy, or developmental plasticity, tends to increase individual inclusive fitness because it provides for more efficient environmental tracking. And not only does this plasticity make culture possible, culture itself, coupled with the epigenetic rules of development, provides for the nongenetic transmission of information that preserves the adaptive potential of these models and rules in subsequent generations. If this information is also often irrelevant to individual inclusive fitness this only reflects the degree of behavioral plasticity that we have evolved and how this plasticity buffers us from much of our environment. On the other hand, if this information is sometimes actually detrimental to inclusive fitness, this may be the price we have to pay for the greater adaptability that this same plasticity gives us. No adaptation is ever perfect, and all adaptations represent a compromise between two or more selective pressures.

One implication of this view of the nature-culture problem as a problem of development is that the reasons for cultural differences in behavior, social organizations, beliefs, rules, and values are less likely to be found in the ultimate causes of behavior (the DNA template) than in the proximate causes of behavior (environmental and historical factors affecting development through the life span). In other words, there are good evolutionary biological reasons why the relationship between genotype and phenotype is not the same in *Homo sapiens* as it is in chimpanzees, greylag geese, scorpion flies, or *Drosophila*.

BIBLIOGRAPHY

Abbie, A. A. and J. Schroeder. 1961. Blood pressure in Arnhem Land Aborigines. *Medical Journal of Australia,* 2:493–496.

Aberle, D. F. 1961. Navaho. In D. M. Schneider and K. Gough (Eds.), *Matrilineal kinship.* Berkeley: University of California Press.

Aberle, D. F. 1963. Some sources of flexibility in Navaho social organization. *Southwestern Journal of Anthropology,* 19:1–18.

Adams, W. Y. 1963. *Shonto: A study of the role of the trader in a modern Navaho community. BAE Bulletin No. 188.* Washington: Smithsonian Institution.

Adams, W. Y. and L. T. Ruffing. 1977. Shonto revisited: measures of social and economic change in a Navajo community, 1955–1971. *American Anthropologist,* 79:58–83.

Ainsworth, M. D. S. 1967. *Infancy in Uganda: Infant care and the growth of love.* Baltimore: Johns Hopkins University Press.

Ainsworth, M. D. S. 1974. Infant–mother attachment and social development: "socialization" as a product of reciprocal responsiveness to signals. In M. P. M. Richards (Ed.), *The integration of a child into a social world.* Cambridge: Cambridge University Press.

Ainsworth, M. D. S. and B. Wittig. 1969. Attachment and exploratory behavior of one-year-olds in a strange situation. In B. M. Foss (Ed.), *Determinants of infant behavior,* Vol. 4. London: Methuen.

Ainsworth, M. D. S., S. M. V. Bell, and D. J. Stayton. 1971. Individual differences in strange-situation behavior of one-year-olds. In H. R. Schaffer (Ed.), *The origins of human social relations.* New York: Academic Press.

Ainsworth, M. D. S., M. C. Blehar, E. Waters, and S. Wall. 1978. *Patterns of attachment: A psychological study of the strange situation.* Hillsdale, N. J.: Lawrence Erlbaum Associates.

Aleksandrowicz, M. K. and G. Aleksandrowicz. 1974. The effect of pain-relieving drugs administered during labor and delivery on the behavior of the newborn: a review. *Merrill-Palmer Quarterly,* 20:121–141.

Alfred, B. M. 1970. Blood pressure changes among male Navajo migrants to an urban environment. *Canadian Review of Sociology and Anthropology,* 7(3):289–300.

Als, H. 1978. Assessing an assessment: conceptual considerations, methodological issues and a perspective on the future of the Neonatal Behavioral Assessment Scale. In A. Sameroff (Ed.), *Organization and stability of newborn behavior: A commentary on the Brazelton Neonatal Behavioral Assessment Scale. Monographs of the Society for Research in Child Development,* 34 (5–6):14–28.

Argyle, M. and M. Cook. 1976. *Gaze and mutual gaze.* Cambridge: Cambridge University Press.

Audy, J. R. 1971. Measurement and diagnosis of health. In P. Shepard and D. McKinley (Eds.), *Environ/Mental: Essays on the planet as a home.* Boston: Houghton Mifflin.

Bailey, F. 1950. Some sex beliefs and practices in a Navaho community. *Papers of the Peabody Museum,* 40(2). Cambridge, Mass.: Harvard University Press.

Bakow, H., A. J. Sameroff, P. Kelly, and M. Zax. 1973. Relation between newborn behaviors and mother–child interaction at 4 months. Paper presented at Biennial meeting of the Society for Research in Child Development, Philadelphia, March.

Barnes, F. 1975. Accidents in the first three years of life. *Child: Care, Health, and Development,* 1:421–433.

Barry, H. and L. M. Paxson. 1971. Infancy, and early childhood: cross-cultural codes 2. *Ethnology*, 10:466–508.

Barth, F. 1966. *Models of social organization*. Royal Anthropological Institute, Occasional Paper No. 23.

Basso, K. 1970. To give up on words: Silence in Western Apache culture. *Southwestern Journal of Anthropology*, 26(2):213–230.

Basso, K. 1979. *Portraits of the "Whiteman": Linguistic play and cultural symbols among the Western Apache*. New York: Cambridge University Press.

Bateson, P. P. G. 1976. Rules and reciprocity in behavioral development. In P. P. G. Bateson and R. A. Hinde (Eds.), *Growing points in ethology*. Cambridge: Cambridge University Press.

Bell, R. Q. 1968. A reinterpretation of the direction of effects in studies of socialization. *Psychological Review*, 75:81–95.

Bell, R. Q. 1971. Stimulus control of parent or caretaker behavior by offspring. *Developmental Psychology*, 4:63–72.

Bell, R. Q. 1974. Contributions of human infants to caregiving and social interaction. In M. Lewis and L. Rosenblum (Eds.), *The effect of the infant on its caregiver*. New York: Wiley.

Bell, R. Q., G. Weller, and M. Wldrop. 1971. Newborn and preschooler: Organization of behavior and relations between periods. *Monographs of the Society for Research in Child Development*, 36(142).

Bell, S. M. and M. D. S. Ainsworth. 1972. Infant crying and maternal responsiveness. *American Journal of Orthopsychiatry*, 19:342–350.

Benedict, Ruth. 1949. Child rearing in certain European countries. *American Journal of Orthopsychiatry*, 19:342–350.

Bernal, J. 1974. Attachment: some problems and possibilities. In M. P. M. Richards (Ed.), *The integration of a child into a social world*. Cambridge: Cambridge University Press.

Bingle, G. J. and J. D. Niswander. 1975. Polydactyly in the American Indian. *American Journal of Human Genetics*, 27(1):91–99.

Bischof, N. 1975a. Comparative ethology of incest avoidance. In R. Fox (Ed.), *Biosocial anthropology*. London: Malaby Press.

Bischof, N. 1975b. A systems approach toward the functional connections of attachment and fear. *Child Development*, 46(4):801–817.

Bloch, A. 1966. The Kurdistani cradle story: A modern analysis of this centuries-old infant swaddling practice. *Clinical Pediatrics*, 5:641–646.

Blurton Jones, N. G. 1967. An ethological study of some aspects of social behaviour of children in nursery school. In D. Morris (Ed.), *Primate ethology*. London: Weidenfeld and Nicolson.

Blurton Jones, N. G. 1972a. Comparative aspects of mother–child contact. In N. G. Blurton Jones (Ed.), *Ethological studies of child behaviour*. Cambridge: Cambridge University Press.

Blurton Jones, N. G. 1972b. Characteristics of ethological studies of human behaviour. In N. G. Blurton Jones (Ed.), *Ethological studies of child behaviour*. Cambridge: Cambridge University Press.

Blurton Jones, N. G. (Ed.) 1972c. *Ethological studies of child behaviour*. Cambridge: Cambridge University Press.

Blurton Jones, N. G. 1978. Natural selection and birthweight. *Annals of Human Biology*, 5(5):487–489.

Blurton Jones, N. G. and R. H. Woodson. 1979. Describing behavior: The ethologists' perspective. In M. Lamb, S. Suomi, and G. Stevenson (Eds.), *Social interaction analysis: Methodological issures*. Madison: University of Wisconsin Press.

Blurton Jones, N. G., R. H. Woodson, and J. S. Chisholm. 1979. Cross-cultural perspectives on the significance of social relationships in infancy. In R. Schaffer and J. Dunn (Eds.), *The first year of life*. London: Wiley.

Blurton Jones, N. G., J. S. Chisholm, M. F. Hall, and R. H. Woodson. nd. Behaviour catalogue. Unpublished manuscript.

Bowlby, J. 1965. *Child care and the growth of love*. (2nd ed.) Baltimore: Penguin Books.

Bowlby, J. 1969. *Attachment and loss*. Vol. I. *Attachment*. London: Hogarth Press.

Bowlby, J. 1973. *Attachment and loss*. Vol. II. *Separation*. London: Hogarth Press.

Bowlby, J. 1980. *Attachment and loss*. Vol. III. *Loss*. London: Hogarth Press.

Brackbill, Y. 1973. Continuous stimulation reduces arousal level: Stability of the effect over time. *Child Development*, 44(1):43–46.

Brazelton, T. B. 1973. *Neonatal Behavioral Assessment Scale*. London: Spastics International Medical Publications.

Brazelton, T. B. 1978. Introduction. In A. Sameroff (Ed.), *Organization and stability of newborn behavior: A commentary on the Brazelton Neonatal Behavior Assessment Scale. Monographs of the Society for Research in Child Development*, 43(5–6):1–13.

Brazelton, T. B., B. Kozlowski, and M. Main. 1974. The origins of reciprocity: The early mother–infant interaction. In M. Lewis and L. Rosenblum (Eds.), *The effect of the infant on its caregiver*. New York: Wiley.

Brazelton, T. B., B. Kozlowski, and E. Tronick. 1976a. Neonatal behavior among urban Zambians and Americans. *Journal of the American Academy of Child Psychiatry*, 15:97–107.

Brazelton, T. B., E. Tronick, S. Wise, H. Als, L. Adamson, and J. Scanlon. 1976b. The effects of regional obstetric anesthesia on newborn behavior over the first ten days of life. *Pediatrics* 58(1):94–100.

Brenner, C., K. Reisinger, and K. Rogers. 1974. Navajo infant mortality, 1970. *Public Health Reports*, 89(4): 353–359.

Bretherton, I. and M. D. S. Ainsworth. 1974. Responses of one-year-olds to a stranger in a strange situation. In M. Lewis and L. Rosenblum (Eds.), *The origins of fear*. New York: Wiley.

Brim, O. G. and J. Kagan (Eds.). 1980. *Constancy and change in human development*. Cambridge, Mass.: Harvard University Press.

Bronson, G. W. 1972. Infants' reactions to unfamiliar persons and novel objects. *Monographs of the Society for Research in Child Development*, 37(3).

Browne, J. C. M. and N. Veall. 1953. The maternal placental blood flow in normotensive and hypertensive women. *Journal of Obstetrics and Gynecology of the British Empire*, 60(2):141–147.

Burton, A. C. 1965. *Physiology and biophysics of the circulation*. Chicago: Year Book Medical Publishers.

Casley-Smith, W. W. 1958. Blood pressures in Australian Aborigines. *Medical Journal of Australia*, 1:627–633.

Caudill, W. 1972. Tiny dramas: Vocal communication between mother and infant in Japanese and American families. In W. P. Lebra (Ed.), *Transcultural research in mental health* (Vol. 2 of *Mental health research in asia and the pacific*). Honolulu:University of Hawaii Press.

Caudill, W. and L. A. Frost. 1973. A comparison of maternal care and infant behavior in Japanese-American, American, and Japanese families. In W. P. Lebra (Ed.), *Youth, socialization, and mental health* (Vol. 3 of *Mental health research in asia and the pacific*). Honolulu: University of Hawaii Press.

Caudill, W. and C. Schooler. 1973. Child behavior and child rearing in Japan and the United States: An interim report. *Journal of Nervous and Mental Diseases*, 157:323–338.

Caudill, W. and H. Weinstein. 1969. Maternal care and infant behavior in Japan and America. *Psychiatry*, 32:12–43.

Chance, M. R. A. 1962. An interpretation of some angonistic postures: The role of "cut-off" acts and postures. *Symposium of the Zoological Society of London*, 8:71–90.

Chisholm, J. S. 1981a. Residence patterns and the enviornment of mother-infant interaction among the Navajo. In T. Field, A. Sostek, P. Vietze, and P. H. Leiderman (Eds.), *Culture and early interactions*. Hillsdale, N. J.: Lawrence Erlbaum Associates.

Chisholm, J. S. 1981b. Prenatal influences on Aboriginal-White Australian differences in neonatal irritability. *Ethology and Sociobiology*, 2:67–73.

Chisholm, J. S. and M. P. M. Richards. 1978. Swaddling, cradleboards, and the development of children. *Early Human Development*, 2(3):255–275.

Chisholm, J. S., R. H. Woodson, and E. da Costa Woodson. 1978. Maternal blood pressure in pregnancy and newborn irritability. *Early Human Development*, 2(2):171–178.

Cohen, B. M. 1953. Arterial hypertension among Indians of the Southwest. *American Journal of Medical Science*, 225:505–513.

Coll, C., C. Seposki, and B. M. Lester. 1981. Cultural and biomedical correlates of neonatal behavior. *Developmental Psychobiology*, 14:147–154.

Collier, M. C. 1966. *Local organization among the Navajo*. New Haven: HRAFlex Books.

Connell, D. B. 1976. Individual differences in attachment: An investigation into stability, implications, and relationships to structure of early language development. Unpublished doctoral dissertation, Syracuse University.

Connolly, K. and P. J. Smith. 1972. Reactions of preschool children to a strange observer. In N. G. Blurton Jones (Ed.), *Ethological studies of child behaviour*. Cambridge: Cambridge University Press.

Cooper, E. S., A. J. Costello, J. W. B. Douglas, J. D. Ingleby, and R. K. Turner. 1974. Direct observation? *Bulletin of the British Psychological Association*, 27:3–7.

Cravioto, J., H. G. Birch, E. DeLicardie, L. Rosales, and L. Vega. 1969. The ecology of growth and development in a Mexican preindustrial community. *Monographs of the Society for Research in Child Development*, 34(129).

Crider, A., D. Shapiro, and B. Tursky. 1966. Reinforcement of spontaneous electrodermal activity. *Journal of Comparative and Physiological Psychology*, 61:20–27.

Crosignani, P. G. and C. Robyn, (Eds.). 1977. *Prolactin and human reproduction*. London: Academic Press.

Cutler, R. G. 1976. Evolution of longevity in primates. *Journal of Human Evolution*, 5:169–202.

Demarest, W. 1977. Incest avoidance among human and nonhuman primates. In S. Chevalier-Skolnikoff and F. Poirier (Eds.), *Primate bio-social development*. New York: Garland STPM Press.

Denenberg, V. 1969. The effects of early experience. In R. Mater (Ed.), *The behavior of domestic animals*. New York: Williams and Williams.

Denham, W. 1974. Population structure, infant transport, and infanticide among modern and pleistocene hunter-gatherers. *Journal of Anthropological Research*, 30(3):191–198.

Dennis, W. 1940a. *The Hopi child*. New York: Wiley.

Dennis, W. 1940b. Does culture appreciably affect patterns of infant behavior? *Journal of Social Psychology*, 12:305–317.

deVries, M. and C. M. Super. 1978. Contextual influences on the Brazelton Neonatal Behavioral Assessment Scale and implications for its cross-cultural use. In A. Sameroff (Ed.), *Organization and stability of newborn behavior: A commentary on the Brazelton Neonatal Behavioral Assessment Scale*. *Monographs of the Society for Research in Child Development*, 43(5–6):92–101.

Dobbing, J. 1974. Prenatal development and neurological development. In J. Cravioto, W. Hambraeus, and R. Vahlquist (Eds.), *Early malnutrition and mental development*. Uppsala: Swedish Nutrition Foundation and the World Health Organization.

Dobzhansky, T. 1950. Evolution in the tropics. *American Scientist*, 38:209–221.

Downs, J. F. 1964. *Animal husbandry in Navajo society and culture*. Berkeley: University of California Press.

Draper, P. 1975. Cultural pressure on sex differences. *American Ethnologist,* 2(4):602–616.

Draper, P. and H. Harpending. 1982. Father absence and reproductive strategy: an evolutionary perspective. *Journal of Anthropological Research,* 38(3):225–273.

Dressler, W. W. 1980. Coping dispositions, social supports, and health status. *Ethos,* 8(2):146–171.

Dunn, J. 1976. How far do early differences in mother–child relations affect later development? In P. P. G. Bateson and R. A. Hinde (Eds.), *Growing points in ethology.* Cambridge: University of Cambridge Press.

Durham, W. H. 1979. Toward a coevolutionary theory of human biology and culture. In N. Chagnon and W. Irons (Eds.), *Evolutionary biology and human social behavior: An anthropological perspective.* North Scituate, Mass.: Duxbury.

Dyk, W. 1938. *Son of Old Man Hat.* Lincoln: University of Nebraska Press.

Edwards, F. M., P. H. Wise, D. W. Thomas, J. B. Murchland, and R. J. Craig. 1976. Blood pressure and electrocardiography findings in the South Australian Aborigines. *Australia and New Zealand Journal of Medicine,* 6:197–205.

Egeland, B. and A. Sroufe. 1981. Developmental sequelae of maltreatment in infancy. New Directions for Child Development, 11:77–92.

Eldridge, N. and S. J. Gould. 1972. Punctuated equilibria: an alternative to phyletic gradualism. In T. J. M. Schopf (Ed.), *Models in paleobiology.* San Francisco: Freeman, Cooper.

Ember, C. 1973. Female task assignment and the social behavior of boys. *Ethos,* 1:424–439.

Erikson, E. 1963. *Childhood and society.* New York: Norton.

Fox, R. 1980. *The red lamp of incest.* New York: Dutton.

Ferreira, A. J. 1965. Emotional factors in prenatal environment. *Journal of Nervous and Mental Disease,* 141:108–118.

Freedman, D. G. 1958. Constitutional and environmental interactions in rearing of four breeds of dogs. *Science,* 127:585–586.

Freedman, D. G. 1971. Genetic influences on the development of behavior. In G. B. A. Stoelinga and J. J. Van der Werff Ten Bosch (Eds.), *Normal and abnormal development of behavior.* Leiden: Leiden University Press.

Freedman, D. G. 1974a. Cradleboard and temperament: cause or effect? Paper presented at the Annual Meeting of the American Association for the Advancement of Science, San Francisco.

Freedman, D. G. 1974b. *Human infancy: An evolutionary perspective.* Hillsdale, N. J.: Lawrence Erlbaum Associates.

Freedman, D. G. 1976. Infancy, biology, and culture. In L. Lipsitt (Ed.), *Developmental psychobiology.* Hillsdale, N. J.: Lawrence Erlbaum Associates.

Freedman, D. G. and T. B. Brazelton. 1971. The Cambridge Neonatal Scale. In G. B. A. Stoelinga and J. J. Van der Werff Ten Bosch (Eds.), *Normal and abnormal development of behavior.* Leiden: Leiden University Press.

Freedman, D. G. and N. Freedman. 1969. Differences in behavior between Chinese-American and European-American newborns. *Nature,* 224:1227.

Freedman, D. G. and B. Keller, 1963. Inheritance of behavior in infants. *Science,* 140:196–198.

Freedman, D. G., H. Boverman, and N. Freedman. 1966. Effects of kinesthetic stimulation on smiling in premature infants. Paper presented at the Annual Meeting of American Orthopsychiatric Association, San Francisco.

Freud, S. 1964. An outline of psychoanalysis. In *The standard edition of the works of Signumd Freud* (Vol. 23). London: Hogarth Press, pp. 141–208.

Friedrich, W. N. and J. A. Boroskin. 1976. The role of the child in abuse: A review of the literature. *American Journal of Orthopsychiatry,* 44(4):580–590.

Frodi, A. M. 1981. Contribution of infant characteristics to child abuse. *American Journal of Mental Deficiency,* 85(4):341–349.

Gadgil, M. and W. H. Bossert. 1970. Life historical consequences of natural selection. *American Naturalist*, 104:1–24.

Giacoman, S. L. 1971. The effects of hunger and motor restraint on arousal and visual attention in the infant. *Child Development*, 42:605–614.

Goodenough, W. 1981. *Culture, language, and society*. (2nd ed.) Menlo Park, Calif.: Benjamin/Cummings.

Goodman, M. 1963. Man's place in the phylogeny of the primates as reflected in serum proteins. In S. L. Washburn (Ed.), *Classification and human evolution*. Chicago: Aldine.

Gorer, G. 1949. Some aspects of the psychology of the people of Great Russia. *American Slavic and East Eurpoean Review*, 8:155–160.

Gorer, G. and J. Rickman. 1949. *The people of Great Russia*. London: Cresset.

Gould, S. J. 1977. *Ontogeny and phylogeny*. Cambridge, Mass.: Harvard University Press.

Gould, S. J. and N. Eldridge. 1977. Punctuated equilibria: The tempo and mode of evolution reconsidered. *Paleobiology*, 3:115–151.

Greenberg, R. E., J. Lind, and V. S. Von Euler. 1960. Effect of posture and insulin hypoglycemia on catecholamine excretion in the newborn. *Acta Pediatrica*, 49:780–785.

Gregg, C. L., M. E. Haffner, and A. F. Korner. 1976. The relative efficacy of vestibular-proprioceptive stimulation and the upright posture in enhancing visual pursuit in neonates. *Child Development*, 47:309–314.

Griswold, R. E. and M. T. Griswold. 1973. *A SNOBOL 4 Primer*. Englewood Cliffs, N. J.: Prentice-Hall.

Griswold, R. E., J. F. Poage, and I. P. Polansky. 1971. *The SNOBOL 4 programming language*. Englewood Cliffs, N. J.: Prentice-Hall.

Hall, E. T. 1969. *Listening behavior: Some cultural differences*. Phi Delta Kappan, March.

Hall, F. and S. Pawlby. 1981. Continuity and discontinuity in the behavior of British working-class mothers and their first-born children. *International Journal of Behavioral Development*, 4:13–36.

Hamburg, D. 1963. Emotions in the perspective of human evolution. In P. H. Knapp (Ed.), *Expression of the emotions in man*. New York: International Universities Press.

Harper, L. V. 1972. Early maternal handling and preschool behavior of human children. *Developmental Psychobiology*, 5:1–5.

Hebb, D. O. 1953. Heredity and environment in mammalian behavior. *British Journal of Animal Behavior*, 1:43–47.

Henderson, E. B. and J. E. Levy. 1975. *Survey of Navajo community studies 1936–74*. Lake Powell Research Project Bulletin 6. Los Angeles: University of California Press.

Hobson, R. 1954. Navajo acquisitive values. *Papers of the Peabody Museum*, 42(3). Cambridge, Mass.: Harvard University Press.

Hoffman, H. S. 1974. Fear-mediated processes in the context of imprinting. In M. Lewis and L. Rosenblum (Eds.), *The origins of fear*. New York: Wiley.

Holt, A. B., D. B. Cheek, E. D. Mellits, and D. E. Hill. 1975. Brain size and the relation of the primate to the nonprimate. In D. B. Cheek (Ed.), *Fetal and postnatal growth: Hormones and nutrition*. New York: Wiley.

Houston, W. R. 1929. The spasmogenic aptitude. *Medical Clinics of North America*, 12:1285–1302.

Horowitz, F. D., M. K. Aleksandrowicz, J. Ashton, S. Tims, K. McCluskey, R. Culp, and H. Gallas. 1973. American and Uruguayan infants: Reliability, maternal drug histories, and population differences using the Brazelton Neonatal Scales. Paper presented at the Annual Meeting of the Society for Research in Child Development, Philadelphia.

Hudson, C. 1966. Isometric advantages of the cradleboard: A hypothesis. *American Anthropologist*, 68:470–474.

Humpheries, P. 1974. *PRIMATE user's manual, version 4.* Department of Psychology, Brunel University, Uxbridge, England.

Huttenen, M. O. and P. Niskanen. 1978. Prenatal loss of father and psychiatric disorders. *Archives of General Psychiatry*, 35:429–431.

Itani, J. and A. Nishimura. 1973. The study of infrahuman culture in Japan: A review. In E. Menzel (Ed.), *Precultural primate behavior.* Basel: Karger.

Jacob, F. and J. Monod. 1961. On the regulation of gene activity. *Cold Spring Harbor Symposia on Quantitative Biology*, 26:193–209.

Jacobson, M. 1969. Development of specific neuronal connections. *Science*, 163:543–547.

Jewell, D. P. 1952. A case of a "psychotic" Navajo Indian male. *Human Organization*, 2(1):32–36.

Jones, F. and E. Dlugokinski. 1978. The relationship of stress during pregnancy to perinatal status and maternal readiness. Paper presented at the First Biennial Meeting of the International Conference on Infant Studies, Providence, R.I.

Kagan, J. 1971. *Change and continuity in infancy.* New York: Wiley.

Kagan, J. 1974. Discrepancy, temperament, and infant distress. In M. Lewis and L. Rosenblum (Eds.), *The origins of fear.* New York: Wiley.

Kagan, J. 1981. Universals in human development. In R. H. Munroe, R. L. Munroe, and B. B. Whiting (Eds.), *Handbook of cross-cultural human development.* New York: Garland STPM Press.

Kagan, J., R. B. Kearsley, and P. R. Zelazo. 1980. *Infancy: Its place in human development.* Cambridge, Mass.: Harvard University Press.

Kaminor, B. and W. Lutz. 1960. Blood pressure in Bushmen of the Kalahari desert. *Circulation*, 22:289–295.

Kaplan, N. M. 1978. Stress, the sympathetic nervous system, and hypertension. *Journal of Human Stress*, September.

Kass, E. M., B. Rosner, S. H. Zinner, H. S. Magolius, and Y-H. Lee. 1977. Studies on the origin of human hypertension. In D. Barltrop (Ed.), *Pediatric implications for some adult disorders.* London: Fellowship of Postgraduate Medicine.

Keith, A. B. 1964. The Navajo girl's puberty ceremony: Function and meaning for the adolescent. *El Palacio*, 71: 27–36.

King, M. C. and A. C. Wilson. 1975. Evolution at two levels in humans and chimpanzees. *Science*, 188:107–116.

Kluckhohn, C. 1944. *Navaho witchcraft.* New York: Beacon-Free Press (1967).

Kluckhohn, C. 1946. Personality formation among the Navaho Indians. In R. Kluckhohn (Ed.), *Culture and behavior.* New York: MacMillan-Free Press (1962).

Kluckhohn, C. 1947. Some aspects of Navaho infancy and early childhood. *Psychoanalysis and the Social Sciences*, 1:37–86.

Kluckhohn, C. 1955. Recent studies of the "national character" of Great Russians. In R. Kluckhohn (Ed.), *Culture and behavior.* New York. MacMillan-Free Press (1962).

Kluckhohn, C. and D. Leighton. 1974. The Navaho. (Rev. ed.) Cambridge, Mass.: Harvard University Press (1946).

Kluckhohn, C., W. W. Hill, and L. W. Kluckhohn. 1971. *Navaho material culture.* Cambridge, Mass.: Harvard University Press.

Konner, M. J. 1972. Aspects of the developmental ethology of a foraging people. In N. G. Blurton Jones (Ed.), *Ethological Studies of Child Behaviour.* Cambridge: Cambridge University Press.

Konner, M. H. 1977. Evolution of human behavior development. In P. H. Leiderman, S. R. Tulkin, and A. Rosenfeld (Eds.), *Culture and infancy.* New York: Academic Press.

Konner, M. J. and C. Worthman. 1980. Nursing frequency, gonadal function, and birth spacing among !Kung hunter-gatherers. *Science*, 207:788–791.

Korner, A. F., T. Gabby, and H. C. Kraemer. 1980. Relation between prenatal maternal blood pressure and infant irritability. *Early Human Development*, 4(1):35–39.

Kunitz, S. J. 1974. Navajo and Hopi fertility, 1971–1972. *Human Biology*, 46(3):435–451.

Kunitz, S. J. 1976. *The relationship of economic variations to mortality and fertility patterns on the Navajo reservation*. Lake Powell Research Project Bulletin 20. Los Angeles: University of California Press.

Ladd, J. 1957. *The structure of a moral code*. Cambridge, Mass.: Harvard University Press.

Lamphere, L. 1977. *To run after them*. Tucson: University of Arizona Press.

Lazarus, R. S., M. Tomita, E. M. Opton, and M. Kodama. 1966. A cross-cultural study of stress-reaction patterns in Japan. *Journal of Personality and Social Psychology*, 4:622–633.

Leiderman, P. H. and C. G. Leiderman. 1977. Economic change and infant care in an East African agricultural communituy. In P. H. Leiderman, S. R. Tulkin, and A. Rosenfeld (Eds.), *Culture and infancy*. New York: Academic Press.

Leighton, D. and C. Kluckhohn. 1948. *Children of the people*. Cambridge, Mass.: Harvard University Press.

Leighton, D. and A. Leighton. 1942. Some types of uneasiness and fear in a Navaho Indian community. *American Anthropologist*, 44:194–209.

Lester, B. M. and T. B. Brazelton. 1982. Cross-cultural assessment of neonatal behavior. In D. Wagner and H. Stevenson (Eds.), *Cultural perspective on child development*. San Francisco: Freeman.

Leutenegger, W. 1972. Newborn size and pelvic dimensions of Australopithecus. *Nature*, 240:568–569.

Levin, R. 1980. Evolutionary theory under fire. *Science*, 210:883–887.

LeVine, R. A. 1970. Cross-cultural study in child psychology. In P. H. Mussen (Ed.), *Carmichael's manual of child psychology*. (3rd ed.) New York: Wiley.

LeVine, R. A. 1977. Child rearing as cultural adaptation. In P. H. Leiderman, S. R. Tulkin, and A. Rosenfeld (Eds.), *Culture and infancy*. New York: Aademic Press.

Levine, S. 1969. Infantile stimulation: A perspective. In A. Ambrose (Ed.), *Stimulation in early infancy*. New York. Academic Press.

Levine, S. 1971. Stress and behavior. *Scientific American*, 224(1):26–31.

Levy, J. E. 1962. Community organization among the Western Navajo. *American Anthropologist*, 654:781–801.

Levy, J. E. 1964. The fate of Navajo twins. *American Anthropologist*, 66:883–887.

Levy, J. E. and S. J. Kunitz. 1974. *Indian drinking*. New York: Wiley.

Lewis, M. 1972. An infant's interaction with its social world: The origin of meaning. Paper presented at the Meeting of the Canadian Psychological Association, Montreal.

Lewis, M. and L. Rosenblum (Eds.). 1974. *The effect of the infant on its caregiver*. New York.: Wiley.

Lipton, E., A. Steinschneider, and J. Richmond. 1965. Swaddling: A child care practice: Historical, cultural, and experimental observations. *Pediatrics*, 35:519–567.

Lovejoy, C. O. 1981. The origin of man. *Science*, 211:341–350.

Løvtrup, S. 1974. *Epigenetics: A treatise on theoretical biology*. New York; Wiley.

Lumsden, C. J. and E. O. Wilson. 1981. Genes, mind, and culture: The coevolutionary process. Cambridge, Mass.: Harvard University Press.

Lynch, G. and C. Gall. 1979. Organization and reorganization in the central nervous system: Evolving concepts of brain plasticity. In F. Falkner and J. Tanner (Eds.), *Human growth*. Vol. 3. *Neurobiology and nutrition*. New York: Plenum Press.

Lynch, M. A. 1975. Ill-health and child abuse. *The Lancet*, 3:317–319.

McAllester, D. P. 1954. Enemy way music: A study of social and esthetic vales as seen in Navajo music. *Papers of the Peabody Museum*, 41(3). Cambridge, Mass.: Harvard Univ. Press.

McGrew W. C. 1977. Socialization and object manipulation of wild chimpanzees. In S. Chevalier-Skolnikoff and F. Poirier (Eds.), *Primate bio-social development.* New York. Garland STPM Press.

Main, M. 1973. Exploration, play, and level of cognitive functioning as related to child–mother attachment. Unpublished doctoral dissertation, Johns Hopkins University.

Mann, A. 1975. Paleodemographic aspects of the South African australopithecines. *University of Pennsylvania Publications in Anthropology,* 1:171.

Marvin, R. and D. Mossler. 1976. A methodological paradigm for describing and analyzing complex non-verbal expression: Coy expressions in preschool children. *Representative Research in Social Psychology,* 7:133–139.

Mason, O. T. 1886. *Cradles of the American aborigines.* U.S. National Museum Annual Report 1886–1887, Part 2, pp. 161–212.

Mason, W. A. 1968. Early social deprivation in the nonhuman primates: Implications for human behavior. In R. Glass (Ed.) *Environmental influences.* New York: Russell Sage–Rockefeller University Press.

Mead, M. and R. Metraux. 1953. *The study of culture at a distance.* Chicago: University of Chicago Press.

Metcalfe, A. 1976. From schoolgirl to mother: The effects of education on Navajo women. *Social Problems,* 23(5):535–544.

Minturn, L. and W. W. Lambert. 1964. *Mothers of six cultures: Antecedents of child rearing.* New York: Academic Press.

Money, J. and A. A. Ehrhardt. 1968. Prenatal hormonal exposure: Possible effects on human behavior. In R. P. Michael (Ed.), *Endocrinology and human behavior.* London: Oxford University Press.

Morgan, G. and H. N. Ricciuti. 1969. Infants' response to strangers during the first year. In B. M. Foss (Ed.), *Determinants of infant behaviour.* Vol. 4. London: Methuen.

Moss, H. A. 1967. Sex, age, and state as determinants of mother-infant interaction. *Merrill-Palmer Quarterly,* 13(1):19–36.

Munroe, R. H. and R. L. Munroe. 1971. Household density and infant care in an East African society. *Journal of Social Psychology,* 83:3–13.

Myerscough, P. R. 1974. Normal pregnancy and antenatal care. In W. Passmore and J. Robson (Eds.), *A companion to medical studies.* Oxford: Blackwell.

Nie, N. H., C. Hadlai Hull, J. G. Jenkins, K. Steinbrenner, and D. Bent. 1975. *Statistical package for the social sciences.* New York: McGraw-Hill.

Osofsky, J. 1976. Neonatal characteristics and mother-infant interaction in two observational situations. *Child Development,* 47:1138–1147.

Osofsky, J. and B. Danzger. 1974. Relationships between neonatal characteristics and mother–infant interaction. *Developmental Psychology,* 10:124–130.

Ottinger, D. and J. E. Simons. 1964. Behavior of human neonates and prenatal maternal anxiety. *Psychological Reports,* 14:391–394.

Parsley, N. J. and F. M. Rabinowitz. 1975. Crying in the first year: An operant interpretation of the Bell and Ainsworth (1972) findings. *Child Study Journal,* 5(2):83–89.

Pederson, D. R. and D. Ter Vrugt. 1973a. The influence of amplitude and frequency of vestibular stimulation on the activity of two-month-old infants. *Child Development,* 44(1):122–128.

Pederson, D. R. and D. Ter Vrugt. 1973b. The effects of vertical rocking frequencies on the arousal of two-month-old infants. *Child Development,* 44(1):205–209.

Petit, G. A. 1946. Primitive education in North America. *Univeristy of California Publications in American Archaeology and Ethnology,* 48:1–182.

Piaget, J. 1950. *The psychology of intelligence.* New York: Harcourt, Brace and World.

Pianka, E. R. 1970. On *r* and *K* selection. *American Naturalist,* 104:592–597.

Plomin, R., J. C. DeFries, and G. E. McClearn. 1980. Behavioral Genetics: A Primer. San Francisco: Freeman.

Prader, A., J. Tanner, and G. von Harnack. 1963. Catch-up growth following illness or starvation. Journal of Pediatrics, 62:646–659.

Prescott, J. W. 1970a. Early somatosensory deprivation as an ontogenetic process in the abnormal development of the brain and behavior. Medical primatology. Proceedings of the second conference on experimental medicine and surgery in primates, New York, 1969, pp. 356–375.

Prescott, J. W. 1970b. A developmental neural-behavioral theory of socialization. Paper presented at the Annual Meeting of the American Psychological Association, Miami.

Prescott, J. W. 1973. Human affection, violence, and sexuality: A developmental and cross-cultural perspective. Paper presented at the Annual Meeting of the Society for Cross-Cultural Research, Philadelphia.

Rabin, D. L., C. R. Barnett, W. D. Arnold, R. H. Freiberger, and G. Brooks. 1965. Untreated congenital hip disease: A study of the epidemiology, natural history, and social aspects of the disease in a Navajo population. American Journal of Public Health, 55(1), supplement.

Raphael, D. 1974. The tender gift: breastfeeding. Englewood Cliffs, N.J.: Prentice-Hall.

Reichard, G. 1950. Navaho religion: A study of symbolism. Bollingen Series, No. 18. Pantheon Books.

Reynolds, T. R. 1979. Residential ideology and practice among the Sheep Springs Navajo. Unpublished doctoral dissertation, University of British Columbia.

Reynolds, T. R., L. Lamphere, and C. Cook. 1967. Time, resources, and authority in a Navajo community. American Anthropologist, 69:188–199.

Rheingold, H. 1961. The effect of environmental stimulation upon social and exploratory behavior in the human infant. In B. M. Foss (Ed.), Determinants of infant behaviour. Vol. 1. London: Methuen.

Richards, M. P. M. 1976. Parents and children in non-accidental injury. Paper presented at a Symposium on Child Abuse, The Royal Society of Medicine, June.

Richer, J. 1974. Direct observation: A reply to Cooper et al. Bulletin of the British Psychological Association, 27:500–502.

Roberts, J. M. 1951. Three Navaho households. Papers of the Peabody Museum, 40(3). Cambridge, Mass.: Harvard University Press.

Robson, K. 1967. The role of eye-to-eye contact in maternal–infant attachment. Journal of Child Psychology and Psychiatry, 8:13–25.

Rogoff, B. 1978. Spot observations: An introduction and examination. Quarterly Newsletter of the Institute for Comparative Human Development, 2(2):21–26.

Ross, H. 1975. The effects of increasing familiarity on infants' reactions to adult strangers. Journal of Experimental Child Psychology, 20:226–239.

Rushforth, S. 1982. Autonomy and community among the Bear Lake Athapaskans. Paper presented at the Conference on Native American Interaction Patterns, University of Alberta, April, 1982. To be published in the conference proceedings.

Rutter, M. 1970. Psychological development—predictions from infancy. Journal of Child Psychology and Psychiatry, 11:49–62.

Rutter, M., S. Korn, and H. G. Birch. 1963. Genetic and environmental factors in the development of primary reaction patterns. British Journal of Social and Clinical Psychology, 2:161–173.

Rutter, M., H. G. Birch, A. Thomas, and S. Chess. 1964. Temperamental characteristics in infancy and the later development of behavioral disorders. British Journal of Psychiatry, 110:651–661.

Ruyle, E. E. 1973. Genetic and cultural pools: Some suggestions for a unified theory of biocultural evolution. Human Ecology, 1(3):201–215.

Ruyle, E. E. 1977. Comment on "The adaptive significance of cultural behavior." *Human Ecology*, 5(1):53–55.

Sameroff, A. 1975. Early influences on development: Fact or fancy? *Merrill-Palmer Quarterly*, 21(4):267–294.

Sameroff, A. 1978. Summary and conclusions: The future of newborn assessment. In A. Sameroff (Ed.), *Organization and stability of newborn behavior: A commentary on the Brazelton Neonatal Behavioral Assessment Scale. Monographs of the Society for Research in Child Development*, 43(5–6):102–117.

Sameroff, A. and M. J. Chandler. 1975. Reproductive risk and the continuum of caretaking casualty. In F. D. Horowitz, E. M. Hetherington, S. Scarr-Salapatek, and G. M. Siegel (Eds.), *Review of child development research*. Vol. 4. Chicago: University of Chicago Press.

Sameroff, A., R. Selfer, and P. Elias. 1982. Sociocultural variability in infant temperament ratings. *Child Development*, 53:164–173.

Sander, L. W., G. Stechler, D. Burns, and H. Julia. 1970. Early mother-infant interaction and 24-hour patterns of activity and sleep. *Journal of the American Academy of Child Psychiatry*, 9:103–123.

Sasaki, T. T. 1960. *Fruitland, New Mexico: A Navaho community in transition*. Ithaca: Cornell University Press.

Scarr-Salapatek, S. and M. Williams. 1973. The effects of early stimulation on low-birth weight infants. *Child Development*, 44(1):94–101.

Schaffer, H. R. 1974. Cognitive components of the infant's response to strangers. In M. Lewis and L. Rosenblum (Eds.), *The origins of fear*. New York: Wiley.

Schaffer, H. R. and P. E. Emerson. 1964. The development of social attachments in infancy. *Monographs of the Society for Research in Child Development*, 29(3).

Schoenfeld, L. S. and S. I. Miller. 1973. The Navajo Indians: A descriptive study of the psychiatric population. *International Journal of Social Psychiatry*, 19(1,2):31–37.

Scotch, N. 1960. A preliminary report on the relations of sociocultural factors to hypertension among the Zulu. *Annals of the New York Academy of Science*, 94:1000–1009.

Scotch, N. 1963. Sociocultural factors in the epidemiology of Zulu hypertension, *American Journal of Public Health*, 53:1205–1213.

Scott, J. P. 1971. Attachment and separation in dogs and man: Theoretical propositions. In H. R. Schaffer (Ed.), *The origins of human social relations*. New York: Academic Press.

Sears, R. R., E. E. Maccoby, and H. Levin 1957. Patterns of child rearing. Evanston, Ill.: Row and Peterson.

Shaw, C. 1977. A comparison of the patterns of mother–baby interaction for a group of crying, irritable babies and a group of more amenable babies. *Child: Care, Health, and Development*, 3:1–12.

Shepardson, M. and B. Hammond. 1964. Change and persistence in an isolated Navajo community. *American Anthropologist*, 66(5):1029–1050.

Shepardson, M. and B. Hammond. 1970. *The Navajo mountain community*. Berkeley: University of California Press.

Shepher, J. 1971 Mate selection among second generation kibbutz adolescents and adults: Incest avoidance and negative imprinting. *Archives of Sexual Behavior*, 1:293–307.

Slobodkin, L. and A. Rapoport. 1974. An optimal strategy of evolution. *Quarterly Review of Biology*, 49:181–200.

Sofue, T. H., H. Soye, and T. Mirakami. 1957. Anthropological study of the eijiko, a Japanese cradle for child. *Journal of the Anthropological Society of Nippon*, 66:77–85.

Sontag, L. W. 1941. The significance of fetal environmental differences. *American Journal of Obstetrics and Gynecology*, 42:996.

Spicer, E. H. 1962. *Cycles of conquest*. Tucson: University of Arizona Press.

Spiro, M. 1954. Is the family universal? *American Anthropologist*, 56:839–846.

Spitz, R. 1965. *The first year of life.* New York: International Universities Press.

Sroufe, L. A., E. Waters, and L. Matas. 1974. Contextual determinants of infant affective responses. In M. Lewis and L. Rosenblum (Eds.), *The origins of fear.* New York: Wiley.

Sroufe, L. A. and E. Waters. 1977. Attachment as an organizational construct. *Child Development,* 48:1184–1199.

Stanley, S. M. 1979. *Macroevolution: Pattern and Process.* San Francisco: Freeman.

Stayton, D., R. T. Hogan, and M. D. S. Ainsworth. 1971. Infant obedience and maternal behavior: The origins of socialization reconsidered. *Child Development,* 42:1057–1069.

Stearns, S. C. 1976. Life-history tactics: A review of the data. *Quarterly Review of Biology,* 51:3–47.

Stern, D. 1974. Mother and infant at play: The dyadic interaction involving facial, vocal, and gaze behaviors. In M. Lewis and L. Rosenblum (Eds.), *The effect of the infant on its caregiver.* New York: Wiley.

Stott, D. H. 1973. Follow-up study from birth of the effects of prenatal stress. *Developmental Medicine and Child Neurology,* 15:770–787.

Strauss, M. E. and D. L. Rourke. 1978. A multivariate analysis of the Neonatal Behavioral Assessment Scale in several samples. In A. Sameroff (Ed.), *Organization and stability of newborn behavior: A commentary on the Brazelton Neonatal Behavioral Assessment Scale. Monographs of the Society for Research in Child Development,* 43(5–6):81–91.

Super, C. M. 1976. Environmental effects on motor development: The case of African infant precocity. *Developmental Medicine and Child Neurology,* 18:561–567.

Super, C. M. 1981. Behavioral development in infancy. In R. H. Munroe, R. L. Munroe, and B. B. Whiting (Eds.), *Handbook of cross-cultural human development.* New York: Garland STPM Press.

Talmon, Y. 1964. Mate selection in collective settlements. *American Sociological Review,* 29:491–508.

Tanner, J. 1978. *Fetus into man.* Cambridge, Mass.: Harvard University Press.

Tinbergen, N. 1951. *The study of instinct.* London: Oxford University Press.

Tinbergen, N. 1963. On the aims and methods of ethology. *Zeitschrift für Tierpsychologie,* 20:410–433.

Tinbergen, N. 1965. Behaviour and natural selection. In J. A. Moore (Ed.), *Ideas in modern biology* (Vol. 6 of *Proceedings of the XVIth International Zoological Congress, Washington, 1963*).

Tolan, W. J. and L. Tomasini. 1977. Mothers of "secure" vs. "insecure" babies differ themselves nine months later. Paper presented at the Annual Meeting of the Society for Research in Child Development, New Orleans.

Topper, M. and C. Begaye. 1978. "Not Navajo life": Clinical anthropology, mental "illness," and psychotherapy among the Navajo. In J. L. Steinberg (Ed.), *Cultural factors in the rehabilitation process.* Department of Counselling Education, California State University, Los Angeles.

Trivers, R. L. 1972 Parental investment and sexual selection. In B. Campbell (Ed.), *Sexual selection and the descent of man.* Chicago: Aldine.

Tung, C-L. 1927. Relative hypotension of foreigners in China. *Archives of Internal Medicine,* 40:153–159.

Tung, C-L. 1930. Blood presssure of northern Chinese males. *Chinese Journal of Physiology,* 4(3):117–130.

Turner, E. K. 1956. The syndrome in the infant resulting from maternal emotional tension during pregnancy. *Medical Journal of Australia,* 43:221–222.

Vermeij, G. J. 1973. Adaptation, versatility, and evolution. *Systematic Zoology,* 22:466–477.

Waddington, C. H. 1953. Genetic assimilation of an acquired character. *Evolution,* 7(2):118–126.

Waddington, C. H. 1968. The theory of evolution today. In A. Koestler and J. Smythies (Eds.), *Beyond reductionism*. New York: MacMillan.

Waddington, C. H. 1975a. *The evolution of an evolutionist*. Edinburgh: Edinburgh University Press.

Waddington, C. H. 1975b. Mindless societies. *New York Review of Books*, August 7, 1975. (Also: In A. L. Caplan (Ed.), *The sociobiology debate*. New York: Harper & Row.)

Waters, E. 1978. The reliability and stability of individual differences in infant–mother attachment. *Child Development*, 49:483–494.

Waters, E., J. Wippman, and L. A. Sroufe. 1979. Attachment, positive affect, and competence in the peer group: Two studies in construct validation. *Child Development*, 50:821–829.

Watson, J. B. 1919. *Psychology from the standpoint of the behaviorist*. New York: Lippincott.

Watson, J. S. 1967. Memory and "contingency analysis" in infant learning. *Merrill-Palmer Quarterly*, 13:55–76.

Watson, J. S. 1972. Smiling, cooing, and "the game." *Merrill-Palmer Quarterly*, 18:323–340.

Weinraub, M., J. Brooks, and M. Lewis. 1977. The social network: A reconsideration of the concept of attachment. *Human Development*, 20:31–47.

Weisner, T. S. and R. Gallimore. 1977. My brother's keeper: Child and sibling caretaking. *Current Anthropology*, 18:169–190.

Werner, E. E., J. Bierman, and F. French. 1971. *The children of Kauai*. Honolulu: University of Hawaii Press.

Witherspoon, G. 1970. A new look at Navajo social organization. *American Anthropologist*, 72:55–66.

Witherspoon, G. 1975. *Navajo kinship and marriage*. Chicago: University of Chicago Press.

Witherspoon, G. 1977. *Language and art in the Navajo universe*. Ann Arbor, University of Michigan Press.

Whiting, B. B. 1976. The problem of the packaged variable. In K. F. Riegel and J. A. Meacham (Eds.), *The developing individual in a changing world*. Vol. 1. The Hague: Mouton.

Whiting, B. B. 1978. The dependency hang-up and experiments in alternative life-styles. In S. Cutler and M. Yinger (Eds.), *Major social issues: A multidisciplinary view*. New York: Free Press.

Whiting, B. B. 1980. Culture and social behavior: A model for the development of social behavior. *Ethos*, 8:95–116.

Whiting, B. B. and J. W. M. Whiting. 1975. *Children of six cultures*. Cambridge, Mass.: Harvard University Press.

Whiting, J. W. M. 1971. Causes and consequences of the amount of body contact between mother and infant. Paper presented at the Annual Meeting of the American Anthropological Association, New York.

Whiting, J. W. M. 1981. Environmental constraints on infant care practices. In R. H. Munroe, R. L. Munroe, and B. B. Whiting (Eds.), *Handbook of cross-cultural human development*. New York: Garland STPM Press.

Whiting, J. W. M. 1973. A model for psycho-cultural research. Distinguished Lecturer Address presented at the Annual Meeting of the American Anthropological Association, New Orleans.

Whiting, J. W. M. and I. Child. 1953. *Child training and personality*. New Haven: Yale University Press.

Wolf, A. 1966. Childhood association, sexual attraction, and the incest taboo: A Chinese case. *American Anthropologist*, 68:883–898.

Wolf, A. 1968. Adopt a daughter-in-law, marry a sister: A Chinese solution to the problem of the incest taboo. *American Anthropologist*, 70:864–874.

Wolf, A. 1970. Childhood association and sexual attraction: A further test of the Westermarck hypothesis. *American Anthropologist*, 72:503–515.

Wolff, P. H. 1977. Biological variations and cultural diversity: An exploratory study. In P. H. Leiderman, S. R. Tulkin, and A. Rosenfeld (Eds.), *Culture and infancy*. New York: Academic Press.

Woodson, R. L., N. G. Blurton Jones, E. da Costa Woodson, S. Pollock, and M. Evans. 1979. Fetal mediators of the relationship between increased pregnancy and labour blood pressure and newborn irritability. *Early Human Development*, 3:127–139.

Yang, R. K., A. R. Zweig, T. C. Douthitt, and E. J. Federman. 1976. Successive relationships between maternal attitudes during pregnancy, analgesic medication during labor and delivery, and newborn behavior. *Journal of Developmental Psychology*, 12(1):6–14.

Zajonc, R. B. 1975. Birth order and intellectual development. *Psychology Review*, 1:74–88.

Zelazo, P. R., N. A. Zelazo, and S. Kolb. 1972. "Walking" in the newborn. *Science*, 176:314–315.

Index

Aboriginal Australian, 136, 137
Adaptability, *see* Adaptation
Adaptation, 1, 2, 6–12, 24–39, 225–232, 244–246
  in development, 225–232
Allometry, 19
Anglo, 44, 97, 104–108, 125–152, 156–161, 173–189, 192–203, 215–223
  cradleboard use, 97, 105–107
  fear of strangers, 141–152, 156–161
  mother–infant interaction, 173–189, 192–203, 215–223
  newborn behavior, 125–140
  sample, 104–108
Apache, 50, 241, 242
Attachment, *see* Attachment theory
Attachment theory, 25–29, 31–39, 87–92, 215–219, 225–232
  anxious/secure, 26–29, 34, 228
  behaviors, 26
  and developmental control mechanisms, 34, 35, 246, 247
  perturbations in, 25–29, 87–92, 215–219
  and social context, 36–39, 225–232
Autonomic function, *see* Temperament
Birth control, 102
Blood pressure, 126, 131–140, 223; *see also* Prenatal influences
  population differences in, 137–138
  pregnancy and newborn behavior, 131–136
Brazelton Neonatal Behavioral Assessment Scale, 97, 113–118, 203–206, 223–225
  methods of, 113–118
Canalization, 32, 33, 91
Catch-up growth, 32, 33, 218
Chach'osh, 54
Chinese, 138, 229, 233
Cosocialization, 225–232
  and incest avoidance, 229–232
Cottonwood Springs, 51–70, 97–104
  birth interval, 102–104

breast-feeding, 102–104
demography, 56–58
domestic life, 68–70
ecology, 51–54
economics, 59–61
history, 54–56
residence patterns, 61–68, 97–104
Cradleboard, 71–91, 96, 163–198, 225, 226
  adaptation to, 225, 226
  Anglo, 97, 105–107
  and attachment, 88–91, 96, 215–219
  and climate, 72, 73, 76
  and congenital hip disease, 75, 82
  in cross-cultural perspective, 71–73
  design, 73
  determinants of use, 172–174
  functions, 72–74, 78
  long-term effects of, 174–198
  and mother–infant interaction, 163–198
  and motor development, 81–83
  physiological effects, 83–87, 164–169, 178, 187, 188
  and proximity to mother, 173, 174, 218, 219
  "swaddling hypothesis," 79–81, 87, 193
  and temperament, 86, 87
  use, 73–79
"Cut-off" act, 145
Dental wear gradient, 20
Developmental control mechanisms, rules of, 30, 33–35, 246, 247
Developmental pathway, 34–36, 39, 40, 217, 219, 223, 224, 226, 228, 231, 237, 243, 246–248
Developmental plasticity, 21, 31, 226, 232, 236, 237, 244, 246–248
Environmental perturbations, 6, 7, 9–12, 14, 19, 22, 24, 28–36, 224, 232, 246
  in attachment, 25–29, 35–40, 87–96, 215–219

cradleboard as, 88–91, 215–219, 225, 226, 228
Environmental tracking, 9–14, 19, 22, 24, 29, 34, 39, 216, 246
Epigenesis, 4–6, 24, 31–33, 136, 139, 140, 246–249
Epigenetic landscape, 31, 32
Epigenetics, see Epigenesis
Essential indeterminacy, 4, 9, 12, 248
Ethology, 93–96, 108–113
  methods of, 93–96, 108–113
  reliability and validity, 109, 110
Fear of strangers, 97, 118–121, 141–161, 221
  and cradleboard use, 152–154
  methods, 118–121
  Navajo–Anglo compared, 141–152, 156–161
  and Navajo handshaking, 143–145, 147, 150, 158
  and residence patterns, 154–160, 221
Flagstaff, Arizona, see Anglo
Gambler's Ruin, 11
Ganda, 37
Genetic assimilation, 23, 24
Gestation, see Blood pressure; Prenatal influences
Hashke'neini, 54
Heterochrony, 19
Incest avoidance, 229–232
Infant state, 115–117, 127–131, 134, 164–167, 169, 171, 173, 184, 187, 204, 217; see also Irritability
Irritability, 127, 129, 130–133, 136, 137, 140, 161, 172, 204–206, 212, 223–225, 232, 233, 237, 243, 244; see also Temperament; Infant state
Israeli kibbutzim, 229
Japanese, 234–236
K-selection, 13–23, 39, 216, 226, 227
Kikuyu, 222
Kin selection, 95, 139, 230, 231
Levels of explanation, 3, 12
Life history strategies, 16
Logoli, 37, 220
MAP (Mean Arterial Pressure), 131; see also Blood pressure
Mexican, 45, 46, 245
Mormon, 54
Mother–infant interaction, 25–29, 36–39, 87–92, 163–213, 215–223

Anglo, 178–189, 192–203
  and cradleboard, 163–198, 215–219
  Navajo, 163–203
  and newborn behavior, 203–206
  and residence patterns, 206–213, 219–223
  perturbations in, 25–29, 87–92, 215–219
  and social context, 36–39, 219–223
Nature-culture dispute, 1–4, 12, 25, 140, 233, 246, 249
Navajo, 42–51, 86, 87, 125–140, 164–169, 178, 187, 188, 203–206, 215–223, 232–246; see also Cottonwood Springs
  anxiety/depression, 47–51
  behavior, 47–51, 238–246
  cradleboard, see Cradleboard
  fear of strangers, see Fear of strangers
  history, 45–47
  mother–infant interaction, 163–203, 215–223
  newborn behavior/temperament, see Temperament
  pregnancy, 126, 130–140
  reservation ecology, 42, 43
  shyness, 50
  social organization, 43, 44
  values, 238–243
  view of Anglos, 241–242
Neonatal cranial capacity, 20
Neoteny, 15–23, 39, 216, 227
Nila, 69, 76, 232, 238–242
Operon model, 5
Oyugis, 38
Paiute, 45, 54, 97, 245
Parental investment, 16–18, 21–24, 95, 140, 229
Parent-offspring conflict, 139
Pickup truck, 44, 61, 65–68, 70, 78, 173, 222
Placenta, 16, 17, 133–135
Pregnancy, see Blood pressure; Prenatal influences
Prenatal influences, 126, 127, 130–140, 223–225
Pueblo, 42–46, 245
Punctuated equilibria, 2
r-selection, see K-selection
Regulator genes, 5, 6
Reproductive strategies, 14, 95

Residence patterns, 38, 43, 61–70, 99–104, 154–160, 206, 213, 219–232; see also Cottonwood Springs; Navajo
    and birth interval, 102–104, 221
    and breast-feeding, 102–104, 221
    and domestic life, 68–70
    and mother–infant interaction, 206–213, 219–232
    nuclear-extended compared, 99–104
Response-contingent stimulation, 26–28, 79, 89, 170
San, 137, 160
Six Cultures Study, 36, 94
Spanish, 45, 46, 245
Spot observations, 121, 122
Strange Situation Test, 26, 27, 34; see also Attachment
Structural genes, 5, 6
Successful response, 7–9, 11, 23–25, 29–31, 36–39, 217, 226, 232, 246

Swaddling, see Cradleboard
Swaddling, hypothesis, see Cradleboard
T'áá bee bóholnííh, see Nila
Tabula rasa, 25, 31, 36, 227, 246, 247
Temperament, 86, 87, 125–140, 203–206, 225, 232–246
    Anglo newborn, 125–140
    and autonomic function, 233–237
    and mother–infant interaction, 203–206
    Navajo newborn, 86, 87, 125–140, 243–244
    and Navajo pregnancy, 130–140, 225
    "Oriental," 233–237
    and values, 232–246
Ute, 45, 245
Uterine depletion, 133, 163
Values, 232–246
Vestibular stimulation, 84, 85, 169
Zulu, 138